# BORIS PASTERNAK

Life and Times of William Shakespeare
Marko the Prince (Serbo–Croat translations)
Goodbye to the Art of Poetry
The Noise made by Poems
Yevtushenko's Poems (translations)

# BORIS PASTERNAK

PETER LEVI

HUTCHINSON

London Sydney Auckland Johannesburg

This edition first published in 1990 by
Hutchinson

Century Hutchinson Ltd,
20 Vauxhall Bridge Road, London, SW1V 2SA

Century Hutchinson Australia (Pty) Ltd
20 Alfred Street, Milsons Point, Sydney NSW 2061, Australia

Century Hutchinson New Zealand Limited
PO Box 40–086, Glenfield, Auckland 10, New Zealand

Century Hutchinson South Africa (Pty) Ltd
PO Box 337, Bergvlei, 2012 South Africa

**British Library Cataloguing in Publication Data**
Levi, Peter, *1931–*
    Boris Pasternak: a new biography.
    1. Fiction in Russian. Pasternak, Boris, 1890–1960
    Biographies
    I. Title
    891. 73' 42

ISBN 0–09–173886–5

Set in Linotronic Bembo by Speedset Ltd, Ellesmere Port
Printed and bound in Great Britain by
Butler and Tanner Ltd, Frome, Somerset

*For Deirdre*
*Matthew and Cressida*

# Contents

# List of Illustrations

# Introduction

The biography of any human being raises problems, because language distributes meaning and value, and the art of biography is an attempt to give meaning to an individual life. By giving one meaning you exclude others. In the case of a poet, biography comes too late, because the poems have already underlined the life with meaning and value here and there, and the lifework of the poet has offered an apparent meaning to his life as a human being. Only push aside these curtains of poetry and you will find the usual human chaos, the hunger for goodness and the habitual craftsmanship by which people make themselves. Poets need to be understood, they want to be believed and not applauded, but it is only in terms of their private lives and of the history of their times that they become credible.

In the case of Boris Pasternak the times were extraordinary and he was so stubbornly, so irresistibly an artist and an individual that the course of his private life reveals a great deal. He was a very great poet, and I have written his life for the sake of the light it throws on his poetry, and on *Dr Zhivago*, a novel different from any other ever written. In a way the story of his development as a writer is simple, and it has been traced many times. The son of a famous painter who knew Tolstoy, a little older than Mayakovsky, dazed by the futurists, amazed and excited by the revolution, criticised by Blok (a poet comparable with Yeats) and self-criticised, reducing himself by experiment after experiment to silence, a poet of snowstorms, who lived by translation and in the end invented *Zhivago*, a marvellous narrative implying faith in life and in resurrection from the dead, where the dynamite in the narrative is poetry, a few simple, personal poems: that is more or less the portrait as we receive it.

Pasternak has a symbolic and real importance for the Russians: he represents what they have believed in and what has survived.

1

Some sense of this importance has given him a special meaning in the west, and no doubt the echo of his international resonance and his Nobel prize has added to the powerful symbol he became in Russia. His poems were known by heart and pasted in typescript between the pages of permitted books; they generated an intense excitement. That is part of his biography, but it has generated confusions among his biographers. There are those who read his life too much in terms of politics, who cannot clear their eyes of political propaganda, and therefore exaggerate until Pasternak becomes a distorted or an impossible figure. 'Do not idealise the writers of my generation', he said to a young friend, 'we were often weak, we hesitated, we betrayed at times.' But there are also those who transfer poetry and literature to a sphere of absolutes, where they are eternal and above mundane meanings. Their mistake is worse because they make the poetry and the spirit meaningless, whereas the political specialists were at least bulldozing their brutal way towards the truth.

While I was writing the *Life and Times of William Shakespeare* it became clear to me that I could never get really close to my subject. Shakespeare retains his mystery, which belongs not to his life but to his poetry: our ignorance about his life is a matter of chance. With Pasternak, because he is close in time, because of an abundance of evidence, photographs, the memories and imitations of his friends, what is left of his house at Peredelkino and of the Moscow he knew, and above all because of poems near to us in time, one feels constantly close to the poet, one catches him in vignette after vignette. After some uncertainty, I find that these things do add up to a life. It is impossible all the same that this biography should cover absolutely everything. A few facts are already irrecoverably lost, and long and painstaking research produces less and less about them; meanwhile books and memoirs continue to appear, in Russia at an alarming rate and in English steadily. Letters exist on a prodigal scale: they have not yet been gathered or catalogued, but Mr Ozerov, a poet who acted as a sort of secretary to Pasternak and was his friend, reckons a complete edition would stretch to ten volumes at least.

Yet this is the time to write about him. I picked on it by chance, though I have loved his poetry since my schooldays or soon afterwards, and have thought of writing about him for twenty years or more. But I was very slow to learn Russian; even now I can hardly stammer a few phrases, though I can read it. The true reason for writing about him is that of all the poets of this century in any European language he is the most invigorating, the most interesting, and has the most to say. Eliot may be more perfect but is less infectious, and Blok is to Pasternak in my view as Yeats is to Eliot, towering but somehow less satisfying. Valéry is a brilliant and Rilke sometimes an inspired poet, but Pasternak is more human. Lorca is in his own way inimitable, but he is a poet islanded in time as Pasternak is not: Pasternak sometimes writes less well than Lorca, but his range is vast and this age belongs to him. His subject-matter and the circumstances of his life make him more fascinating than George Seferis or David Jones, with whom in other ways I would judge him equal. He was better than Auden or even Robert Lowell, whom he inspired. He is intolerably difficult to translate, but we need to know what his poems mean, and we need to know what he signifies. Why is it that even at a first reading in a bad translation he makes one shiver? How is it that Eliot leaves one with the sensation of music perfectly composed that can never be invented again, only replayed, while Pasternak opens windows? One admires Eliot, but Pasternak makes one want to join in.

So I have read his works, and every translation I can get hold of, and as much literary history and Russian history as I could find, and all the books about him or touching on him I could discover. Mayakovsky, Yesenin, Khlebnikov, Tyutchev, Fet, Akhmatova and Tsvetayeva, and of course Pushkin, are easily enough available, and so in prose are Bulgakov, Zemyatin, Ehrenburg, Paustovsky, and classics like Chekhov and Tolstoy and Gorky. I read enough Lenin to know him, and came to see what Pasternak admired in him. I went to Moscow as a guest of Mr Stabnikov and the Union of Writers, and spent some time at Peredelkino with Zhenya Yevtushenko, my friend for nearly thirty years.

It is best to acknowledge my indebtedness for interviews as they occur in this book, but I was particularly fortunate to know Lydia and Josephine Pasternak, the poet's surviving sisters, in Oxford, and to meet his son, Zhenya Pasternak, on a visit there with his wife. Anne Pasternak, Lydia's daughter, gave me help with the family tree. Sir Isaiah Berlin spent an afternoon giving me vivid memoirs of the poet and a valuable discussion of Russian literature. I got perceptive help from Robin Milner-Gulland and from Richard McKane, who made me a special translation of Pasternak's poem 'Marburg', among others. I owe years of encouragement and enthralling conversation to Sir Dimitri Obolensky, and I was helped constantly by Mike Shotton and by Professor John Bayley, of St Catherine's College. I could not have written this book without the generous support of my friends Andrew and Margaret Hewson, of my lively and far-sighted publisher, Richard Cohen, and of the *Spectator* and the *Independent*. My large debts to other writers and translators will be sufficiently obvious, but no one except me can begin to understand what I owe to my dear wife Deirdre or to Matthew and Cressida.

# 1

## Family and Boyhood to Sixteen

In the middle and late nineteenth century Odessa was the third city of Russia, second only to Moscow and Leningrad, then called Peterburg, or in English Petersburg. Moscow was already heaving with industry: the factory that overshadowed Tolstoy's town house still flaunts from its chimney-top a shattered iron banner saying '1859', and heavy cast-iron plates still decorate the pilasters that line the street wall beside the magnificent wrought-iron gates of the Demidoffs, masters of iron who had begun the serious exploitation of the Urals in the eighteenth century. Moscow was still unselfconsciously Russian all the same; the vogue for the 'old Russian' style of architecture, which is still to be seen in certain railway stations and in the original part of the Tretyakov Gallery, belongs more to the 1890s. It has something in common with the archaising style of Pont Street, and appears to the outsider very queer indeed.

Leningrad has been credited, since its creation from nothing by Peter the Great in the early eighteenth century, with being modern, and open to the west, conjured as it were with a visionary sword from granite and ice. Until Lenin went to Moscow in 1918, it was the capital city of Russia. But Moscow, with its ancient markets and the old subdividing gates that shut off district from district at night, with the stuffed bears in the windows of the coachmakers' and the overflowing flower market and the trade of half Asia, was more central to Russian life. Even today it has immense reserves of character. The tinkle of the Kremlin's silver bells must once have sent many a drowsy emperor to sleep, and even today, after the appalling devastations of Stalin, who plucked out churches like a torturer pulling out teeth, the city is full of extraordinary churches. The fortified monasteries that once surrounded it and now stand in their graveyards in the suburbs are unforgettably beautiful. In the 1880s it must all have been magical, more glamorous than Paris and more beautiful than London and with better and more sparkling architecture from the 1820s, though the comings and goings of the Tsar doubtless made it pompous in the London manner. The best witness I know in English to what it was like at roughly that time is Maurice Baring, but the poet Pasternak and his younger brother Sasha are better still.

Odessa was a world away. An oil-painting of 1880 by Aïvasovsky in the Pushkin literary museum shows how grand it was, with its sea-front of tall white buildings. It was growing as fast as any port in the world at that time, though its position on the Black Sea does not guarantee it a riviera climate: it is just a sea-washed extension of continental Russia, with the same extremes of heat and cold. If the Pasternaks went back there for holidays, that was from loyalty and nostalgia. Socially it must always have been a mixture. It was the setting for Pavstovsky's gentle memoirs and a background for Chekhov when Yalta was a village. In the seventies it was just beginning to have a musical and artistic life of its own. As American Negroes still rise from the slums as the English used to do, by boxing, southern Russian Jews of that generation sought to rise by music. The little world where Leonid Pasternak was born was not the fine white sea-front of the oil-painting but an old courtyard towards the edge of town, half a caravanserai, just the setting in fact for one of Isaac Babel's stories about Odessa's Jewish quarter and its criminals. Odessa itself is all but a character in Babel's writing, just as Moscow as it was and as it became is like a character in Boris Pasternak's poetry.

'In Odessa,' wrote Babel in a posthumously published piece, 'there is a poor, crowded and much suffering Jewish ghetto, a very self-satisfied bourgeoisie, and an extremely fascist city council. There are negroes, Englishmen, Frenchmen and Americans. Odessa has known prosperity, and now it's in decline – a poetic, rather carefree, and very helpless decline.' But in 1880 the decline had scarcely started, and the Pasternak family when we first catch sight of them had physically broken out of the ghetto, which was essentially urban. And the sun and the sea and the swimming at Peresyp were equalisers in their elemental way.

The history of Jewish emancipation and rising in the social scale is almost always a story of absorption into a nation and the forgetfulness of one's origins. I would not go so far as to call this the loss of roots, but one cannot enter into a new culture without losing something of the old one. Leonid Pasternak became an artist of great brilliance, much favoured by Tolstoy and collected by the royal family. He lived and died a Russian citizen, but his life was spent all over Europe, mostly in Moscow and in Germany, and finally in Oxford. As a painter he was an internationalist trained in Munich: on Tolstoy's walls he ranks with Gué and Repin and Serov, the greatest Russian painters of their generation, but his sketches are thrillingly full of life, and closer in style to Constantin Guys. Although it was forbidden to Jews to reside in Moscow, he was important enough to get away with it. His son Boris grew up there, and thought of himself as a Russian. It irritated him to be called Jewish or be recalled towards Jewishness by his father – which happened, I am told, as Leonid grew older outside Russia. Boris Pasternak thought of himself not as a Jewish but a Russian poet. This so infuriated the Israelis that *Dr Zhivago* is one of the few books that have ever been forbidden in Israel.

The name Pasternak is the Russian word for a parsnip, and seems as common in Poland as in Russia. By ancestry, Leonid's family and his wife's were Sephardic Jews who had settled in south Russia in the eighteenth century. Leonid's father Osip was a synagogue cantor: his mother, of whom a portrait survives, was an illiterate countrywoman with a passion for flowers, particularly roses. In her picture she looks old and dignified and full of sorrows. Leonid Osipovich was born in 1862, the fifth of six children; three died at birth and his brother David, who drew very well, at seventeen. His younger sister Asya learnt the piano. She married a Freidenburg and went away with him to live in Leningrad. Some of Leonid's memoirs take the form of warm letters to her about their childhood memories. The synagogue cantor was a severe and practical man, who saw no future in any painting except house painting. Young Leonid was given a circus poster by David, and (for want of anything better to do) he was colouring in the hindquarters of a horse when he was caught, and the poster was burnt in the stove. Whenever he was found drawing afterwards there was always a sneer about painting filthy behinds; his sketches were ruthlessly destroyed. All the same, Osip's fortunes had clearly taken an upward turn, because Leonid's early memories are of 'Gryuzdov's house', where the family rented a wing and a courtyard on the outskirts of the city.

The place was famous for the cheapness of its rooms. The whole area was 'very provincial, almost like a village'; you could see the sea from it, and a hamlet called Romanovka. This probably lay east of the port, since the west was a long string of shack-like seaside villas where the middle class lay 'on couches in their white socks' under the sky. The Pasternaks had a kitchen and two little rooms, approached by a rickety wooden staircase in the open air. There were no servants of course, and Mrs Pasternak baked her own bread. Leonid's sharpest memories were of falling downstairs, which he did quite often, and of the glamorous smell of an Odessa fair, a peculiar compound of honey-cakes, fresh leather boots and sheepskin jackets. He remembered the gypsies making camp, and a wonderful cake shop where Osip Pasternak commissioned an awe-inspiring confection for a government official, who was probably their landlord, but on the whole 'my father accustomed us to a simple, severe, joyless way of life from our childhood. As he used to say to himself, the purpose of our upbringing was to accustom us to misfortune; we were to depend on nobody and nothing, we were never to be in debt. . . . We never had any fun.'

Yet the courtyard itself seems extraordinary. Opposite the gateway stood a hut between stables, where some hysterical cocks and hens lived, cocks on the stove and hens underneath, like the little Pasternaks in their mother's kitchen. In the next-door rooms lived two half-mad drunken brothers who had once owned the entire establishment. The yard was full of the carts and oxen and horses of the peasants, except at times like Christmas and Easter, when it would stand empty and a little eerie. Osip Pasternak rented 'the courtyard with corner wing, which had eight numbered rooms for small landowners who would arrive in their huge unwieldy carriages and tarantasses straight out of Gogol.' A *tarantass* is defined as a roofless, seatless, springless, semi-cylindrical tumbril. It is what the Pasternaks used to go to the fair in Odessa: they were too excited to mind about the bumps. The dung in the yard was cut into bricks and piled in pyramids to dry. That is where the children played Cossacks and Robbers.

Leonid remembered the two drunken brothers as hardly emerging from their squalid den; he says they never cooked and never ate, only drank. The truth is that, although the world he describes may be less exciting and less action-packed than the Moldavanka district of Isaac Babel, it is surely as low, and similar in its social construction. Ephraim Rook the carter, who crashed out at night under his cart, and Benya Krik the drayman's son would have recognised Gryuzdov's house. Mendel Krik the drayman was more brutal than Osip Pasternak's clients perhaps, and Babel wrote about him with the wide-eyed wonder of a middle-class boy 'with spectacles on his nose and autumn in his heart', but Osip knew such people.

The chief difference is that the Pasternaks were good Jews, and going up in the world, though by steps almost too small to discern, while those Babel describes, even aside from his touches of Damon Runyon, were stuck at something below working-class level. Yet one can learn a lot from Babel. His Lyubka keeps an inn. 'Wild peasants from Nerubaysk and Tatarka crawled under their wagons and fell into a wild and loud-echoing slumber. A drunken apprentice staggered to the gate. Wrinkled German colonists who brought wine from the Bessarabian border lit their pipes, and the smoke-rings from their bent stems began to grope their way through the silvery bristles on elderly and unshaven cheeks.' One has the sense of a great seaport: the mate of an English ship with smuggled silk, tobacco and cigars from Aden, the news of prices at Constantinople, olive oil from Marseille, coffee beans, Malaga from Lisbon, French sardines, the new tea from Dutch steamers, the ships that crowded the bay. It was a city that no one forgot. When Leonid Pasternak, as a married man in his forties, at last saw Venice, with the boats swaying offshore, the first word he said was 'Odessa'.

If I have dwelt rather long on Odessa, which to me is naturally mysterious, and which was doubtless changing in the late nineteenth century as fast as our world is changing now, I have done so because 'Life, like autumn silence, is always deep in detail', as the poet says somewhere. Leonid Pasternak's ideal as a painter was to be 'laconic . . . fresh . . . incisive', which has something in common with his son's different achievement. And it may be that Leonid's rise to fame was possible only in Russia, and only from a bubbling cauldron like Odessa. Russia has been intent on modernising herself since 1700, though often with one step forward and two steps back.

The Pasternak family in Leonid's and Asya's generation, in Boris's and Sasha's generation, and down to this day, has been drawn into that process and has even flourished by it. Let a small example serve. To the poet's brother Sasha, the early Odessan aeronaut S. I. Utochkin (1874–1916), who flew from Moscow to Petersburg in 1911, remained a hero of modernity for ever (though Babel recorded of him that he was out of his mind and wrecked by cocaine or morphine, after a crash in Novgorod province), and this enthusiasm for the air, which Sasha picked up from his motor-cycling Freidenberg cousin Alexander, can be traced to an earlier generation, when Michael Freidenberg flew a balloon over Odessa market. Leonid painted the posters, and his sister Asya was in charge of the tickets. That sort of thing is how the modern world really began. Young Freidenberg was a close, early friend of Leonid Pasternak and married his sister Asya, although Osip disapproved of his wildness; and he was a success in Petersburg as Pasternak was in Moscow. His son Alexander was Sasha Pasternak's friend on the summer holiday beaches of Odessa, and his academic daughter Olga's correspondence with Boris is often the fullest and most reliable witness we have to the poet's life.

Leonid's emergence into the light appears startling and spasmodic because his memoirs are so fragmentary, but its graph is regular enough. He drew and painted as a child in spite of opposition, and his first patron was a yard-keeper who gave him five kopeks for a hare hunt with borzois. The yard was a teeming, swarming place that overflowed with life and stank of manure; only the little Pasternak flat was an oasis of severe order. To the end of his life he could smell the horse harness and tar, and hear the lowing of oxen and the snorting and neighing of horses, with the penetrating shouts of human quarrels. Leonid's drawing was noticed at primary school, and became notorious at the Richelieu High School, where it took a satiric turn. This school took some boarders, including landowners' children who were older than the other boys and disinclined to learn; one of them was still sitting among the children at twenty. Leonid rather liked these amiable, Dickensian characters, but he was destined to advancement, and he was transferred to Odessa High School. He appears to have left both his previous schools on his own initiative by playing truant, having hated them for unnamed reasons. But at the third he was taken up by the French master, Liote, who told him of artists and of galleries, and of a painter called Gigout whom he knew at home in Besançon. When Leonid was fifteen, Liote in his uniform brought the Mayor of Odessa, Marazli, to visit him at home.

Michael Freidenberg, 'a young man with intelligent open

features and laughing eyes', who was sub-tenant in one of the Pasternak rooms, got to know the boy and used him for the art magazines he edited, first *The Beacon* (a supplement to the *Odessa Herald*), then *The Little Bee*. He was a friend for life; 'he believed in my natural gift and became the closest of all my friends.' Leonid already showed the bullied boy's passionate hatred of injustice, and a compassionate curiosity about human misery which was essentially visual. Of his mother, the principal quality he observed was her compassion. Later in life, when he met Gorky, he found that Gorky already knew his drawing of a *Bossiak*, a destitute man hanging about the Odessa docks, first published in the *Bee*. His illustration to Tolstoy's *Resurrection*, *After the Flogging*, is a mature and terrible work in the same spirit: the flogged man is half-fainting and Christlike, and even one of the warders is like an old, grieving Jew. His *Wounded Soldier*, a Red Cross poster for the 1914–18 war, was an important and very popular image of a similar figure, gasping against a wall. The Tsar hated it; no soldier of his would stand like that, he said; they would stand at attention. When Serov and Pasternak were famous and established painters, they habitually made savage cartoons which could not be shown or reproduced. Leonid's son Sasha treasured one to the end of his life, of the Grand Duke who commanded Moscow, torn to pieces and carefully put together again.

As a sixth former Leonid received free tuition at the Odessa School of Drawing, which was founded in 1865. His father would not have sent him there, since he was still opposed to his becoming an artist. Indeed, he was always amazed that commercial Odessa should nourish such a place, but that same generation of M. Morandi, architect, patron and director of the School, founded a conservatory and an opera house, and their students in some numbers became artists on at least a national scale, feeding the hungry patronage of Moscow and Petersburg. Diaghilev's discovery of the arts of southern Russia was about to burst on the world. It was all part of the frenzied pace of Russian development. Whatever was not suppressed or persecuted, and a lot that was, grew in profusion with the rise of the great cities and the merchant classes. Leonid's valuable pages on the history of Russian art in his time are as fascinating to read now as the biography of Tolstoy or Chekhov: they are a neglected source, and not only for his own career and his family's history. I think of him as an old man in

Oxford after the grief and turmoil of his life, recording what he remembered, and wandering between the Ashmolean Museum and his house at Park Town, which is still Russian inside the front door. His reputation is only that of a *petit maître*, but it will rise.

He left school in 1881, and to please his parents he entered the medical faculty at Moscow, with the idea of getting into the School of Painting at the same time. But he was too late to register, and the next year the only place went to Countess Tolstoy, so he went to Munich and was taken in there by Yevgraf Sorokin. At Moscow, though he did well at anatomy, he found dissection repulsive, so he transferred to law, but in order to travel abroad he registered for law at Odessa, where travel was permitted, provided he came back annually to pass an examination. In 1885 he graduated, and served his time in the artillery of the Russian army. This was when he met the pianist Rosa Kaufmann, whom he was to marry. They met at the house of a journalist famous for his trenchant, pseudonymous pieces about art and current affairs, a friend of Rosa's Jewish family. After the army, Leonid had his eye on Paris. He had no wish to stand in Rosa's way as a concert pianist, but he was planning a great painting of garrison life; he therefore left her in Odessa and moved to rooms in Moscow. These were in the Lyubyansky Passage, and by no means grand, but there he painted *Letter from Home*, which was bought before it was finished or publicly exhibited by P. M. Tretyakov, the greatest and most discerning patron in Russia, whose monument is the Tretyakov Gallery. His collections cast much light on the art of those times.

Leonid exhibited at the annual Black and White exhibition of the Society of Art-lovers, where his charcoal drawings caused a sensation; the technique was learnt at Munich and rather new to Russia, and his freshness and skill were apparent. S. I. Shchukin (1854–1937) bought the head of an old man and Tretyakov bought a number of drawings. Shchukin turned later to French art, of which he made an important collection. In 1912 he had Matisse come to arrange a 'Matisse gallery' in his house: a large, opulent Edwardian room with stucco Pans on the doorways leering at the obscener works of the master. The other great collector of post-Impressionists was Morozov, a second-generation textile baron who committed suicide, having insured his life for a huge sum to go to the Communist Party through Maxim Gorky. The art world was not a lake without ripples. Leonid Pasternak's friend the painter V. A. Serov had advised these powerful patrons in their early days, but he broke with them. He greatly disliked the Petersburg World of Art (Mir Isskustvo) movement, which promoted French painting from about 1900; he hated Matisse's colour sense; he found cubism hard to swallow. Serov was a brilliant and conscientious painter all the same, and Leonid Pasternak shared his taste and his limitations. By the time Leonid was forty-two, in 1904, the work of his generation was essentially done.

Leonid married Rosa after a year in Moscow, in February 1889. His friendship with Serov, whom he already knew, was cemented by the pre-existing friendship of their wives at the Odessa conservatory. Rosa had been a child genius. She was born in 1867, and according to an account of her youth quoted by her son Sasha from 'a certain Buchman', written in 1885, she was giving concerts at the age of eight and nine, to some acclaim. Her life was in some ways a calamity, but she sustained it with extraordinary fortitude. She was taken up by a distinguished teacher called Tedesco until at thirteen she was noticed by Rubinstein. He toured Russia with her, she played with Sarasate the violinist, but fell violently ill with typhoid before the climax, a solo concert at Petersburg. A year later she was about to begin a foreign tour when the news of Tedesco's death sank her back into illness. From 1883 to 1889 she studied at Vienna, and at that stage she met Leonid. As a married woman she suppressed her art for the sake of his, and herself for the sake of her family. As the children began to grow up, she did play again in public from 1907 to 1911, but then she fell silent, for reasons that we shall see. Sasha Pasternak believed that 1907 and 1908 were his parents' happiest years.

The younger Serovs were important friends and allies with whom Leonid's roots were intertwined. Old Serov had been a composer well known in Odessa, and his wife Vera, whom Leonid met at Munich, wrote an opera, *Uriel Akosta*, of which he specially enjoyed 'the male chorus from the Jewish Synagogue service'. The Serovs were friends of the Wagners; their son, V. A. Serov the painter, told Leonid in later life 'that the only Bayreuth impression to stay in his memory was how he used to ride on Wagner's gigantic St Bernard dog'. V. A. Serov was a pupil of Repin. He lived in Repin's house and was brought up by him when his own father died. It appears that he and Leonid first met in Odessa, where he used to visit his mother's family, whose name was Simonovich; it was in their house that Olga (whom Serov married) was brought up.

Boris Pasternak was born on 29 January 1890 in a flat in Oruzheinyi Lane, a road now scarcely recognisable, because one side of it has been utterly demolished and the other largely rebuilt. What remains of its courtyards gives the impression of a red-brick rabbit warren two or three storeys high. He wrote his prose memoirs three times – once in *Safe Conduct* (1931), dedicated to Rilke and influenced by him; once in his *Essay in Autobiography*, after Stalin's death in 1953, commemorating a number of dead friends; and finally in his *People and Situations*, intended to go with a volume of his poems in 1956, but revised later and printed in the magazine *Novy Mir* seven years after his death, only in 1967. All three of these documents deal with his early life, and they overlap in several areas. His early memories are no doubt an important source of his verse, but by the time he recorded them formally they were distinctly malleable, not to say mythologised. His brother Sasha was three years younger, and wrote with a younger brother's emphasis and the slightly different viewpoint created by the three years' gap. They grew up as a tightly knit family, with plenty of room by modern Moscow standards, but in cramped conditions by the standards of professional families of the day.

Boris recalled the district around Oruzheinyi Lane as 'rather disreputable', and later 'most disreputable'. It included such slums as Tverskie and Yamskie Streets, the Truba, and the Tsvernoi Lanes. It is now ordinary and looks middle class, but it is easy to believe him. At midday the mounted police recruits drilled in front of the Znamensky Barracks. What he remembered best was the stuffed bears in the coachmakers' window, the sodden footpaths heaped with fallen leaves in the seminary park, the fights and games of the seminarians in their hours of recreation, and the vaulted archway under his family's flat that led to a courtyard of horse-cabs. It all sounds normal enough, and much like some Paris equivalent, except perhaps for the seminary, which has left no trace. But he writes that 'as a result of all this rubbing shoulders with beggars and pilgrims, and of nearness to the world of the rejected and of listening to their stories of troubles and hysterics, I was filled too early and for life with a compassion for women, and a still more anguished pity for my parents who would die before me'. The condition is clearly real, but they left that district when he was three, and the symptoms he describes are not abnormal for a sensitive elder son in a Jewish family; they need not be the result of the terrifying life of the streets. The most comfortable of his early memories was of a kindly, shaggy, stooping giant, the publisher Konchalovsky, and the sketches on the walls of his flat, by Serov and Vrubel and his own father. The truth is that he was born on the edge of a ring of boulevards that encircle central Moscow, only a mile or two from the Kremlin; Tverskie and Yamskie lie a little further out and seem to have been a red-light district.

His father prospered, old Gué called him his successor, and he became a professor. When Boris was three and Sasha was born they all moved to an official flat in Myasnitskaya Street (now Sergei Kirov), opposite the General Post Office, then a beautiful old building which had survived the great fire during Napoleon's occupation of Moscow in 1812, though today it looks modern and humdrum enough. Not far away the Malakov tower still stands, a rococo church tower painted pink and gracefully ornamented with white stucco angels, unique in the beautiful awkwardness of its ornamentation. It was probably near here, in the small church of St Florus and St Laurus, that the poet's nanny, who was called Akulina Gavrilovna, had him baptised. No one seems to have noticed particularly, and she was a simple Christian country girl who thought it no harm. People used to make a mystery of this event, but there is no doubt that it happened. The poet spoke about it in later life. She used to sing over him as a child:

> Sleep baby, sleep darling
> when you grow you shall sleep,
> and your daddy will paint no more,
> he'll hire men for his painting,
> sleep baby, sleep darling.

The church of St Florus and St Laurus was separated from the School of Arts only by a winding lane. It has gone now, and left only an empty parking lot. The School of Arts is dusty and locked up with padlocks, but it is now exposed on two sides as if it stood at the head of the street. A seventeenth-century watercolour reveals the vanished church as an undistinguished building, but a four-square fortress with three windmill-shaped domes once stood behind it: presumably a fortified monastery. The ancient gate called Myasnitskaya stood at the head of the street, which is still the most surprising series of art nouveau buildings I have ever encountered. Next to the School of Arts is an old tea warehouse, embellished from top to toe in a Chinese style. In any other city in the world it would be a place of pilgrimage; John Betjeman would have raved about it. The School of Arts itself is adorned with no news of Pasternak but has a banal bronze relief of a bearded artist called Aleksei Savrasov. As a building it remains imposing, with a pillared semicircular balcony on the corner, and tall blank windows behind which the Pasternaks had their flat. On pavement level at one side some huge old windows mark the position of what was once Prince Trubetskoy's sculpture studio.

Leonid Pasternak worshipped and loved Tolstoy. Just before Easter in 1893, he met the great old man in the School of Arts where he was soon to teach, at an exhibition of the important group called the Wanderers, after their travelling exhibitions. It was a blazing bright day in early spring when the sun was hot and the air still snowcooled, an air thrilling with energy and hope, in which you could see the glint of a gilded onion-dome five or ten miles away as the sun rose. The paintings were being uncrated and hung, venerable old painters from Petersburg were striding about in their fur coats, the noise was formidable. Leonid's *Débutante* was in position and he was hanging about timidly on the sidelines. The old painter Savitsky, who knew Pasternak had already been working for a magazine on some new illustrations for *War and Peace*, offered to introduce him. His agony of shyness is sharply registered in pages he wrote forty years later. Tolstoy came gliding along in his grey peasant shirt, hands stuffed into his belt, and to the young painter's amazement, when Savitsky mentioned his name in front of the *Débutante*, Tolstoy interrupted: 'Yes. Yes, I know the name. I have been following his work.' He knew the *Letter from Home* and some drawings; Pasternak was invited to tea on Friday with his unpublished drawings for *War and Peace*.

So he presented himself at the suburb of Khamovniky, up the broad stairs (felt-covered to mask the noise of children sliding on tin trays) and past the cuckoo clock and the big white bust of Antinous with its hyacinthine hair and mesmerised eyes, to the large drawing-room, the only good room in the house. When the old man saw the drawings, he called to his daughter Tatyana to come quickly. She was a painter, a pupil of Repin. 'This is such a strange thing,' he said. 'They bring the squirrel nuts when it's lost its teeth. When I wrote *War and Peace* I dreamed of illustrations like this. It's wonderful, just wonderful.' 'Many times,' writes Leonid, 'I have heard this word on his lips and to this day it is fresh in my memory, and I can still hear that special Tolstoyan *Wonderful.*' They became friends and intimates. He went often to Yasnaya Polyana, painted and drew Tolstoy many times, made a bust of him, was drawn by him, drew a conversation piece of 'the serious corner' of his living-room in the country (the children's corner has less club-like furniture) and illustrated *Resurrection* as it was written, with all the excitement that implies.

Over the *Resurrection* illustrations we must pause. But before we discuss them comes Boris Pasternak's earliest clear memory. In November 1894 he woke crying to the sound of music which for some reason upset him. 'Late in the night I was aroused by such a sweet, nostalgic torment as I had not experienced in the same degree before. . . . The music drowned my cries and it was not until the end of the movement that anyone heard me. Then the curtain that divided the room in two was pushed aside. My mother came in and calmed me down. She may have carried me into the drawing room or perhaps I only saw it through the open door. The air was filled with cigarette smoke; the candles blinked as if it stung their eyes.' His mother was playing a trio by Tchaikovsky, *For a Dead Artist*, with a cellist and a violinist from the Conservatory, for a little crowd of ladies, who 'leaned out of their shoulder-high dresses like flowers out of flower-baskets', and gentlemen in frock-coats. Gué was there, but the principal guest was Tolstoy. It is probable that he knew the secret of Tchaikovsky's suicide.

Boris Pasternak was used to the piano, 'but the voices of strings, particularly strings combined in chamber music, were unfamiliar and as disturbing as real voices.' He remembers what the music was, and realises that Tchaikovsky had died in November the year before, and Anton Rubinstein that year. What he fails to recall and possibly never knew is that his father recorded the concert as he listened to it, in one of his most brilliant coloured sketches. The lamplight is not the general glow of the electrified twentieth century, but a sharper and more individual beam, as it so often is in his drawings. He discerns only the expressive figures of the soloists in action, the vaguer bulk of the piano, and, unmistakably but almost in shadow, the bearded figure of Tolstoy. The sketch is dated 22 November 1894, and appears to have been given to Tolstoy immediately, so it is not the sketch that Boris is remembering so long afterwards. That is now in the Tolstoy literary museum in Kropotkin Street, where Sophia Andreevna, Tolstoy's granddaughter and the poet's friend Yesenin's widow, was director for many years until her death in 1959. The Tchaikovsky trio symbolises a great deal for the Pasternak family: his mother began to play again in public, but after playing this music at a memorial concert for Tolstoy on the first anniversary of his death she never played in public again. It was a poignant introduction of the theme of death, and if there is such a thing as a calling to be a poet or an artist, I think that Boris Pasternak dated it to that night of the concert when Tolstoy came to their house.

The *Resurrection* illustrations, which he certainly knew well and admired all his life, present a stranger entanglement with the past. From his earliest prose notes towards fiction, which were written in boyhood, one of Boris Pasternak's themes is railway trains, the moving lights and the clouds of steam. The death of Zhivago and the tram are a late variation on it, and a tram that falls silent, abandoned by its driver in a revolution, is the ominous end of his brother Sasha's autobiograqphy, *A Vanishing Present*. (The book had been longer but its original ending was censored.) One of Leonid's drawings for *Resurrection* shows Katiushka in clouds of steam running after the train. In the scene in church a child in a sailor suit and a woman like Boris Pasternak's nanny hold candles. 'A candle burns, only a candle burns'? I believe that the flogged man is Christlike, with an implication of the 'fool of God' who figures in Orthodox Russian mysticism and who Russians suggest provides at least a component of Zhivago himself. These suggestions are as uncertain as the flicker of candlelight, yet I did find the *Resurrection* drawings highly suggestive of the poet's work, as well as of Tolstoy's. There is also a charming portrait of Tolstoy's family (1902–3), commissioned by a foreign publisher but retained by the Grand Duke Aleksei, the Tsar's brother and the School's patron. And there is a remarkable self-portrait of Leonid that belonged to Tolstoy. It is as wholly un-Jewish as Pushkin's neoclassic self-portrait is un-Negroid. Yet Leonid painted a splendid rabbi or cantor in oils as late as 1909.

The children were brought up with the smell of oil paint and turpentine, and they were constantly being sketched. One forgets how much of the experience of childhood is glimpsed through a window. In Moscow the windows were double and tightly sealed for the winter. The first lighting of fires in the stoves and testing of chimneys in autumn was a ritual; so was the getting of fur coats and hats and boots out of their mothballs. Below the windows, history passed by: the funeral procession of Alexander III in 1894 with the tolling of the bells of three or four hundred churches, and the coronation celebrations for Nicholas II in 1896. There were more ordinary rituals: the uncrating of paintings in the spring, the blessing of horses in Yushkov Lane beside the church of St Florus and St Laurus every autumn, the elaborate checking of clean laundry, and the ritual of tutors and lessons. Boris was taught in German at first, because he was supposed to go to the Peter and Paul Gymnasium, which was attached to the Lutheran Church and attended by Jews as well as Russians and the German children for whom it was founded. But on the whole the family lived and entertained in cheerful, Bohemian confusion, and day by day, hour by hour, there was music. The children's favourite games were exhibitions of art, Chemists and Doctors, and the illustration of one another's stories. Out of doors the whole of Moscow resounded to the yells of Cossacks and Robbers.

The courtyard of the School of Arts was still a large garden fringed with poplars: it was part of one of those old Moscow estates which in the eighteenth century had market gardens, stables, outbuildings, fishponds and more servants than one can imagine, each with a specialised job and a place to do it. The School had been set up in 1832 and, as a college in 1843, amalgamated with a college of architecture in 1863; by 1900 it was short of funds, building in its own garden, letting flats and contriving cast galleries and exhibition halls. To the children this meant the ruination of their playground, and Sasha in particular records it in sad detail. In *Spektorsky* it enters recognisably though confusedly into poetry. Moscow had got through the middle nineteenth century with a population of well under 400,000, and what was happening now was part of its expansion. There were fifteenth-century palaces in the Kremlin, but until about 1900 there was almost no residential building above two or three storeys, and this includes hotels. By 1906 one could telephone, and earlier still one could switch on an electric light.

It is hard to take Boris Pasternak's earliest memories of women literally as a record, though it is true that Tverskie-Yamskie, which means Tver coach service streets, was a district containing entire streets of brothels. But at the age of eleven, in 1901, he was taken to the circus, where he saw a procession of ladies from Dahomey, and got his first clear impression of what women look like: 'sealed in by suffering and a tropical drum parade'. He was steadily growing up. When he was ten, travelling south in the heat of the summer with his father from the Kursk station towards Odessa on the line that passes through Tula junction a few miles from Yasnaya Polyana, they met a stranger anxious to stop at Tolstoy's special halt. This turned out to be the young Rilke, passionately in love with Russia and all things Russian, travelling with Nietzsche's old mistress Lou Salomé to visit the old man. Trains would drive slowly to let the passengers watch Tolstoy haymaking in the fields, but he appeared less in Moscow now, being too old and for political reasons too famous and too popular. In itself the tiny incident of the foreigner in the hot carriage means little enough, because Leonid Pasternak went everywhere and knew everybody, but in retrospect it became important. Boris was overwhelmed with gratitude to Rilke and for Rilke's influence in later life. He translated six or ten poems by him: Christopher Barnes has written a thesis about this relationship and Zhenya Yevtushenko believes their styles are oddly close. There is no doubt that Rilke stimulated him as a youth, but I think having met a famous foreign poet was part of that enchantment. 'Although I knew the language perfectly, I had never heard it spoken as he spoke it.'

In 1901 Boris entered the Moscow Fifth Gymnasium in the second year. He became crazy about botany and botanical names; even at games of Chemists and Doctors with Sasha he had specialised in Latin mumbo-jumbo names for drugs. At school he learnt a little Greek. Sasha followed him to the same school, in Povarskaya Street, a few steps from Arbat Square. The school, or rather its less élitist successor, is still there. A few houses away stood a building where the first Moscow Soviet met in the 1905 revolution. The poet Mayakovsky, who even as a schoolboy was a one-man revolution, was in the same class as Sasha; Boris knew him only by sight at that time. Boris was awkward in movement, and distinctly rebellious in temperament; 'he seldom took part in pranks,' says Karlov, his schoolmaster, 'but always joined in if they were threatened with punishment.' He was industrious, but more careless than accurate, and Karlov observes that the parting of his raven-black hair was never straight. His walk to school was right through the centre of Moscow, skirting Red Square and the Kremlin, past the old university and several other buildings of extraordinary splendour. In winter the coaches ran silently, and snow and fur coats diminished the roads to one-third of their summer width. In spring in those days the icebergs roared and smashed on the Moscow river. Little Sasha found a secret place to watch them from a bridge.

In 1903 Leonid Pasternak took a country cottage from May to August, the Russian school holidays, near Maloyaroslavets on the Bryansk railway (now called the Kiev line), on the estate called Obolenskoye after its Obolensky owners. No great house stood there, no church, no farms, only three cottages on a wooded hill, and the railway halt, writes Sasha, 'used only by holiday people and goods trains: big trains scornfully snorted through, enveloping the platform in steam and dust.' The old park was overgrown with pine trees. The railway crossed a small, clear river called the Puddle on an iron bridge with brick piers; beyond it you could see a village or two and some biggish houses. The Pasternaks once saw an accident there that held up an express for hours; Boris used that and the landscape for the suicide in *Dr Zhivago*.

Boris was collecting a herbarium for his holiday task, and Sasha, who was only ten, was trailing along behind him, doing the same. According to Boris, they just strolled across to the next cottage, where Scriabin happened to be staying, but Sasha insists convincingly that they were playing Red Indians. 'If it was very hot we stayed in the forest. Prowling in a new direction through the undergrowth one day, on the trail of nothing in particular, the silence only intensified by squirrel chatter and the rare chirp of a bird, we suddenly heard a snatch of piano-playing far away. . . . We wriggled towards it with hardly a sound. At the forest crest our way was barred by an abandoned shrubbery, impenetrably overgrown: in a sunlit grassy plot beyond stood a dacha like our own.' The children made a hide, and Boris observed at once that whoever it was must be composing at the piano, not just playing. It was Scriabin, composing his *Divine Poem*; soon afterwards their father met him. Boris records only sunlight in the woods, moving shadows, and the twittering and calling of the birds. 'And just as lights and shadows alternated and birds cried and flittered from branch to branch, so fragments from the *Third Symphony* or *Divine Poem*, composed in the next house, carried and resounded through the woods.'

They became close, as holiday families will, and it was under Scriabin's influence that Boris Pasternak decided to become a musician. But in that same summer he had an accident which determined a great deal of his future, since it saved him from two world wars and a revolution, by leaving one of his legs slightly shorter than the other. What happened is simple enough. The veranda of the Pasternaks' cottage looked out far across the water-meadows to a skyline of forest. Leonid Pasternak determined to paint a herd of horses being driven to their night grazing. He saw his picture in epic terms, like the galloping of Scythian hordes. Every night they watched a cavalcade of peasant girls riding bareback on what Sasha somewhat wildly calls 'a herd of unbroken horses'. What Leonid Pasternak intended is no doubt not a million miles from the engraving of a herd of horses with peasants or gypsies by Rosa Bonheur, which hangs to this day in the rather dim place of honour in Scriabin's dining-room.

Boris and Sasha often went with their father to watch and to sketch, and got to know the girls. They wore kerchiefs of red, blue and bright yellow, long plaited hair and very full skirts. 'Everything blazed and billowed in the sun. . . . The last light died.' Boris longed to ride in this romantic cavalcade. Finally he beat down all the arguments raised against this adventure, and the family let him go. Alas, the horses were not led as usual by a girl they knew on a bay mare, but by a black stallion: a horse neighed at it somewhere in the meadows and the whole herd stampeded. The horse Boris was riding began to buck, and of course he fell off. They found him alive and conscious but in a state of shock, feeling no pain. Luckily there was a doctor in the cottage at the time, his leg was set at once and a surgeon fetched the next day. Meanwhile, on that same disastrous holiday, a girl they knew fell into the river, and a student was drowned trying to save her, and she attempted suicide several times by jumping from the same cliff. In the end she went out of her mind. Once, as Leonid drove homewards he saw the red glow and flare of a fire, which he thought was the end of his family.

Fortunately it was not. The worst permanent result, apart from Boris being slightly lamed, a condition that is rather a help than a hindrance to a young poet, was that Leonid's picture was never painted. In the 1920s the brothers found a big brown window-blind, half ripped and half rotten, which had once covered a window at Myasnitskaya Street. It was a pastel sketch of the horses, nearly life-size, abandoned in 1903.

Sasha has a younger brother's stern criticism to make of Boris, however much he loves him. Boris, he writes, was passionately devoted to his father, bitterly resented the fate of 'that unfinished masterpiece', and rightly pointed to his mother as the victim of her family. Sasha was an expert in the sufferings of artists, and a kind and just man whom we should take seriously. 'From his child-hood, my brother was distinguished by an inordinate passion to accomplish things patently beyond his powers, ludicrously in-appropriate to his character and his cast of mind.' Sasha notices that in everything he hated failure. When he was badly beaten at a game he invented, he minded more than most boys would. When a German urchin sneered at him he gave up playing the German. When he found that he lacked perfect pitch in music he dropped his career as a composer like a hot brick. There is a truth in these pointed criticisms, but it is only a truth about adolescence. He was slow to find his true vein, but when in the end he found it he did not hesitate. Hence, so late in the day, *Dr Zhivago*. 'I shall still write my novel, in the twenty-fifth hour of the day.'

From 1903 to 1909, that is from the age of thirteen to nineteen, 'for six years I lived for music'. It was not a passing craze. He could strum and even compose before that summer, but it was Scriabin who awakened his passionate ambition. Scriabin was a diminutive man of thirty-one whose fingers scarcely covered an octave. He had been brought up by aunts and a grandmother, since his father was a diplomat in Turkey, and his mother had died when he was a baby. He had married in 1897, but by 1903 that was going badly. His wife Vera, a pianist, got on well with Mrs Pasternak, while Leonid liked wandering along the old Warsaw road with the composer, whose eccentric walk is variously described as the flapping of a bird and the skimming of a stone. They agreed about almost nothing, since Scriabin was an anti-Tolstoyan who believed in Nietzsche, and at that time was planning *Mysterium*, a philo-sophic opera about his hero which was never finished. In 1905 he took up with Madame Blavatsky. (I was much surprised to be asked by an exquisitely well-dressed young man in the Scriabin Museum whether I had 'any news of English theosophic circles'.) He abandoned his wife and four young children for an admirer who was the niece of her piano professor, and by 1909 was composing his *Prometheus* for performance with a display of synaesthetic colours, though it was performed without them in Moscow in 1911. His development from the charming derivative to the powerful progressive was immediate. He believed in the regeneration of the world by cataclysm and saw the 1914–18 war as a step in the right direction. Nirvana would spring from his own Promethean creativity, and would combine all the arts and appeal to all the senses. This preposterous man would seem an alarming influence on any impressionable adolescent, but Rosa and Leonid Pasternak were extremely tolerant people.

Scriabin was absent from Russia for most of Boris Pasternak's affair with modern music. But his personality represents the extraordinary disorder of the arts which was a symptom of the uncontrollable energy of the times, and existed in every direction. Boris Pasternak's generation were extremists. 'More than anything in the world I loved music; more than anyone else in music: Scriabin.' And, in spite of what may be said in his disfavour, Scriabin was a most interesting musician, a pusher-down of boundary fences, a man of swelling imaginative ambition. Apart from one or two queer gadgets, such as a kind of motor tyre of coloured light-bulbs which he got from Cambridge, his Moscow rooms are charming. The house is in a quiet road between the old Arbat and the new, and by no means grandiose. Since these are rooms that Boris Pasternak visited one studies them with interest; they are quiet, darkish and Edwardian in feeling. Scriabin used a standing desk and a shabby old rocking-chair. The piano room had two terrible pictures of naked ladies, one of them 'after Correggio'. He was comfortably off, and commissioned some art nouveau furniture, but the old looks more comfortable. The books are intellectually adventurous and unreadable. It is all perfectly in period and the scale is so modest that the awkward schoolboy visiting the great composer fits in precisely.

Boris neglected his mathematics and his classics to work out fugues under the desk. His class defended him and his teachers did not seem to mind his refusal to extend his natural abilities. He spoke wonderful cooing Russian in a style he probably picked up a little later from the symbolists. He fell in love more than once. Let it be stated once and for all that no biographer has traced all his affairs, and I have no wish to do so. He was intensely emotional and intimately personal in all his dealings with women. He was not exactly flirtatious, because his engagement in their lives was genuine. I used to think that every upheaval of the heart went with a great upheaval of style, and there are some cases of that, but it is not a general truth. I asked his son Zhenya about it, and he answered that his father showed symptoms of love whenever he had time or whenever he was otherwise disengaged, having trained himself to work extremely hard all his life, like an athlete in training. I believe that to be the answer, though not when he was an adolescent. But, once having loved, he seldom, perhaps never, fell out of love, and suffered very much from the resulting complications.

In 1904, in the year he fell for a certain Vera, Russia went to war with Japan. The conflict, which at first sight appeared a remote imperial squabble, marked the serious emergence of Japan into the modern world and set in motion a train of events which led to the Tsar's death and the revolution. In 1894 the Japanese claimed a war indemnity of £25 million from China. They also took Port Arthur from China fearing that the weakness of Korea might otherwise attract the western imperial powers. Russia, Germany and France mobilised their navies and forced the Japanese to withdraw, with another £5 million from China as a consolation. But the Japanese were enraged, and spent their money on a brand new navy which they bought from English shipyards. In 1898 the Russians leased Port Arthur from China, thus acquiring an ice-free naval base. Two years later they occupied Manchuria on the occasion of the Boxer rebellion. In 1902 they refused to withdraw; they were protecting their new Trans-Siberian railway, which still takes five days from Moscow and is one of the wonders of the world. They put troops into Korea and traded actively. One must remember that transport from Kamchatka (for example) was still by sleigh and teams of twenty or thirty dogs. In February 1904 the Japanese opened hostilities by bombarding the Russians in harbour at Port Arthur.

The war took an idiotic course. The Russians lost every battle, and fell back steadily through Manchuria, but their army was never destroyed. The Japanese were better at almost everything, but they ran out of men and money.

Meanwhile the Russian Baltic fleet sailed 20,000 miles to the relief of Port Arthur. They were overloaded, and lost in a haze of coaldust. At the Dogger Bank they mistook Hull trawlers for Japanese torpedo-boats. There were constant breakdowns and near collisions. At Tangier they cut the French telephone cable with an anchor. By the time they got to Madagascar Port Arthur had fallen. The mixture of tropical heat and Marxist ships' libraries produced a rash of mutinies. After seven months they arrived at Tsushima Strait, where they were blown out of the water by Admiral Togo. America arranged the peace conference, the principal fruit of which was that the Japanese decided that their true enemies were not the Russians really but the Americans. A few days after a treaty was signed, Togo's flagship mysteriously blew up at anchor.

In Russia the repercussions were more severe. The revolution of 1905 led to the two revolutions of 1917, and the starvation, pestilence and civil war that followed. It is interesting that Lenin attributed the 1905 revolution in Russia largely to the influence of Tolstoy, and its failure largely to the same influence. Tolstoy's opposition to the war had been implacable, though he owned in private to a flicker of patriotism which made him grieve for the fall of Port Arthur to the Japanese. Publicly, he wrote, 'I am neither for Russia nor for Japan but for the workers of both countries who are deceived by their governments and made to take part in a war which is against their well-being, against their conscience, and against their religion.' His ideas pervaded the Moscow atmosphere as if they had been practicable: he appeared to be neither for nor against revolution, owning only to an old sage yearning for the kingdom of God on earth, and yet he was part of its process. Lenin's article, 'Leo Tolstoy as the Mirror of the Russian Revolution' (September 1908) criticises him powerfully, yet at the same time justifiably claims him as a John the Baptist.

For Boris Pasternak the dramatic events of 1905 were deeply formative; he sees them clearly as a poet, secondly in retrospect in his personal memoirs, and lastly, in the second chapter of *Dr Zhivago*, as a novelist. Since there is some danger of confusing fact with fiction and poetry, it is important to notice the order in which things happened before returning our attention to the Pasternak family. The background to the revolution is best understood through the lavish and interesting exhibition at the Museum of the 1905 Revolution in the Presnya district of Moscow, an old working-class area of terrible textile mills (crowded dormitories and a thirteen-hour day) and furniture factories. A few hovels and some old people survive to bear witness to what the district must once have been; in the museum you learn enough to last you a lifetime about whips and fetters and weapons and the youth and innocence of the early Marxists.

On 9 January 1905 Father Gapon led a crowd of thousands carrying icons but no political placards to beg for relief from the Tsar, who ordered his Cossacks to open fire on them. A year of strikes and mutinies followed. The Grand Duke Nikolai was appointed military dictator, though it was obvious he could do nothing; Russia became a constitutional monarchy, but a century too late. The Grand Duke Sergei, patron of the School of Arts, was assassinated at the gates of the Kremlin in February. In late summer the new battleship *Potemkin* mutinied off Odessa: Petty Officer Matushenko, one of its leaders, fled abroad, but he was tempted back to Russia in 1907 and promptly hanged. Father Gapon was hanged as a spy by Social Revolutionaries in Finland in 1906. A large part of the Bolshevik leadership at this time were *agents provocateurs* employed by the government. In June at Lodz, which lay within the Russian empire, railway and textile workers mounted an armed rebellion. In October a railway strike led to a general strike in Russia. At Moscow in October the funeral of Baumann, a student revolutionary, drew crowds of many thousands. On 9 December the government had the Fiedler Technical Institute bombarded with artillery, since it was used as a drill-hall and assembly place by the students. Finally, on the 10th the district of Presnya barricaded itself against cavalry, and held out against the army for a week. The barricades, some of which were photographed, were pitiful but effective. Water was constantly poured over them so that they became smooth walls of ice. One on the crest of a hump-back bridge (now rebuilt as a monument) was held against dragoons. The end came with a serious artillery barrage starting at four in the morning. Most of the district was levelled to the ground, and the massacre that followed was merciless.

Sasha Pasternak was eleven, but his memory is very clear, and he is an excellent witness to feelings. All through the autumn of 1904 strikes had increased and become more threatening, until the climax of Bloody Sunday, 9 January 1905. The people sang psalms and went to the Tsar as their father and their patriarch, led by Father Gapon, 'the Tsar's secret agent and *agent provocateur*, as it later turned out'. Schoolchildren of Sasha's age became immediate supporters of some kind of revolution, those of Boris's age more so. One day in February, the family were deep in breakfast conversation about the perfect forms of nature and the lines of beauty and art, and Sasha was watching the ribbed dome of the Polish cathedral, as it kindled with rose-coloured light against the rising of the winter sun. There was an almighty bang, which Leonid, having served in the artillery, knew was an explosion and not a gunshot. That was the death of the Grand Duke in the gateway of the Kremlin. The strikes got worse and so did the repression. The schoolboys were in turmoil; little Sasha spent hours copying out Social Democrat pamphlets by hand for secret distribution by an old friend of his mother's. She was caught and exiled, bequeathing to Sasha a typewriter so primitive that it was quicker to copy by hand. This dangerous instrument of revolution was promptly hidden by his mother, and never came to light again.

For the summer of 1905 they all went to an estate at Safontyevo, where the landowner foresaw a confrontation with the villagers, and pointed (to their surprise) to his rifles and his revolver. 'In Moscow they hadn't dreamt of such things', and Sasha's mother still wandered placidly through the village, doing good as usual. The landowner was a lawyer; he returned early to Moscow and tried hard to make Leonid take over his rifles. He did insist on leaving him the revolver and some ammunition. Leonid shot a crow with it in the woods with his boys; then they slunk guiltily home. In September in Moscow the pace increased. Children had imitation revolvers, but students, many of whom of course the Pasternak family knew and liked, had real ones: they took lessons in shooting and the manufacture of bombs. The Fiedler students were joined at their secret meetings by 'booted workers in grubby jackets', and later still by soldiers, 'their arms laid aside'. Sasha and Boris were thrilled to be in on the secret. By the end of September you heard occasional shooting, 'like the rattle of dried peas'.

On 17 October a proclamation from the Tsar was issued, an unlikely document part imperial and part forward-looking, which convinced nobody; the very next day Baumann of the Fiedler

Institute was shot dead at a meeting devoted to reading it. He was buried on 30 October. The whole of the Pasternak family and the whole staff crowded the balcony of the School of Arts, as the funeral passed down Myasnitskaya, ten abreast, for hour after hour. Sometimes they sang the Requiescat, sometimes a revolutionary hymn about those who fell as martyrs. At the head of the procession came the coffin, carried by men, ahead of that a gun-carriage strewing fir branches now and then under their feet, and in the very front no priest and no icon, but a man in black, waving a palm-branch in time with the steps of the crowd. As the crowd returned in groups the way it had come, they were attacked with sticks, whips and gunshots. The head of the School of Arts, Prince Lvov, had a barricade built in the main hall; there might well have been a pogrom. One of Leonid's notes for a drawing recorded a wounded girl on the balcony, leaning on a pillar and speaking to the crowd in the street. Dragoons are charging the crowd and shooting at the girl.

Leonid was in touch with Gorky at this time about new satirical magazines. I do not know when the incident of the wounded girl happened, except that Boris and Sasha were kept out of the way. Boris says the university and higher technical schools were looted, stones and hoses were made ready to defend the School of Arts, and 'every now and then' a crowd would enter it from the street to hold meetings; speakers would address overflow meetings from the balcony. At night the School's private guard kept watch. One night Boris disappeared for so long that his father was setting out to look for him when suddenly he arrived, utterly bedraggled but beaming with pride and happiness. He had met a crowd running away from a mounted patrol, got caught against a fence and whipped around the head and shoulders by a dragoon. Meanwhile the School's stokers had gone off to a meeting and a pipe had burst and made a skating rink of the Pasternaks' flat, the only rooms still inhabited. Boris and Sasha had two sisters, Josephine and Lydia. Lydia, the last and youngest child who was only three, became seriously ill. As Boris records his memory of Moscow in that month, 'Stray bullets whistled down the empty streets, and mounted patrols charged with soundless fury over the untrodden snow.'

The School was shut, but there was a general rail strike and anyway it was impossible to leave. The family doctor was luckily cut off from home in their flat, so he could concentrate on Lydia, who had double pneumonia. Five days before the crisis, which she passed with the doctor's help and some spoonfuls of champagne, the Governor-General had threatened to bombard the School and reduce it to ashes as the Fiedler Institute had been reduced. Prince Lvov consulted Leonid, but the threat did not materialise because the revolutionaries, realising their whereabouts were known, simply flitted in the night. Sasha is unable to distinguish one night with its frightful noises from another; we know only that the general strike went on formally until 1 January 1906, and that by then the Pasternak family had left Moscow by rail for Berlin. Leonid had an exhibition there in the spring of 1906.

Boris had already been to Petersburg on his own, perhaps the previous winter (his brother doubts the date). One of his mother's sisters was married to the head of the goods station there on the Nikolayevsky line, which had served Moscow since the 1850s, so Boris had travelled with a warrant to a city that was a 'stone book', as he said. 'For days on end I wandered about the streets of the immortal city, as though with feet and eyes I was devouring a magnificent stone book.' He spent evenings in the theatre and he was intoxicated with the newest books. He read the early works of Hamsun, who was the rage, and Polish novels, and the Russian symbolist Beliy, and he saw some Chekhov. He was growing up so fast that it is hard to keep track of him, because everything was happening at once. It was through this railway uncle that he got to know the railwaymen of the Brest station at Moscow. He told stories about them to Ida Vysotskaya, a childhood girlfriend; he was physically excited by the railway trains of those days, and his friends the railwaymen figure of course in *Dr Zhivago*. To this day Russia depends more on railways than on roads, which can be hazardous. In 1906 a first-class carriage had not only its samovar and its restaurant car but its piano, its library and its bathrooms, all of which are recorded by Maurice Baring, who just at this time travelled backwards and forwards between Moscow and Petersburg for a week third-class, to see what people thought about the revolution. The Pasternak family attitude speaks for itself: they were Tolstoyan pacifists, though removing themselves to another country may be a particularly Jewish reaction. They had a cousin in Vienna and no doubt others further afield. Berlin was full of both Russians and Jews in 1906.

For the children Berlin was an adventure, of which Sasha Pasternak is the fullest chronicler, as indeed he is of all the excitements of childhood, small and great, from magic lanterns and the waterfalls of the thawing gutters to revolution itself. His being three years younger is an advantage here, and his un-disturbed recollection of the eyesight of childhood, which Boris shared but exhausted in his comparatively early works, was entirely expended on his memoirs. It is typical that Sasha's chapter 'A Year in Berlin' begins with a section in the Old Coriander Shop. Not a piece of fruit or a nuance of smell escapes him; it has all been hoarded for sixty years.

The Berlin train was a sober brown, standing in mist and clouds of steam, but travelling fast, with its windows frosted over. From a city of paraffin lamps, just transformed into bulbs called 'pears' of twenty-five candle power, they were suddenly transferred to full electricity, slot-machines for cigars and cheap scent and sugared almonds, mechanical luggage lifts and motor cars. Even in 1921 the vacuum cleaners and gas cookers of Berlin were new to the Pasternaks. It was a contrast that makes some sense of Lenin's formula hatched in Switzerland, 'socialism and the electrification of Russia'. Moscow seems to have had no intervening period of gaslights as Berlin and London had.

Boris describes more than he can have seen at the time, since the frost was thick on the windows. Even Sasha's imagination was dazed. 'With strident icy wheels, like some dragon, a Fafner of Wagnerian opera breathing clouds of steam, smoke and freezing mist, our hot-bellied, frost-whitened train crawled slowly under the vast roof of the station. It was already getting dark. Lamps were coming on, and their deathly yellowish-green light seemed to make the icy air still colder'. The boys were at first scornful, then amazed at portable fires in their hotel rooms. They moved to a boarding house, then the boys alone moved to a little ground-floor room in a fruit shop round the corner. They called it the Old Coriander Shop in memory of Dickens and his Curiosity Shop. It was the last paradise of their boyhood; Sasha sometimes served behind the counter, and Boris taught music to his landlady's daughter. But in Berlin Boris became at last the elder brother, the gap between sixteen and thirteen is final, and they were no longer equals, no longer just a couple of little boys.

Boris was dominated by Wagner. He hated his exercises and

lacked technical skill; he improvised, seeing himself as a composer. The sound of his improvisations distressed his little sisters. He had been taking lessons in theory and harmony from Y. D. Engel, who was well known in Moscow as a critic and a composer. Engel was not an easy master, and music was a fearful obstacle course for the boy. In Berlin he got his own copy of a fat tome on theory by Riemann, and continued his demanding lessons by post. Sasha found the travails and throes of composition a bit difficult to live with, while the landlady's daughter had to bear the brunt of Boris's new-found learning. He liked the solo piano but disliked trios and quartets and stringed instruments. The two of them went to a lot of symphony concerts, usually in the morning: Beethoven, Brahms, Wagner overtures and Richard Strauss. They also went to churches to hear the organists practising Bach.

By the end of their time in Berlin, Sasha thinks no earlier, Boris was becoming excited by poetry, both in German and in Russian. That is quite normal at the age of sixteen, but of course whatever we can learn of the poets he preferred is important. It is also important that he was a reader then, not a writer. Boris never collected books: on the whole he read them and simply dropped them. The books so carefully recorded by his visitors late in his life were mostly recent gifts from publishers and well-wishers. The only books he was careful to bring home from Berlin were a herbarium and some palaeontology, and the only book he is known to have treasured for most of his life was a small cheap edition of Blok. But in Berlin it was mostly prose that delighted him, and Hoffmann's stories overshadowed his own early prose. Indeed, the influence of their laboured over-brilliance and intensely 'artistic' style makes early Pasternak extremely difficult to read, as later in life he came to see.

It is hard to expect any other beginning of a writer of his generation. What was his experience of life, after all? Mostly of symbolist writers both in prose and in verse, or such painters as his father's pupil Larionov, in the forefront of the avant-garde in a stiff, winged collar. He was enormously impressed by the aged, grieving, passionate Tolstoy, but Tolstoy was an old man of peculiar opinions and his father's god. In later life Boris sought and obtained at times the approbation of Gorky, but Gorky was often absent, and his approbation was a kind of pressure which Boris Pasternak on the whole did well to resist. The adolescent Boris was

TOP LEFT: Leonid Pasternak's drawing of the composer Scriabin
BELOW LEFT: One of Leonid Pasternak's sketches of Leo Tolstoy in old age

TOP RIGHT: Leonid Pasternak's romantic picture of the poet Rilke
BELOW RIGHT: Leonid Pasternak's drawing of Professor Cohen of Marburg

a natural victim of writers like Hoffmann and Kleist and of a musician like Scriabin. This vulnerability to the influence of his day is part of his talent because it is part of his ambition. Greatness, which as a writer he achieved abundantly, was a very slow growth.

Blok is another matter. 'Blok was part of my youth, as of the youth of others of my generation. . . . He had all the qualities which go to make a great poet – passion, gentleness, dedicated insight, his own conception of the world, his own gift of transforming everything he touched . . . his swiftness, his wandering yet attentive glance, the quickness of his observations.'

> The sweeping snowstorm
> swings into the streets:
> a hand reaches out to me,
> somebody smiles to me.

The stanza, which he quotes in the fifties, might almost be from a poem of his own written about 1917, but Blok wrote it in 1907. He was a young poet of twenty-seven in 1907, only ten years older than Boris, but he was immensely popular. He cherished the common Russian symbolist obsessions with a mysterious woman or goddess or *Ewig–Weibliches*, with imminent apocalyptic catastrophe, and with a messianic figure who might easily be the artist, but his pessimistic power and seriousness, as well as his power of observation which thrilled Boris Pasternak, mark him uniquely. He was one of those few poets who have a great deal to say. It is hard now to imagine the excitement of reading him as a young man only ten years younger. Had he survived, he and not Pasternak would have been the greatest poet of this century, and there are native Russian speakers who think he was precisely that. No one so strongly conveys the sense of a wasted life and a lost generation.

> Let the croaking raven fly:
> on our death-beds we lie dumb,
> God, God, let those more worthy
> see Thy Kingdom come.

# 2

## Youth and Folly – he becomes a young poet

Life is continuous: it is not divided into chapters. But its transformations are as unlikely as Ovid's *Metamorphoses*. At the age of sixteen the future is taking root, but the humus of childhood still holds it hidden. Boris Pasternak in Berlin was a normal, sensitive adolescent, a brilliant linguist concentrating on his music. He had already written a piano sonata in 1905 and a prelude in December 1906, which so far as I know remain his only completed works. His lack of perfect pitch had no huge significance, and, although all writers about him repeat criticisms of his technique in perform- ance, those are from an artificially high standard: he was a competent and even a brilliant amateur pianist who until the end of his life occasionally delighted to play works for two pianos with professionals. He was fastidious and shy rather than vain, he was awkward with girls, unable to dance because of his lameness, and accustomed to shooting sideways glances from his eyes like a nervous horse. That is what Ida, the daughter of the wholesale tea merchant, and his cousin Olga from Petersburg say. I like the observation about the horse, because there was always something equine about his appearance. The criticism of vanity appears to be based on Sasha's assessment, which after all is only a younger brother's, and taken up by critics who write like housemasters: at sixteen Boris Pasternak was beyond the grasp of that kind of analysis. We hear of his mother trembling at a window as he was improvising, but I am not convinced that she was horrified by his performance on that particular occasion, or by his music in general. Any alienation that did take place was to do with his poetry, his increasing need for privacy from his family, and possibly his increasing interest in Christianity, which appears to have happened over the next two or three years. All the witnesses to it derive from what he said about it himself in later life.

After the winter in Berlin came a long summer holiday at Goehren auf Rügen, on an island in the Baltic, a resort that they picked on for its beautiful name. It was approached by a train ferry of swimming carriages: 'the silence was startling, the peace absolute'. Boris Pasternak was the most Muscovite of poets, to whom the working-class speech of Moscow and its street life were second nature. His first reaction to the foreignness of Berlin was to adopt every mannerism and accent of a Berliner. Many excellent linguists are like that. But the long summer holidays of his youth were an important breathing space. He was at home in the country and quite capable of living like a peasant. Goehren had a wide sandy beach with parasols and basket-work chairs, on the eastern side of the rocky northern promontory where the village lay, but Sasha and Boris used to run down a dusty footpath to the west and the fishermen's huts, where they 'revelled for hours in the forbidden pleasures of naked bathing'. They were the only Russians on the island, until Engel arrived from Moscow with his family; he loved children and joined in their games like an equal. Leonid drew, Rosa played the piano, and Boris took lessons from Engel on the beach, which Sasha observed as 'a daily, joyful Golgotha'. Boris demanded too much of himself, and suffered accordingly, but not without moments of triumph, when 'they were no longer master and pupil but two musicians together, interrupting each other, humming and whistling like a pair of drunks'.

The Pasternaks stayed on into stormy weather, when the beach approaches were plastered with official notices forbidding swimming. Sasha and Boris would sit in a cave watching the stormy sea, where a little while before they had played at shipwrecked sailors and at aborigines. In late November they came home to Moscow. For Rosa it was the beginning of a new stage of life, perhaps her and Leonid's happiest. She began to play professionally again, liberated first in Berlin when her two sons left the nest. What she loved most were the quintets of Schubert and Schumann, and the Moscow flat resounded with them. She began to rehearse a repertory of violin sonatas by Grieg (new to her) and Mozart and Beethoven. In the season of 1907–8 she played in public. At home there were long, impassioned conversations about art and architecture and natural growth and form. Sasha was inspired at fourteen to a desperate and doomed attempt to become a violinist; in the end he became an architect, but an architect destined by the times to observe Stalin's destruction of Moscow, a subject on which Muscovites speak with intense passion to this day.

It was from 1907 that Boris dated the general explosion in the arts which we know as modernism. The truth is that the new movement in the arts had more names and sects and warring sub-sects than deserve to be catalogued. It occurred sooner or later in all European countries, but I suspect that it originated in France, in Paris, though not among Parisians but through the Norman Braque, the Pole Apollinaire and the Spaniard Picasso. In Russia it was tied to the arts and crafts movement by the patronage of S. Mamontov, who founded an arts and crafts colony at Abramtsevo in 1875 but lived long enough to see cubism and post-Impression-ism. Patrons as well as artists wanted to be modern, to be new. By 1908 Serov and Pasternak found the new generation of their students intolerable and unteachable. It included that wonderful painter and to our eyes very restrained modernist, Goncharova. A great deal of what went on by 1910 and 1911 in Moscow, and still more so in Petersburg, was mere fizz and juvenile display, but the atmosphere was certainly electric. It may be important to remember that these were boom years: agricultural and industrial production were increasing by extraordinary percentages every year, so was population, particularly urban population. Politics from 1905 to 1914 were like a disturbed ant-heap, with reform after reform introduced too late. Stolypin as Prime Minister was the last chance, but he was killed.

In 1907 the Pasternak boys were still at school, and there was a new boy from the Caucasus in Sasha's class: Vladimir Maya-kovsky, a big, surly fourteen-year-old known as the One-Eyed Polyphemos. Boris at seventeen was on the dreamy side; he worked out fugues and counterpoints in Greek and mathematics classes, but his friends shielded him and teachers forgave him, for the sake of his music. Still, he was good at examinations, perhaps because he worked feverishly at the last moment, as he did later at university. On the strength of his music, he was taken up by a kind of futurist sub-group called Serdarda, a gang of ten or a dozen artists of different kinds: 'as the guests arrived I provided musical sketches of each of them'. No one knew what the word 'Serdarda' meant: a poet and bass singer called Arkadyi Gurev had overheard in on the Volga, and it was felt to have the right resonance. They used to meet in the flat of a poet and painter of excellent taste, great

enthusiasm and incurable amateurishness called Julian Anisimov.
It was one of the members of this group, Sergei Durylin, who saw
something worth attention in Pasternak's early verses, probably
around 1910 or 1911. The date is hard to pin down, but Sasha
Pasternak gives some telling arguments, and actually found some
torn-up fragments of verse, written in black ink with the very hard
pen (a *Eureka*) that his brother then preferred. The other members
of the gang included S. Bobrov, A. Kozhebatkin, editor of
*Musagetes* (1912), and S. Makovskyi, editor of *Apollo*, both of
which we would call 'little magazines'.

In the next few years Pasternak drifted from one group to
another, but it is interesting that the nonsense-word Serdarda
(which probably belongs to one of the numerous minority
languages of the river Volga) hints at a link with the same attitude
to words that produced the verbal fireworks of the poet
Khlebnikov (born in 1885) and of Kruchenykh, who was still more
extreme. Yet Khlebnikov was a very advanced futurist indeed. His
theories were extremely daring, and his sanity was sometimes in
question. The formalist Gumilev said of him that 'his images are
convincing by their absurdity, his thoughts by their paradox.'
Personally I find him charming, and inspiring in short doses,
though I have never attempted to make sense of those of his poems
consisting entirely of neologisms or nonsense-words. The aim of
this possibly far-fetched analogy between Serdarda and futurists
like Kruchenykh and Khlebnikov is to indicate an awareness of
words for which in English we would have to point to James Joyce.
Pasternak admired Khlebnikov and helped to edit his works after
his death. Mayakovsky admired him too but felt he was not for
poetry readers, rather for fellow futurists and philologists. The
study of the sound-patterns and the formal theory of poetry was
further advanced in Russia at that time than it was then or is now in
England, largely because of the symbolists. Among Boris
Pasternak's generation, between 1912 and 1922, no holds were
barred in poetry or in any other art. In the resulting confusion a
number of poets sank, but Boris swam. The organising maestro
who orchestrated the modern movement in Russian poetry was an
untalented pupil of the School of Arts, who infuriated Leonid
Pasternak by giving a famously scandalous lecture in Petersburg
against Puskhin while he was still a student. From 1920 until his
death not so long ago he lived on as a nonentity in New York. He

was called David Burliuk: he did for futurism in Russia what Pound did for modern poetry in the west. Paintings by him survive, but they are less thrilling than the works of Pound.

Of course the usual development of poets is from the preceding generation. One can usually say of the poetry as of the whole history of a given century that it inherited the problem of the last generation and created those of the next. To some extent this is true of Boris Pasternak. He knew some of the old Moscow poets through his father. V. Ivanov (1866–1949) was typical of them. He was an old pupil of the greatest of all classical scholars of the nineteenth century, Mommsen, and between 1905 and 1911 he was uncrowned king of the symbolists. His poetry had a majestic and archaic tone which none of the young aimed to reproduce. He was fifty-one in 1917, and left Russia for Italy a soon as he could, in 1920. He died in Rome, a Roman Catholic, at the age of eighty-three. Pasternak speaks of him with respect and curiosity but he was scarcely an influence. In Pasternak's last years at school it was Rilke who was important to him. He found two of Rilke's books, luckily two of the better ones, on his father's bookshelf, they thrilled him, and he introduced Rilke to Serdarda, who of course had never heard of him. When the visiting Belgian poet Verhaeren was having his portrait done by Leonid, Boris was employed to keep him talking, so he asked his opinion of Rilke, which produced an expression of lively admiration. Boris translated some Rilke for the Serdarda group. Rilke was at that time his idea of what poetry could do, what it should be like.

Here I am forced to be autobiographical. I am not in general an admirer of Rilke's work, but when I was very young someone showed me the poem 'Autumn Day', which I know by heart to this day. It had the effect on me that Auden had on his contemporaries. I was deeply excited by it, and at that time probably only my lack of German prevented me from becoming an addict. More recently I have found it very hard to see why there is such a fuss about Rilke. Isaiah Berlin said to me, 'It's purely an English affair.' I see that a young poet with an international reputation was a dazzling apparition in Moscow, and that the Russians were amazed at his learning Russian so swiftly and thoroughly. Then the German language was thrilling to Boris Pasternak, and Rilke's reverence for Tolstoy predisposed Moscow to like him. And he was an aesthete to the fingertips; indeed, that is what kept him from the first rank of modern writers: his subject is beauty rather than reality. That is what appealed to an adolescent, both to Boris Pasternak and to myself. His poetry at its best has a crisp economy of surface, which his prose never has, and a mysterious depth.

> Sir, it is time, the summer was so gross,
> let fall your shadows on the sun-dials
> and in the meadows let the wind go loose.

> Command the last fruits to be full and fine,
> give them just one or two more southern days,
> draw them to their fulfilment and then chase
> the last sweetness into the heavy wine.

> Who has no house now shall not build one.
> Who is alone now shall be long alone,
> shall watch and read, shall write long letters
> and on the boulevards restless shall go
> this way and that way, when the dead leaves blow.

'Autumn Day' is from *The Book of Pictures* (1902; second edition 1906). What Pasternak read to Serdarda was 'Mir zu Feiern', 'Celebrating Myself'. Later he introduced Anisimov to *The Book of Hours* (1905), which Anisimov had translated complete by 1913. Pasternak himself translated several poems from *The Book of Pictures* between 1911 and 1913. In 1929 he translated some more Rilke (for reasons that we shall see later). He came across the two books on his father's shelf, which Rilke had sent with inscriptions, long after they had arrived. 'They shook me by the same indistinct, unconditional gravity, the same directness in the use of language as had first astonished me in Blok.' What Verhaeren said later, in 1913, was 'He is the best poet in Europe, and my beloved spiritual brother.' It was not precisely the Russian side of Rilke – though that side certainly existed (he had lived in the country with a Russian poet called Drozhzin, and translated Chekhov, and had a love affair with the Russian language) that struck Boris Pasternak so deeply, but rather something central to poetry, something almost conservative, and at least as old as Baudelaire. It was not an exotic adventure, but a serious experience of what poetry is, for which he was precisely ready. Without it, one does not know what might have become of him in the whirlpools of futurism. It was his twenty-first birthday present, delivered a little early, from his father's generation.

As for his music, that was in some way an ideal preparation for a poet, but I have wondered whether the mother's balalaika which Zhivago carried most of his life yet never learns to play may not be a symbol of Boris Pasternak and his mother's music. 'Rilke looked on the descriptive and psychological discoveries of the novelists of his time (Tolstoy, Flaubert, Proust and the Scandinavians) as intimately linked with his own poetic language and style,' wrote Pasternak in retrospect. He then translated 'Der Lesende' and 'Das Schauende' into Russian (in 1954) to show what he meant, rather as I have translated 'Autumn Day'. The implication that Rilke was determined to win back for poetry some of the skills of prose and some of the ground lost to prose is interesting because it appears that Pasternak digested that lesson. One of the things that makes his early poetry hard to approach, unless one takes it with extreme simplicity and directness, is that it reads like pieces of diary or novel and is full of just those unlikely observations of reality that a novelist could use. It is almost as if a great novelist was lost in him, as in the Eliot of *The Waste Land*, but for much of his life Boris Pasternak was not mature enough to be a great novelist.

In his last autobiographical work, *People and Situations*, which was posthumously published in 1967, he wrote that Rilke was still quite unknown in Russia, because the few attempts to translate him had been unsuccessful. That was no one's fault, the translators produced the sense of the poems and not their tone, 'but with Rilke everything depends on the tone.' That is a just estimate of Rilke's influence on his own lyrics: still, of all the numerous foreign influences on Pasternak at different times of his life, including the whole bewildering range of his translations, the two that most closely define his early and his late style are Rilke and Shakespeare. As a young man he was excited by the musicality and mystery of Rilke's tone, by its gravity and sense of autobiographic revelation; but it was not enough to last him a lifetime.

> I read for a long time. While a storm of rain
> all afternoon obscured the window-pane.
> Nor did I notice wind raging outside . . .
> . . . Now I look up from all that I have read,
> all is great, nothing's unrelated.

> All I live inwardly is outward there,
> and without limit either there or here,
> but that I weave myself deeper in it . . .
>
> After days of mild decay
> now the storm is in the trees,
> my window shakes at the rough play,
> and things I hear horizons say
> now without friend I fear,
> no love, no sister dear . . .

These are fragments from the two poems Pasternak translated: it will be seen that the personality, the adolescent drama, might almost be his own. The second contains the wrestling angel that touches Jacob's sinews into music as it wounds him. Jacob the loser 'goes forth upright in resurrection, / great from that hard creative hand / which embraced and finished him.' It is not as good a poem as Charles Wesley's 'Wrestling Jacob', but it said something important to Boris Pasternak at the age of seventeen.

In January 1909 Scriabin returned to Moscow, to the not inelegant little house near the Arbat where he died of a poisoned boil or tumour on the lip in 1915. Pasternak says Scriabin's Superman was just another case of the Russian yearning for extremes. Music should be super-music and everything on earth should transcend itself. What he loved and remembered best was the Scriabin of the middle period who had been his daily bread: Scriabin from the third to the fifth sonata. 'For me, the most startling developments occur when an artist is so bursting with what he has to say that he has no time to think, and utters his new words in the old language without caring whether it is old or new. . . . Scriabin introduces a note of such utter naturalness into his work, the kind of naturalness which is decisive in any work of art.' In late middle life he put his old idol higher still: as Dostoevsky was more than a novelist and Blok more than a poet, so was Scriabin more than a composer.

As soon as Scriabin arrived, he began rehearsals for his *Extase du Printemps*, a title which sounds (as Pasternak noticed) like a box of French soap. The young poet attended, walking miles through the fog, 'a foggy broth . . . ice cold kvass and spring onion soup . . . limp tongues of church towers, fingers of icicles . . . the church of

St Nikita whipped egg and cognac.' The music was 'man's first colonization of the world discovered by Wagner for chimeras and mastodons . . . scared from the scene by kettle-drums, and by cascades of chromatics from trombones as cold as fireman's hoses.' Too much of this – and it does go on for paragraphs – is like a wayward version of Dylan Thomas, but one sees what he means.

Young Pasternak was thought of as a promising pupil. He could conceive of no life but music; all he had to do now was to study orchestration. Only his lack of perfect pitch worried him, and that played an important part in the catastrophe that followed. His mother possessed it, but it is not necessary for composers and in retrospect he felt it was not the lack of it but his own obsessional worry about lacking it that meant music was not for him.

He put himself to the test with his throat shut and his tongue dried up with nerves, not in the small room with the small piano and the arty naked ladies, but in the big living-room with the grand piano and the upper-class chairs. He was nodding and smirking and wiping his forehead. Spring steamed outside, the samovar steamed inside, Scriabin smoked a cigar. 'I was still agitated while I played my first piece, at the second I nearly bested it, at the third it gave way entirely to that onrush of something quite new, quite unforeseen. Scriabin raised his head, raised his eyebrows, smiled in time with the music.' When Boris had finished, the composer said it was not right to speak of musical gifts in the presence of so much more. 'You are destined', he said, 'to add your word to music.' He sat at the piano and replayed the bits he liked best, but he played them in the wrong key. Boris decided to ask him about perfect pitch. If he said that like Boris he lacked it, all would be well. If he just said it didn't matter, that would be all right. But Scriabin made excuses, he told the old story of how Wagner lacked it, and Tchaikovsky, and how a thousand piano tuners possessed it. He did not admit that he lacked it until years later.

They paced up and down the room. He put his arm round the boy's shoulders, he walked arm in arm with him. (Scriabin was a very small man and Boris was nineteen, so the second of these manoeuvres would have been easier.) He told him of the harm of improvisation to which he was wedded. He warned him how and when and with what purpose to compose. He offered the mind-bending complexity of his own latest works as models of simplicity, and condemned the simplest of sentimental romances as examples of complexity. Hearing that Boris was due to read law at the university he told him to change at once to moral philosophy, and Boris did so the very next day. It was dark in the room and the streetlights were lit outside. It was time for Boris to go home. He idolised Scriabin even more: he had kept his secret, and the secret of how he must once have overcome his own juvenile misgivings; he retained his mystery. 'As I bid him goodbye I did not know how to thank him. Something rose within me, striving to get free. Something wept, something rejoiced.' That was how he gave up all ambition to be a composer of music.

Boris had left school with the coveted gold medal, and enrolled himself at Moscow University. His intellectual life was largely bound up with Serdarda, and then with the groups that followed it. But his student life is a story of its own which has a climax, and is better treated without interruption, so before I deal with that I shall describe a single event which has at least a symbolic significance as the end of a world. It was dramatic and to the Pasternaks unforgettable.

In 1910 the household and family of Leo Tolstoy had sunk into a terminal civil war, with frightening explosions of quarrelling and every sort of emotional outburst. His wife attempted suicide more than once. A religious manipulator called Tchertkov was attempting to get hold of Tolstoy's manuscripts and literary rights, and set about discrediting his wife in order to do so. People spied on one another, everyone kept diaries and read one another's. Yasnaya Polyana was a fairly small house, and full of egos. At the end of October, Tolstoy ran away from home. He was eighty-two and weak: he had been nine years old at the death of Pushkin; in his twenties he had fought against the British in the Crimea. He got as far as Astapovo, a railway station about a hundred miles away, about two hundred from Moscow, and there he took to his death-bed in the station-master's small house. He lingered long enough for all the parties to the quarrel to catch up with him. Tchertkov took over, disciples and journalists thronged the station, his wife was excluded from the station-master's house but she camped out in a special train. There was a Pathé news camera. The church sent envoys, to secure a death-bed conversion. Leonid Pasternak was sent for to draw the old man dying, and Boris went with him.

The rights and wrongs of what happened at Astapovo can still be argued in several directions. Martine de Courcel's version in her

*Tolstoy*, has perhaps the most sensitive nuances, though A. N. Wilson's has a reasoned clarity. Leonid Pasternak was greatly distressed by what he witnessed. He preferred to remember Tolstoy happy, as after all he often was. 'And when I was young . . . and when the Caucasus was young . . . and when the pheasants were young . . .' Leonid was passionate in his defence of Countess Tolstoy, and appalled by those who attacked her. So, I am glad to say, was Gorky. It is only recently that biographers have begun to come round to his view. Unfortunately Leonid never wrote the definitive account that he intended. His notes end: 'Must write here about Sonia and the tragedy of Lev Nikolaevich. Death, death-mask, Mikhailo. Trip with Borya to Astapovo . . . Astapovo. Morning. Sofya Andreyevna at his bedside. The people's farewell. Finale of a family tragedy.' Sonia and Sofya are the countess, and Lev is Tolstoy: she was allowed to see him only when he had lost consciousness.

Tolstoy died on 7 November 1910, but Boris Pasternak confuses that sad day and a journey that he remembers well with one of the most important events in his own early life, a paper he read on 'Symbolism and Immortality' in February 1913, the climax of his student years and the only fruit of his passion for philosophy, which followed the one for music. His memory about dates was not good, but it is strange that these two became entangled in his mind. 'In those days, leaving the city was much more noticeable than it is now. . . . From early morning and throughout the day the carriage window was filled with the view of a flat expanse of fields. . . . The ground was already silvered by the first frosts, the meadows fringed with the gold of the birch trees still unshed. The sleeping ploughland rushed past the carriage windows, unaware that its last great hero had died, a man noble enough to have been Tsar, a man of subtle mind; seduced by the most refined pleasures, the most spoilt of spoilt darlings, lord of all lords, had nevertheless out of love and compassion for this land followed the plough dressed as a peasant.'

He tells us what his father had left unwritten about the death-bed. The crowd had been told to leave, a modeller was coming 'from Merkurov's' to make a death-mask, and the two Pasternaks entered an almost empty room. The countess came to Leonid with her face tear-stained, saying what she had suffered and that 'You must know how much I loved him'. Boris goes on: 'A mountain the size of Mount Elburz lay in that room, and she was one of its peaks. A towering thundercloud filled that room and she was one of its flashes of lightning. Yet she did not know that the mountain peak and the lightning had a right to silence . . . she had no need to enter into arguments with the Tolstoyans, who were in reality the most unTolstoyan creatures on earth . . . the squabbles of those pygmies.' But she did try to justify herself, calling Leonid to witness how she loved her husband best, and understood him best, and would have cared for him best. 'Oh God, I thought, how far can a human being be driven – and the wife of Tolstoy, too.'

'It was no mountain lying there, but a wrinkled little old man, one of those created by Tolstoy himself. . . . It was somehow natural that Tolstoy should find his last rest, like a travelling pilgrim, beside the railway . . . along which his heroes and heroines still rushed whirling past.' He thought Tolstoy's special gift, like Tyutchev's intensity, Lermontov's passion, Chekhov's poetry and Dostoevsky's imagination, was his unique originality. He saw events and phenomena 'in the definitive finality of each separate moment, as a kind of comprehensive statement that stood out in relief, a kind of vision that we only have in rare moments'. Something like that might be said of the poetry that Boris Pasternak would write in the next ten years, before he was thirty. 'To see things in this way, our eyes must be guided by passion.' Even in the labyrinth of philosophy, to which he devoted himself for three or four years, he did not lose his passion, which became visionary as he became a poet. I cannot imagine a poet more ideally educated for his art than he was. The art itself was a slow, natural growth, but he was now twenty, and it was beginning to appear, as much in his criticism of life and of art as in his poems.

He refers to Moscow in his first year as a student, a year in which he crossed and recrossed the city, as 'My Moscow, mine as never before'. Serdarda used to meet at Julian Anisimov's, 'through the slush to the timber-built Razgulyai quarter of Moscow, a damp-sodden tangle of the old world, of inheritance and youthful promises, to return home later on that night quite stunned by the rooks in that upper room under the poplars.' At home 'the sun rose from behind the post office, then settling down like a fruit jelly, it set over Neglaika. As it gilded our flat, after dinner it reached into the dining-room and the kitchen.' The 'rooks' are surely those hooded crows that perch on lampposts near the river and congregate among the graveyards and battlements of the Don monastery and the Novodevichya convent, and Razgulyai is not far from the Kazan Station and the Yaroslav Station, just beyond the great ring of boulevards that define inner Moscow. As for the wooden buildings, there are still wooden houses in that direction in Moscow, but those that survive are extremely smart-looking, and painted and decorated like Regency pavilions. The Razgulyai area was a good tramp from Myasnitskaya, but it was not the end of the earth. It has a cathedral and lies about as far from the Kremlin in one direction as Tolstoy's slightly suburban town house in another.

Julian Anisimov lived in the attic of a surviving wooden building in the grounds of a new block of flats perhaps five storeys high: the wooden building belonged to his father, who was a general. He had weak lungs, spent the winter abroad, and 'used to hold gatherings of young people who shared his interests'. They would gather in good weather in spring or autumn, to read aloud and draw, to argue, to drink tea with rum in it, and to eat. Anisimov was a connoisseur, a patron and a linguist; Boris made many friends there. One was Sergei Durylia, who wrote under the name Kaevsky and wooed him towards literature, a kindly man who supported a mother and an aunt by tutoring; and there his old schoolfriend K. G. Loks introduced him to the poetry of Annensky, having discovered some quality in common between them.

Annensky was headmaster of a grand secondary school and a classicist who translated the whole of Euripides into verse. His original poetry in Russian is like a scarcely penetrable garden of roses, wildly abundant within strict forms, thrilling and tempting like a new Tyutchev. The resemblance to Pasternak is indeed striking, and Annensky is the most unjustly neglected of all modern poets in Russia. He began to publish at the age of forty-five and died at the age of fifty-three in 1909. He knew French poetry and there are traces of nineties-style sadness in his brief poems, but he was too original to be easily placed as a symbolist, a decadent or anything else. I am doubtful of the extent or depth of his influence on Boris Pasternak, who seems to have imbibed his influences in a purer, stronger form and who greatly admired Tyutchev. He often declared that Pushkin, Tyutchev and the crisp and formal Baratynsky (a sort of Russian equivalent of the Greek Kalvos with a more brilliant talent) were the best Russian poets of the nineteenth century. All the same, acquaintance with Annensky's poems, which came as a surprise to him as to everyone else, marked a beginning and an opening out of which he was conscious.

Annensky was a Siberian from Omsk, which may account for his originality. Another friend of Anisimov, Guryev, whose bass voice Pasternak greatly admired and whose warm-hearted clowning he liked, was from Saratov in the south. He was an opera singer with an actor's temperament, but he also wrote striking poetry and drank a good deal. S. Bobrov came too; he was reputed to be the Russian Rimbaud and 'collaborated' with Pasternak on his earliest work, being one year older. That was when they had both joined Centrifuge, a sub-group of futurism. The Anisimov circle was less advanced and earlier Bobrov lent it a touch of period authenticity by writing science fiction and translating Bernard Shaw. It is worth noting that Pasternak was inclined to call his own generation inwardly orientated on art and philosophy and more or less non-political at this time. We know from Maurice Baring that in 1906 ordinary Russians began to talk politics for the first time, and of course we can see in retrospect the speed of events, but circles like Serdarda also existed. *Apollo* was based in Petersburg but *Musagetes* was in Moscow. Its editorial office was an important literary centre through which Beliy reigned over literature. He was a poet and his prose was admired, though today it demands a strong-headed reader. All the same his *Silver Dove* and his *St Petersburg* are rather wonderful: he is an old wizard who still almost convinces. He was a theosophist like Scriabin and a friend of Rudolf Steiner; when the revolution overtook him he declared that he was still a theosophist but a Marxist theosophist. It is hard to conjecture how thickly or for how long the fog of theosophy enveloped Boris Pasternak, but it was certainly present in the atmosphere he breathed.

He was reading Kant and Hegel at university, though he does not seem to have attended many lectures either as a philosopher or as a historian. He was personally acquainted with the greatest Moscow historian of the day, whose portrait his father painted, but his view of history so far as he had one was Tolstoyan. As for modern politics, he despised his own boyish revolutionary zeal, and he might as well have been cultivating the walled garden of the classics. Russians suggest that his essential formation was through the Moscow school of the philosopher Trubetskoy, and it is true that Hegel in particular distils a finely spun darkness which pleased the academic men of the day in Moscow as in Oxford, but I do not believe Boris Pasternak took any notice of them: his own evidence is that he did not. Kant on the other hand gives one a more rewarding kind of headache. His famous paper on symbolism and immortality, which is lost, was a bold attempt to apply Kantian reasoning to a new area. He thought old Trubetskoy was like an elephant in a frock-coat, 'delivering his brilliant lectures on a note of what sounded like entreaty, almost a beseeching'. The *Logical Investigations* of Husserl, which were translated into Russian in 1910, may well be a source of Boris Pasternak's own philosophic views, because the idea of something impersonal in subjectivity without a self inside it flourishes in Husserl and occurs in Pasternak's early verse. But there is no evidence that he read or was at all conscious of him, and the problem of the self in Pasternak's poems is not as queer or as deep as it looks to philosophers. The first person of lyric poems is like the first person of a dream.

In the summer of 1911, as soon as Sasha Pasternak had finished his last school exams, the family moved to an upper flat in a two-storey building at 14 Volkhonka Street, much closer to the university and to the Kremlin. The new flat was still provided by the School of Arts. It was very close to what is now called the Pushkin Gallery, a remarkable art gallery assembled mostly from private collections since 1917. In those days it was a cast gallery, consisting of a magnificent collection of plaster casts, mostly classical; Tsvetaev, father of the poet Marina Tsvetaeva, left it a fine library. The flat in Volkhonka looked out on the Cathedral of Christ Saviour, with its terrible nineteenth-century sculptures now at the Don Monastery across the river and its vast bronze figure of a nineteenth-century Tsar by Trubetskoy the sculptor. The cathedral had taken forty years of the nineteenth century to build. This flat was part of an estate that used to belong to Prince Golytsin, and shows it in the quality and style of its architecture; it was now controlled by the School of Arts, but the cast gallery and its art collection were not open to the public. The Pasternaks had been longing to move for six months: they now had seven rooms and nine windows. Josephine was eleven and Lydia was nine.

That year they spent their holiday at Odessa, no doubt in one of those villas in the sand dunes that Babel knew. Josephine and Lydia had never seen the Black Sea before. Boris had become secretive, because he was writing his first experimental poems without telling anybody. He still seems to have played the piano, but he began to separate from his family, he fluttered his wings towards leaving home. He was twenty-one, so that seems normal to us, but not to that family, which he still loved. He still shared a room and even a light and a table with Sasha, but Sasha noticed nothing at the time. Boris speaks in *Safe Conduct* of hiding 'signs of a new immaturity'. When he suddenly went home to Moscow, Sasha was sent to tidy his room, and found a lot of little piles of paper, some of them pale-blue library slips, full of writing columns. He gathered them up and they were taken back to the city, but Boris showed no interest in them. They were found fifty years later, and turned out to be his earliest surviving attempts at verse. At the time he took a room of his own, first in one place then another, always just round the corner from Volkhonka. His mother was hurt and his father therefore very angry. But he was free. His Serdarda friends began to figure more closely in his life. Yet by 1912 he had tied himself to another father-figure, and won the approval of Professor Cohen, an old man he hero-worshipped as he had worshipped Scriabin: the results were going to be even more painful.

The most aristocratic pupils at the university could afford to buy textbooks and the source books that lie behind textbooks; they did not therefore bother too much about lectures. A graduate student called Mansurov lent Boris such an enormous treasure-trove of books he could hardly fit them all into a taxi. They were enough to see him through his finals. But it is more important that this Mansurov had two friends who were also his kinsmen, a young Nikolai Trubetskoy and a young Dimitri Samarin. Even at school, where Boris first knew them, they had turned up for exams but worked mostly at home. 'The three young people had a family look. Tall, gifted youths, with eyebrows joined together in a single line and voices as resounding as their names, they dropped in at the university as an inseparable trio.' They were keen on the philosophy taught at Marburg, and so indeed was their uncle Trubetskoy the elephantine. Marburg philosophy had more than a toehold in Moscow, and like other universities of its kind it liked to take in promising foreign pupils and send them home as apostles. Nikolai Trubetskoy ended as professor of philology in Vienna; Samarin had a bad time during and after the war, dying in the twenties; Mansurov's fate is unknown to me.

Samarin is the one who interests us, since he knew Marburg personally and persuaded Boris to go there. His family were distinguished conservative thinkers for several generations, labelled 'Slavophiles' but more cultured and more articulate than most of their adversaries. They owned an estate near Moscow, called Peredelkino. Their house was quite small, lost deep in the pinewoods where it still stands. The only trace of Samarin ownership today is that the lake is called the Samarinsky Prud, Samarin's Pond. After the revolution most of the estate was given to the Writers' Union, who live there half lost among the same trees in pleasant wooden houses, rather Swiss in feeling. The Samarin house, classical like the tiniest and prettiest of English country houses, became a convalescent home. Had Pasternak stayed there or visited there with his friend before 1914? Nothing could be likelier, since a train stops nearby, but no direct evidence exists. He lived on the writers' estate for many years at the end of his life. He was apparently conscious of the irony of its former ownership, because he wrote a poem about a wounded soldier in the forties waking up there and recognising it as the house of his childhood. Still, it is better to be pedantic, and to point out that a convalescent home is not quite a hospital: the hospital is big and signposted and used to be a TB sanatorium for children; the Samarin house is deeper in the woods. If he had really stayed there he might not have confused the two. Russians I have asked say it was socially not improbable that he knew the house.

He remembered Samarin all his life. 'Philosophy, dialect and Hegelian scholarship were in Samarin's blood as a hereditary gift. He was disorderly, absent-minded and almost certainly a little mad. The eccentricities which startled his friends when the mood was on him made him impossible to live with. He was always quarrelling with his relations.' In 1921 Samarin got back to Moscow from Siberia, 'dishevelled, stripped of sophistication and full of all-forgiving understanding'. The civil war had tossed him to and fro for a long time, he was distended with undernourishment and crawling with lice, he caught typhus and died of it. I believe that his experience in Siberia, his transformation there, and Boris Pasternak's love for him, played a part in the civil war adventures of *Dr Zhivago*, which was mostly written on the old Samarin estate. Today the view there is beginning to change. The first Moscow buildings, like the white tents of a nomadic invader, have appeared on the horizon. A mysterious and hideous little factory has popped up in the valley below Pasternak's house. The beautiful old green path that led from the village church to his grave was asphalted so that Nancy Reagan would not have to get out of her car.

Dimitri Samarin excited Pasternak about Marburg as a centre of philosophy in a summer coffee-house on Tverskie Boulevard which for some mysterious reason remained open without customers in the winter. Its popular name was the Café Grec. Boris was there by chance 'in that bare pavilion' with Samarin and his Servarda friend Loks. The weather was just turning warm, there was a hint of spring. In the university, most people were excited by Bergson, some liked Husserl; Pasternak remembers them and Shpet their leader, but he was not a Husserl fan. Marburg supporters had no leader except through personal contact with Trubetskoy, but the cult was promoted by the ungainly student Samarin, extemporising as the mood took him on Hegel or on Cohen. He was like Tolstoy's Nekhlyudov. He had only one tone, which was loud, neither a shout nor a whisper. It is best to present him in the Café Grec in Pasternak's own words in *Safe Conduct*, in which for fear of the regime he pretends to have lost sight of Samarin after 1914.

'Samarin had appeared and hardly had time to sit down and join us before starting to philosophise. Arming himself with a dry biscuit, he used it like a choirmaster's tuning-fork to beat out the logical divisions of his argument. A piece of Hegelian infinity stretched out across the empty café, made a series of statements and negations. Probably I mentioned the theme I had chosen for a doctoral thesis, and he leapt at once from Leibniz and mathematical infinity to the dialectical kind. Then suddenly he started talking about Marburg. This was the first account I heard not of the Marburg school but of the town itself. I was convinced there was no other way to talk of its antiquity or its poetry.' One can see that Samarin was irresistible. He suddenly remembered he was there for a different reason, woke the owner, dozing behind a newspaper, but found the phone was out of order. 'He stumbled away, out of that ice-cold aviary, even more noisily than he arrived.'

Boris was able to take off for Marburg because the German summer semester corresponds to the Russian summer holiday. It was a thrilling adventure. Marburg lies some 250 miles west of

Berlin, only fifty east of Bonn, and fifty north of Frankfurt. Its river runs down to Koblenz. In those last idyllic days of Europe it was a small town of great beauty, happy in its countryside, and with the enormous prestige of the German university system. The mainstay of that was the seminar, a close collaborative workshop of a scholar with great authority, who would govern it severely, with students of every degree of seniority. The seminar of Theodor Mommsen was the seed-ground of scholarship all over Europe: at that time it was about to revolutionise Oxford through the legal historian Paul Vinogradoff. The seminar of Hermann Cohen at Marburg had analogous candle-power. The sand of the arena was intellectually speaking blood-sprinkled. On the other hand, simply wandering off to Marburg for a semester was far more acceptable in Germany than it has ever been in England. Rosa Pasternak paid with the astounding and completely unexpected present of 200 roubles in April 1912. She told Boris to take it and travel.

In Russia the snow was still melting, but in Poland the apple trees were in blossom. In Berlin he bought Professor Natorp's hand-book on logic, 'aware that next day I was to see its author in real life', a droopy-headed, gloomy-looking sage with a watch-chain, whom you would not take for anything but a professor, probably of logic. Cohen's predecessor Friedrich Lange has always earned a few inches in the encyclopaedias of the Soviet era, because he wrote a history of the idea of materialism, but Hermann Cohen is a more serious proposition. He was the most distinguished Kantian teacher in Europe. If Boris Pasternak had come two years later, or continued to come, as he would have done if philosophy had continued to be his career, he would have met, perhaps taught and certainly influenced the young T. S. Eliot, who was in Marburg in the summer of 1914. The outbreak of war surprised him there and finally trapped him in England. In 1911 or 1912 Rupert Brooke was writing *Grantchester* in Munich, and Eliot was finishing *Prufrock* at the same café tables. Pasternak and Eliot are both philosophic poets: the difference between them is very interesting, both by temperament and in philosophy. Part of that difference is Professor Cohen.

Marburg is nearly as far beyond Berlin as Berlin is beyond Warsaw, so the young poet passed an uncomfortable night in an uncompromising third-class compartment, mostly alone. He was

entranced by western Germany; it stirred his imagination to a point
where his attempt to recapture it in prose is difficult to understand:
'the train stretched the chain-mail marvel of its ten riveted coaches.
The leather joints of the corridor sections billowed and sagged like
a blacksmith's bellows . . . the leaping paws of the wild vines
barely showed black against the stucco work . . . I was hit again by
the hurricane with its echoed trace of coal and dew and roses.' He
was enraptured; he began counting the names that flashed by, the
Harz mountains, Goslar 'leaping from the woods on a smoky
morning', Göttingen and at last Marburg. He was so excited that
he left some of his luggage in the train, and only now began to
identify the intellectual Marburg with its history and both of those
with the silent, sun-struck place, perching over its plain. Marburg
had an old importance for Russia, not only because of its Protestant
integrity but because Lomonosov – the fisherman's son under
Peter the Great, founder of most of the sciences and some of the arts
in modern Russia – Lomonosov, whose poetry is still read, had
come to Marburg to get an education. Boris suddenly realised that
although Lomonosov stayed for five years there must have been a
moment when he arrived, knowing nobody, with a letter to
Christian von Wolff, a pupil of Leibniz.

Samarin had told him about a cheap hotel, one of the last houses
on the Giessen road. His room had a tiny balcony overlooking
someone else's kitchen garden, where the body of an old horse-
tram was being used as a henhouse. The further view was solidly
and prosperously agricultural, with long barns and enormous,
gleaming cart-horses. At the green foliage of his window Boris
read Leibniz and Descartes in French. In the evening above the dull
wheeze of the spirit-lamp you could hear the jingle of electric bells
at the level-crossing beyond the river. When an express went by, a
man in uniform came out with a watering can to lay the dust. He
was alone in Marburg. That is the key to his time there and his
deeply etched impressions of the place: he was alone, he felt
intensely and he worked very hard. Among his rhapsodic
evocations of Marburg history he speaks of Elisabeth of Hungary
whose tomb was in the church. He spent time where philosophers
gathered, on a particular café terrace, with philosophers well
known in their day, like Lanz and Gorbukov, a revolutionary
Spaniard who declaimed Verlaine, some English girls and some
Danes and (already in 1912) some Japanese. He wrote a paper on

Boris Pasternak drawn as a child by his father. All the children were used to being continually sketched, particularly on winter evenings. He is eight years old.

The Pasternak family are going on holiday, Leonid and Rosa and the Nanny with Boris, pleased with his uniform, his younger brother Sasha the architect, and the baby Josephine. About the time they met Scriabin.

Leonid Pasternak with his wife Rosa, the pianist, painted in Germany by Leonid. His self-portrait shows a brave front, her portrait is subtler and perhaps more moving.

The Tolstoy family at tea at Yasnaya Polyana, in 1892. *The Kreutzer Sonata* was published a year ago, he was still hard at work, but over sixty and feeling his age. The Countess sits with her surviving children, but already the family looks divided. Leonid Pasternak first met the Tolstoys about this time.

ABOVE Scriabin as a travelled and accepted composer, not without touches of flamboyance. He was a tiny man whose fingers could hardly encompass a scale on the piano.

ABOVE RIGHT Alexander Blok in his handsome and successful youth as the greatest symbolist poet in Russia, during the nineteen hundreds.

LEFT Gorky in 1921, elderly and a tough nut, the senior Russian writer and adviser of the young. The authorities did a series of deals with him, but in the end they poisoned him.

Leibniz for Hartmann, and another on Kant's *Critique of Practical Reason* for Cohen.

Hermann Cohen had a shock of white hair and spectacles. In 1912 he was seventy, and he died in 1918. His father was a synagogue cantor as was his mother's father. He went to the Jewish theological seminary at Breslau. As a philosopher, he kept the study of Kant alive and exciting, though he has been severely criticised recently by Julius Ebbinghaus. Towards the end of his life he wrote about religion as a Jew, and there is a story about his visiting Russia in an attempt to prevent conversions to Christianity, but that does not directly affect the Pasternak family. He accepted from Kant that time and space are categories of our experience in advance of all experiences, but he took vigorous action to avoid the resulting paradoxes. In his urge to establish the validity of consciousness he felt one could rely on the fact of the existence of science. Modern science would not have been possible if Kant's categories had not been taken for granted. He got his chair in 1876; in 1902 he published a subtle book that leans in spite of itself towards Hegel: he certainly believed that in order to make sense of Kant one must go beyond him.

Morality depended for Cohen on a pre-existing category of justice that had itself to be justified by the fact of the existence of law. It seems to me extremely likely that Boris Pasternak, in imitation of Cohen, dallied with the idea that aesthetics depend on our category of the beautiful, which can be justified by the fact of the art of poetry. Still, he was more interested then in symbolism and immortality, or the immortality of symbolism and of men through symbolism. On Jewish national or racial questions Cohen taught that Jews were Germans because the prophets shared in the ethical ideals of Kant. This odd view was published in 1880; Pasternak may well have found it sympathetic. Cohen now went on to claim that Karl Marx had an equally close kinship to Kant, to the prophets and to himself, a view that has a resonance for Pasternak's generation but was not popular with the German government or the Marburg faculty. In 1912, therefore, Cohen resigned, and in spite of Paul Natorp's support his pupil Ernst Cassirer was disallowed as his successor. Cohen was deeply hurt and retired to Berlin, where he wrote moving theological works as a member of a Jewish institute. He died personally convinced of the existence of a saving God who was beyond his philosophy and for whom pure philosophy had no room.

In his classroom Cohen was the most beguiling kind of teacher. He 'would lift his head and step back as he talked about the Greek system of immortality, flourishing a hand towards the Marburg fire-station as he interpreted the image of the Elysian fields. . . . He would make a stealthy approach to pre-Kantian metaphysics and coo away in a show of paying court to it, before suddenly uttering a rasp and giving it a frightful scolding with quotations from Hume. He would cough and then fall silent and show that the performance was over with a peaceful, quiet "And now, gentlemen".' It was Chesterton who discovered that one goes to school in order to study the masters, because one learns nothing else there. The same is true of education at the highest level. Cohen would ask difficult questions about philosophers with a wave of his finger, and a German phrase usually translated as, 'What does the old philosopher mean?', but its true translation is closer to 'What is the old boy up to? What is he getting at?' Beliy had once been a pupil of Cohen's but got on with him less well, and wrote a baddish poem about his fingers twisting like bison horns and the hair falling over his marble brow into eyes of azure steel. Pasternak clearly admired Cohen as a human phenomenon and stood in awe of him as a philosopher. But he was also absolutely terrified of him as a teacher.

He recites with a mixture of awe and glee the severities of the old monster as an examiner: 'What is apperception?' 'To – er – grasp through and through.' 'No, Sir, it means *failed*.' He put Pasternak on to read Kant in his seminar, and just at the unexpected moment shot his question, 'What is he getting at?' 'One was required to rap out the answer immediately, with one noun, like a soldier.' What was worse, Cohen was deaf in the right ear, where Pasternak was sitting. He frowned and flapped his hand, Pasternak tried to elaborate, Cohen prodded the air for someone to volunteer the correct answer. These answers got worse and worse. Cohen turned back to Pasternak and drily and quietly said the word he had offered first time. Luckily there was a storm of defence. When he understood, he patted Pasternak on the shoulder and asked him where he was from and how many terms he had been in Marburg. Then he gave a snort and a frown and asked him to carry on reading, but he kept interjecting. 'Quite true, quite right. Do you see that? Yes, yes. Ach, ach, the old boy.'

Taking a walk with him was a mixed pleasure. 'Strolling next to you with frequent pauses and leaning on a stick was the very soul of mathematical physics . . . in an ample frock-coat and floppy hat, this professor was to some degree filled with the same precious essence which in times gone by was corked up in the heads of men like Galileo, Newton, Leibniz and Pascal.' He disliked talking much on his walks; he just listened. The chatter of Cohen's companion was always disjointed by stepped pavements. He would listen, suddenly halt and say something, then push off with his stick. Still, however all this may have felt, it appears that Boris Pasternak became a favoured pupil, even something of an intimate. The ultimate accolade of Marburg philosophy was an invitation to Sunday lunch with the Cohen family. It meant you had a future as a professional philosopher. Cohen had more than taken over from Scriabin, but Boris Pasternak cut and ran and for the second time found a new vocation.

What happened is complicated. Boris was very deeply excited by Marburg as a place. He was passionate, confused and lonely. He was in love, and that was going badly. He was on the edge of writing his first serious poetry, and already writing poems. In *Safe Conduct* he treated Marburg at comparatively enormous length; he also wrote a good deal about girls and the sort of adolescent crisis in which one suddenly takes a train for a foreign city. But one of his most famous mature poems is 'Marburg'. He always liked it but he virtually never stopped working at it, so there are a number of variants or versions. It is as if Marburg or what happened there were the deepest subject of his poetry, as if Marburg were uniquely able to explain what being a poet meant. There are some remarks about art in among the account of that summer in *Safe Conduct* which to him were precious insights. They do not seem to have much in common with the poem 'Marburg' but they seem to be part of what he was thinking about at that time, when he was still a philosopher, and not his later thoughts as a memoirist or as a mature poet. Another factor at Marburg which led to the explosion is that friends close to his family were involved, as we shall see, and the incident closed with his taking flight back to his family.

The girls confirm that his account of what occurred was substantially correct. The most telling analysis is by Olga Freidenberg, in a few pages of her diary which were published with her letters in 1912. She was now his second string; he returned to her and made unsuccessful advances on the rebound from his rejection by Ida Vysotskaya. Olga was his first cousin. They had spent childhood holidays together at Odessa, at Maloyaroslavets and in Estonia at the seaside. They had written to one another since 1910 when they were both twenty, they had been on the edge of an affair more than a year earlier, and when they rediscovered one another ten years after the 1912 episode they at once became close friends and remained so for the rest of their lives. Ida Vysotskaya had been tutored by Boris, they were close family friends and Jewish, and they were often in and out of one another's houses. Mr Vysotsky was a wholesale tea merchant, born in Myasnitskaya Street, where he still lived. Boris and Ida were more or less childhood sweethearts; he had noticed her when he was fourteen, and Ida remarked later that they were 'practically brought up together'. Boris, being a little older, tried to excite her about Greek at a time when he had a passion for it. Ida's governess kept a watchful eye on him: 'she knew better than I did that the geometry I was bringing into the house at such unearthly hours was more Abelardian than Euclidian.' That was when he was eighteen; the hour was generally daybreak. The French governess and a Swiss nanny coalesce as Mlle Fleury in *Zhivago*. Mr Vysotsky was a patron of modern art and of Leonid Pasternak. The children used to have long conversations lamenting the vulgarity of the modern world, particularly about sex, just like Zhivago and Tonia. Ida had a younger sister who travelled with her, but in this story the younger sister remains a silent character; we know her name was Josephine and that she was a nice girl.

Ida was a lovely girl and well brought up, says Boris, spoilt by her old nurse from infancy. His feelings about her are muddled up with his theories of art and of philosophy. 'Art is concerned not with man but the image of man', which is greater than men and can be generated only by movement, by transition. If a man speaks the truth, 'Time passes by as he speaks, and in that time life moves on. His truth lags behind and is deceptive. . . . Now in art his mouth is gagged. In art man falls silent and the image speaks out. And it emerges that only the image keeps pace with the progress of nature . . . from the far distance one can imagine lyrical truth as the form in which humanity is gradually built up from generations . . . the mere perceptibility of the present is already the future. And the future of man is love'. If this should appear to an austere reader to be the merest burbling, which goes well beyond the bounds of disciplined philosophy, the reader should remember that poetry in feeding on philosophy transforms it, and this passage represents the process of digestion; also, that philosophy feeds on love, and neglects poetry at its peril. All the same, what Ida said of Boris was that 'he did not like going out. He did not dance because of his stiff leg. He was a timid lad who could be very brusque.' His shyness did mask a high view of himself, one supposes. 'I call it vanity disguised as modesty,' Olga wrote to him. A few years later he still appeared in public as 'the most tongue-tied of poets', according to Ehrenburg.

Ida and her sister were spending the summer in Belgium. Ida had been in England for a month or two, at the University of Cambridge, and writing long letters to Boris about the beauties of English poetry. The sisters decided to visit him at Marburg on their way to meet their family in Berlin. Ida gave him the works of Shakespeare and told him he had to study English. They stayed three days, which he spent in their company, delirious with happiness. He was intoxicated by their laughter and by the impression they made. They stayed at the best hotel, he showed them everything and took them to some lectures. The evening before they were due to leave, the old dining-room waiter said to Boris, 'This is really your last meal before the gallows, isn't it?' When he went to the hotel next morning he bumped into the younger sister, but something in the wildness or the seriousness of his manner made her retreat swiftly into her room and lock the door. He told Ida in considerable agitation that things could not go on like this and she must decide his fate. 'Apart from my insistence, there was nothing new in any of this.' She backed away until her back was to the wall, then she refused him.

There were noises in the corridor. They heard a trunk being dragged out of the next-door room. The station was only five minutes' walk away, but when they got there Boris was unable to say goodbye. The express from Frankfurt to Berlin loomed into the station when he had only said goodbye to the younger sister, not to Ida. They were off, and the train was moving. Boris ran along the platform beside it as it gathered speed and leapt for the step of the last carriage. The guard had him by the shoulder, the two girls came rushing out of their compartments with money for his ticket, and the party continued all the way to Berlin. The day faded, evening came on, and the sonorous roof of the Berlin station covered them. There they were going to be met, but the girls preferred not to be seen with Boris in his emotional state. He melted into the crowd. Night fell and it was raining, he had no luggage, no papers and no hat. There was no train to Marburg until morning. He was turned away from several lodging-houses, until he found one humble enough to let him in if he paid in advance. There he spent the night sitting on a chair by his room window with his head slumped on a table. The morning was misty but the mist cleared. After his sleepless night, he was in a strangely exalted state. 'I was surrounded by things transformed. . . . The morning had recognized my face and arrived just to be with me and never leave me. . . . Life's laconic freshness was revealed to me.' He travelled back to Marburg in comfort by the morning train, having borrowed the money from Ida Vysotskaya.

About a fortnight earlier Boris had delivered two papers, one for Paul Natorp's seminar and the other for Hermann Cohen's. Both had been thought well of, and they had asked him to develop his arguments in more detail and re-present them at the end of the summer. In fact, at Marburg he was the shining new star in the heavens of philosophy. He had been working with redoubled fervour on his assignment. What he liked most was not the logical skeleton but the actual writing. 'I had rooted in me a certain vegetable thought habit . . . any secondary idea would unfold endlessly and begin demanding nourishment and attention . . . literary references . . . an increasingly bookish incrustation of bookish quotations.' His landlady received him grimly and his excuses for absence drew still more mocking looks. She gave him two messages that had come, one a letter to say Olga Freidenberg was in Frankfurt, and the other a card asking him to lunch at the Cohens on Sunday. It was then Saturday; he chose to go to Frankfurt on Sunday morning. His books and notes lay all over his room like an organic growth in which you could trace physically the shape of his arguments; the landlady had orders not to disturb it on any account or the order of his thoughts would be lost. Now he went to his room and tidied away everything. For the rest of his life he liked to write his poems in an empty room, at an empty table without books or superfluous papers.

The landlady was scandalised at his going off to Frankfurt instead of lunch with the professor, and really shocked at the tidying away of all his books, but she looked up the train for him, and offered him wooden congratulations on accomplishing his difficult task. He records her as a civil servant's widow, but in fact her husband was a vet. She and her daughter both had alarming goitres, probably due to the continual intermarriage of close relatives in some isolated village. Boris is a bit hard on her and knows it. Years later in 1923 he took her a large walnut cake. But this was definitely the end of philosophy and the end of Marburg. 'The value of the town lay in its school of philosophy: I had no further need of it.' He was fermenting with his new views of art and aesthetics, with creativity as the meeting-point of energy and symbolism, but the issue now was not philosophic, it was practical. Later he suffered a difficult quarter of an hour with Cohen, in which his apologies were accepted in dead silence and he announced his retirement from philosophy. In July he heard the old man give his last Marburg lecture at the celebration of his seventieth birthday. Leonid Pasternak had sketched him with his stick and floppy hat, expounding to reverent students in the early summer. Now he was leaving as an embittered man.

That Sunday in June, Olga Freidenberg was sitting in the restaurant of her hotel in a wide-brimmed summer hat with roses on it, about to eat roast beef *au jus* and feeling extremely grown up. 'Suddenly the door opens and a dazed-looking figure walks towards me over the long carpet. It is Borya. His trousers are practically falling down, his dress is careless in the extreme, but he rushes to hug and kiss me.' She was embarrassed and left with him at once. They walked the streets all day; in the evening when she was hungry he fed her with sausages at a chop-house. He saw her to the station. He went on and on talking, 'while I remained as closed up as a stoppered bottle.' He said nothing about his proposal to Ida Vysotskaya and Olga knew nothing about it. All the same, 'somehow I did not like him this time. Not only was I indifferent but I recoiled from him, I found him garrulous and insubstantial.' As she had already written, he was a brother to her, but as a lover she was repelled by him. 'When he fell in love with me I found him difficult, unpleasant, even repulsive, hard as it is to say so.' At first she had been in some kind of trance, but practical questions cooled her and his letters had stifled her. She had thought of 'a dusty apartment, Borya and I alone in six or seven rooms. He would give me tea from a dirty teapot. How could I bathe? What would Aunt Rosa say when she found out?'

The Pasternak family were touring Europe, but for Boris the situation continued fraught. 'Despite everything,' wrote Olga on 28 June, 'I am very happy that I saw you, even though history will label this meeting of monarchs a failure.' In her diary she wrote, 'I promised the Pasternaks I would visit them in Marina di Pisa. Uncle's household greeted me with joy, only Borya was distant. Obviously he had undergone great personal growth . . . he had nothing to say to me.' The two of them went to Pisa together; Olga wanted to be impressed and then to forget, but Boris, guidebook in hand, studied every detail, like a good German student. He drove her mad and they had a quarrel in which she walked off. 'We no longer spoke to each other. From that day on, Borya did not utter a single sound meant for me alone.' Olga was exhausted, longed to get away, and began behaving impossibly. She lived through an extensive correspondence, and swarms of blue envelopes and telegrams followed her everywhere. One quite innocent but (as usual with her) bizarre rendezvous by telegrams alarmed Rosa, so Olga snatched at the opportunity to take offence and leave.

The main characters in the drama met again at a spa called Kissingen on Ida Vsotskaya's birthday, in a party that included all the Pasternaks, a famous Moscow actor and an opera singer. One should remember that tea in Russia was both a necessity and a luxury, and extremely profitable, so Vsotsky was as near to being upper class as a Russian Jew could be. Fabergé himself designed a silver tea caddy in the nineties in the exact shape of a packet of tea tied up with string and sealed with a paper band like a box of Havana cigars. The birthday was on 1 July. The Josephine that Boris was liking has to be Ida's sister, because Josephine Pasternak was only twelve. 'Delicate, grown up, dear Josephine' was nicer to him than the others. 'My God, how boring these disquisitions of yours are,' said Olga. 'Try to live normally,' said Ida. 'Anyone who hasn't eaten or slept properly is subject to all kinds of crazy ideas.' 'Poor Borya', said Josephine, 'you are all mixed up', and she cried. But the break was not final; he went on seeing Ida from time to time. One evening in 1914 he brought Mayakovsky to see her to recite his poems. The end came only when she married, in 1917. In February, she got engaged and in December she married a banker from Kiev. They got away through Siberia to western Europe. Boris still loved her in a way: he saw her in Berlin in 1922 and 1923 and in Paris in 1935, and it was through her that he corresponded with Rilke. But Boris never really stopped loving any woman he had ever loved. Ida hazarded the view that only her marriage in 1917 set him free to become a great poet. Apart from the fact that there were other stirring events in 1917 besides her marrying the banker, 'Marburg' was first printed as the final poem in *Above the Barricades*, poems from 1914 to 1916.

The process of becoming a poet began at once to absorb all his energies and ambitions. He worked incessantly at his poems, read a great deal, and moved in a circle where he was more successful than he had been with the young women. He seems to have thought of making a living by tutoring, but he also had a stab at translation and at the theatre. From Serdarda and the *Musagetes* group he went to join Lyrika, and in the end the sub-branch of futurism called Centrifuge. The *Musagetes* group had many interests, but he could not bear the computer-like attitude to verse that Beliy promoted; he restricted himself to the group studying aesthetics and symbolism under Lev Ellis, and a neo-Kantian philosopher group under E. Stepun. In spite of his protestations in *Safe Conduct*, and in spite of the epigrammatic bronze tablet now to be seen at Marburg, he had not really said goodbye to philosophy. On 10 February 1913 he read the Ellis group his famous paper on 'Symbolism and Immortality', the full form of which is now lost. It goes on cropping up in his work, even in Zhivago, but I see no sense in discussing it further. There are enough clues to it in *Safe Conduct*. It was about this time, early in 1913, that he joined the breakaway group called Lyrika with Anisimov, Sergei Bobrov and Nikolai Aseev.

Of the young poets of those days he wrote later that only Aseev and Tsvetayeva laid foundations on which they could build securely. He met Tsvetayeva here and there, but they were not close until long afterwards, and the judgement is less interesting for being retrospective. What people happen to go on to write is not a proper criterion for dismissing what others fail to go on to write. Aseev was a most sympathetic character, because he was a fine craftsman and an honest friend to Boris Pasternak, but little more than that. He was less than a year Pasternak's senior, which in this era of swift successive change gives him some significance as a

closer contemporary than most poets. He wrote an enthusiastic
preface to Pasternak's early verse in 1913. He has had less than
justice from western critics because he always wrote after 1917 like
a loyal commmunist, and was robustly anti-American after 1945.
Like Pasternak, he became a futurist, but without losing his way.
He got a Stalin prize for a poem in honour of Mayakovsky in 1941.
He was a Slavophile patriot. Pasternak was pleased to praise such a
poet, and to leave open the possibility that one might write like that
and be like that, and still be a decent poet: he chose (if he chose it)
his own path for personal reasons. He was always a friend of
Tikhonov, six years his junior, who wrote epic ballad-like verse
about modern events down to the siege of Leningrad in the forties.
To dismiss such poets today because they failed to write about the
Gulag is like dismissing Pasternak because he failed to celebrate the
genuine triumphs of Soviet industrialisation in the 1930s. We are
free to prefer him to his friends, of course, and when he praised
Tsvetayeva and Aseev in the same breath we are free to surmise
that he means to refer to the acceptable possibilities of modernism,
and no doubt to make his view look solid by coupling the suspect
Tsvetayeva, who was living abroad, with Aseev who was a safer
name as well as a respectable poet close to him.

We have poems of his continuously from 1912 onwards, though
more than most poets he was constantly attempting to shed the
burden of his early work in later life, by revising it or simply by
dropping it. He was usually most violent against his most recent
past. At the time of *Zhivago* he was inclined to dismiss his poetry in
general, but he worked hard and eagerly at new *Collected Poems*
after the death of Stalin, and he never stopped writing poems until
the end of his life. When he spoke to Isaiah Berlin and gave him two
typewritten chapters of *Zhivago* in 1946, he did reject his earlier
verse, but the verse he rejected by name was only *On Early Trains*,
his most recent collection. He begged Akhmatova not to read that.
The times made it constantly tempting to seek for a new
breakthrough and hope one had found it. When Tolstoy wrote *War
and Peace* nothing was altering very fast; the big Russian crisis in
Tolstoy's eyes was that of Pushkin and his friends in 1825. In
Pasternak's lifetime the pace of the sheer alteration of consciousness, let alone objective events, was of hurricane force. We have
seen him in his youth, trying to keep his footing in a flood-tide of
modern life, and establishing the ground of his early poetry. But

consider his first adult encounter with futurism in the person of Vladimir Mayakovsky.

Pasternak's friend Bobrov, to whom he dedicated an early book, was a dedicated amateur of literary polemics and a troublemaker who did plenty of harm. He aimed to protect Pasternak's futurist purity, and to detach him from the patronage and admiration of the earlier generation. It was Bobrov who alienated Anisimov and V. Ivanov from the young poet, whose trainer, as it were, he set up to be. Pasternak translated Kleist's *Broken Jug* for Gorky's journal *The Contemporary*; when this work was severely handled by its anonymous editor, Bobrov spurred him on to write an intolerably arrogant letter to the editor in May 1915. Later Pasternak discovered he had been corrected by Gorky himself. He wrote a generous and grovelling apology, and they were reconciled, but for years he was overcome with embarrassment at the thought of his first letter. In May 1914 Bobrov engineered a confrontation between Pasternak and Mayakovsky in a café in the Arbat, which was supposed to produce a real battle.

The Arbat, now called the old Arbat, had a number of cafés, some of which have not survived, but there is still one quite small coffee-house nearly opposite the post office and close to some flats where Pasternak once lodged, perhaps 200 yards from Scriabin's house, of the right atmosphere and date. Its door has the most wonderful art nouveau metal decoration of any shop in Moscow. I like to think it was there the historic meeting took place. Both sides of the intellectual duel arrived with friends. Pasternak already knew the poems that were going to be in Mayakovsky's *Easy as Mooing*, and he had heard a thrilling public reading of Mayakovsky's tragedy entitled *Mayakovsky*, which was as early as December 1913. Boris encountered 'a handsome youth of gloomy aspect with the bass voice of a deacon and the fist of a pugilist, who was inexhaustibly and lethally witty'. There was no duel; they fell immediately into a deep mutual admiration and intimate friendship. No one but Pasternak has ever called Mayakovsky handsome exactly, but he was outstandingly impressive to look at. I remember an old Russian émigré in Cambridge weeping with nostalgia in the early 1960s at the memory of 'Mayakovsky in his yellow shirt', leaping on to café tables to recite, before the 1914–18 war. What reminded him was a performance of Zhenya Yevtushenko, of whom within an hour he became an enthralled fan.

All those young people, including Pasternak, were fond of writing manifestos: it was a disease of the day, or a disease of youth, like chickenpox. Poets swan about in shoals like small fishes, taking their divisions and alliances all too seriously. In that little world of poets Mayakovsky was definitely somebody: he had a right to take himself seriously, and so had Pasternak. This was the time when Lyrika dissolved and Pasternak and a few friends joined Centrifuge: if they had been Londoners and not Muscovites, they would probably have been Vorticists. Mayakovsky was twenty years old, but while in some obvious ways he was more grown up than the others, in other ways he never did grow up. He was a personality of the boldest originality and the most striking confidence. There is no doubt that he was a great poet; I for one have never read him without satisfaction and pleasure. I admit that part of the pleasure is his entertainment value, which makes him pleasing to read about as well as to read, but the satisfaction of his poetry is more intense, and his letters are thrilling.

He was born at Bagdadi in the Georgian forests, where his father was a forester. He taught himself to read, and justly hated what early schooling he got. At eleven he used to walk two or three miles to fetch the post and the papers, which he read on the way home. His sister Olga began to bring home left-wing political books and pamphlets when he was twelve. In 1905 his school went on strike for five days, and was then shut down for another four because the boys sang the 'Marseillaise' in church. In February 1906 his father, whom he worshipped, died of blood-poisoning, and his mother moved the family to Moscow in the hopes of negotiating a pension, which in the end she achieved. In Moscow he was Sasha Pasternak's classmate, and Sasha has left an impressive portrait of him at the age of fourteen. He was big and strong and hid an inner sweetness; his greatest treasure was his watch-chain, plaited for him by his father out of horse-hair. In 1906 he was in a circle of Social Democrat revolutionaries, and when some of them were exiled in 1907 he began serious party work. He was arrested in 1908 and sentenced to be under surveillance. He was also expelled from school because his fees were not paid. He was arrested again in 1909 but let out too soon to escape by tunnelling as he intended. In July he was caught in a police trap, described as 'a troublesome prisoner', and released to his mother's care. He was then sixteen and a convinced Bolshevik.

The symbolists were no use to him: 'It turned out one could not write in the same way about something else.' At sixteen he settled to study, attending art school, and spoke at Serov's funeral in 1911. He went hungry and lived on his earnings. In 1911 he took up with David Burliuk, and came under the influence of Rimbaud, by way of Livshits in Petersburg, a family friend of Pasternak's cousin Olga. Futurism, he thought, arose not just from the linguistic experimentalists of about 1910 or from the new painters like Larionov, who is credited with painting on sacking with a dry brush as early as 1905, but from 'Rachmaninovian boredom, our school boredom', the entire classical boredom. School boredom is an important sub-theme; it recalls Jarry in France, whose *Ubu Roi* began as a satire against a schoolmaster and has a certain schoolboy flavour. But Mayakovsky is using living bullets; he believes what he says, just as Rimbaud did at sixteen, and is therefore never thought of as a schoolboy.

The relationship of Mayakovsky and Boris Pasternak is not rightly expressed as a polarity of opposites, though they had their differences later in life. It is a significant alliance, which ripened before the revolution. The chance of their going through the same schooling, however briefly, and Mayakovsky's love of Leonid's friend Serov, let alone the immediate friendship they struck up in the café in the Arbat, point to the similarity as well as the difference of their backgrounds. It is obvious to a modern reader that Boris Pasternak belonged by nature to Mayakovsky's world more than he ever could to Ida Vysotskaya's or Professor Cohen's. The fact that both of those were doomed, and that for a few moments Russia was going to give the illusion of being a Mayakovskian invention, has nothing to do with this. Boris Pasternak had found his *métier*. Yet the futurist manifestos are distressing nonsense: Gorky, Blok and Bunin (who is still the ace up the sleeve of Russian literature) 'need only villas on a river bank: thus fate rewards tailors.' The futurists were to administer 'a slap in the public taste' (the title of the pamphlet). That was in 1913, when Mayakovsky began to dress to attract attention. He had sisters, nice modest girls who worked for the post office and loved his performance, though they never had a penny from his royalties. His adoring mother sewed his strange tunic just as he ordered it. In February 1914 Marinetti gave a lecture in Moscow, dismissing the Russian futurists as art students, primitivists and barbarians, but he was wide of the mark. In spite of all the posing and the intricate quarrelling, they were a new force in poetry. With no Great War they would have taken Europe by storm.

They looked like circus performers and to some extent that is what they were at this time. 'I will make myself black trousers', declaimed Mayakovsky, 'out of the velvet of my voice.' His voice was loud, resinous and on the harsh side. But he had a very soft, affectionate tone which he reserved for women, and according to Ehrenburg one man only, Boris Pasternak, whom he defended at a public reading with 'amorous passion'. Mayakovsky used to quote a particular quatrain of Pasternak's with very high praise. It came from 'Marburg'.

The lasting value of futurism is underestimated at the moment, or under attack. It was memorably sketched by Bruce Chatwin in an essay on the collector George Costakis, reprinted in 1989. 'Man had a Promethean mission to hack up the earth and fashion it to his taste. The position of mountains and other inconvenient geographic features were "far from final". . . . The avant-garde hadn't counted on the Bolshevik uprising, but they were the only group of artists in Russia to welcome it. They behaved with customary lack of caution, but superhuman energy. . . . The uniqueness of the Russian situation encouraged in them an almost Messianic belief in the power of art to transform the world.' The belief and the energy go together. They are essential to the strength of Boris Pasternak's work, as of Mayakovsky's. They are all that matters: dogmas and politics matter much less.

# 3

## The Young Poet

In 1912 Boris Pasternak began to write poems that were printed. We are not able to date them precisely; the progress of any young poet is always to some degree irregular, and it will not do to record it as a graph. In 1914 he produced his first book, *Twin in the Clouds*. About a third of poems in it were reprinted in the poems of his *Early Period* which he selected himself years afterwards for his complete poems. He already had five poems in the group anthology of Lyrika which came out in 1913: the group dissolved early next year and he joined Centrifuge. I have made working versions of two of these, which are impressive examples of his style when it was new. They bear out what he claimed in his autobiography, that he and Mayakovsky were working at this time on converging lines. The sharp particularity of his imagery makes translation difficult, because he precisely controls and exploits every resonance of individual Russian words. But his literary relationship with Mayakovsky in the years before 1917 was intimate, and to my mind there is no saying which of them learnt something from the other or from someone else. Rhyme and half-rhyme are essential to his effects, which in Russian are noticeably dazzling at this time. It is said that Mayakovsky 'invented' some of these devices, and yet Pasternak's style is as personal as if it issued like the soul, naked and complete from the hand of God.

> February. Take ink and weep.
> Write of it in storms of tears
> while black spring burns away
> the thunder of the slush.
>
> Take a fly. For sixty pence
> through the rattle and bell-clang,
> travel where the pouring rain
> drowns out inkdrops and teardrops,

The young poet Boris
Pasternak idealized by
his father, rather in the
manner of his
contemporary Rupert
Brooke; but note the
long jaw.

Where like incinerated pears
from skies full of branches the rooks
tumble into puddles and
drop desolation in deep eyes.

The earth is black under the thaw
and the wind furrowed with bird-cries
and certainly and suddenly
verses drip weeping from the pen.

Early Pasternak is particularly clean and pure, the impression of
every image is crisp, and however strange it may be the echo of its
special sound and meaning spreads through the surrounding lines

like an image in Tennyson's *In Memoriam*. It prepares us for what is
to come. The burnt pear, the gleaming rook, the reflection of the
black bird in the snow-puddle lead to the gleaming black weeping
of that pre-war ink. The rattle of the cab, the hint of incineration,
rooks and the furrowed wind are a perfect background to the final
line. What is he weeping about? He is weeping his poem in the early
spring as if he were Heine grieving over love: it is extremely
generalised. But the thaw weeps first, weeps more, is part of
nature, and he is identified with and excused by the force of nature.
Vysotskaya has become as disincarnate as a theme in music.

> Like copper globs of cinders
> the garden scatters beetles in its sleep.
> Level with me, level with my candle
> hang worlds in blossom.
>
> I pass into this night
> as if into a new revelation
> where the poplar rots to silver
> blotting the bright edge of the moon:
>
> and an orchard like apple-surf,
> a pond like a secret revealed,
> and a garden that hangs on piles
> and holds the sky in front of it.

He seems wandering about with a candle, in the garden on a
summer night, and the garden has an upside-down appearance in
the pond. Worlds in blossom and an apple-surf and the poplars in
leaf suggest the summer of 1913, a time that he spent reading
Tyutchev carefully and completely. The wonderful image of the
poplar is very crisply phrased, and the whole thing has the
mysterious or hidden sweetness of Annensky's garden or of
Tyutchev himself, the notes of a thrush in the forests of the
nineteenth century. The images are very hard to reproduce in
English, because they are so exactly defined yet in our experience
they do not exist. The poplar tree is fine, even brilliant, though
perhaps not as strange to us as it is meant to be, but the candle is
bizarre to us and 'poetic', where it is meant to be ordinary, and the

coppery colour of the numerous beetles is quite lost to us, an image from the other end of Europe.

As he advances, moving among other things towards the over-stylish style of his early prose, Pasternak becomes even harder to produce in English, mostly for similar reasons, yet the crispness of incision, the surgical exactness, remains the same, if only one can keep up with it. In a poem from *Above the Barricades* he is on a river-boat.

> It froze. Clamp of jaws,
> leaves shivered like mad
> in a sparkle of blue duck-feathers
> across Kama it dawned . . .

The jaws crunch into the ice, I suppose. He used a similar phrase half a lifetime later about the boats in the winter ice where Tsvetayeva died. But the astral part of the poem is based on a complex interplay of glow-worms and reflected lights, diving star, icon-light. There are smells and a 'mighty epic in the reeds'. Relative movement – the appearance, as one moves in a train or river-boat, that motionless things, lights in particular, are moving – makes the poetry for a moment as difficult to disentangle as the prose: this theme of the paradoxes of perception is in its extreme form his only vice, but the virtues of concreteness and realism that compensate for it are incomparably valuable, even where we lack the exact experience.

> And morning broke in a blood-bath,
> a flood of blazing oil, to drown
> the stateroom gaslights of the ship
> and the pale streetlights of the town.

It is hard to imagine any such poet in English at that time. Some poets seem in retrospect almost inevitable, like developments of the language itself: Gray and Dr Johnson in English, Racine in French and Brecht in German maybe. But if Boris Pasternak had not existed you could not possibly imagine him. He is as lively as Lowell, as hungry as young Eliot, he has a vigorous energy like that of Yeats, and a simplicity which is noble, the specially Russian gift from Pushkin and Tyutchev. He has the Byronic dash of

Lermontov. Pasternak is by his poetic nature a young futurist: the movement may have debauched other talents but it liberated his. The point is that he is not only or simply a futurist. He will take what liberties he chooses with language and verse-form and with the perception of reality; in 1914 he is only at the beginning of that road, but the liberties he takes are productive. He is not canny, but fruitful: he sees what will work, he grasps at opportunities that he alone sees. Symbolism is out of date almost at a stroke, the drawing-room curtains have rotted or worn through. The poet is fully himself and himself alone, and if he wrote a mass of poetic juvenilia to reach this mastery he tore up or threw away or abandoned it. The poem 'Adlestrop' by Edward Thomas has always moved me as a new note mysteriously caught, even though at the time it remained lonely and unimitated. But consider this by Boris Pasternak.

> Poetry I will take my oath
> by you and end hoarsely crying
> you are no noise of liquid throats
> but summer in a third-class train
> a suburb settlement, not a refrain.

He is the poet laureate of railway journeys. Even in prose: 'Chunks of an approaching rumble came flying out of the fog and hit us in the face like stones; . . . like stone moths the stations rushed past.'

Surely the great summary poem of his early period is the one called 'Marburg'. I love that and have often been tempted to accept its perfected surface as what he most deeply wanted to achieve, an experience emptied and transformed into monumental poetry that appears to exist for its own sake, an icon of the world and not a sheaf of snapshots. It lacks the bravura of 'Improvisation':

> I was feeding the flock of keys
> by hand, to the beat of wings.
> I stood on tiptoe . . .
> Night gargled like phlegm in throats of ponds.

But 'Marburg' is a beautiful and a full piece of construction. It is better and more tranquil as a poem. The experience that went into it is abnormally well documented, and part of its importance as a poem is that it was exemplary for Pasternak for what a poet can make of his life. Here it is, then, as perfectly as I believe it can be translated, by Richard McKane, in a version he generously undertook for this book.

MARBURG

I trembled. I caught fire and burnt out.
I shook. Right now I proposed to her,
but, too late, too frightened – and she refused me.
Her tears make me sad, but I am more blessed than a saint.

I went out to the square. Consider me
to have been born again. All the small things
were alive and, giving me no role,
rose before me in all the significance of parting.

The flagstones burned, and the forehead of the street
was suntanned, and the cobblestones looked
at the sky and the wind rowed through the lime trees
like a boatman. These were all similes.

I somehow managed to avoid their looks.
I did not notice the way they greeted me.
I wanted to know nothing of their riches.
I was running away so as not to howl.

I couldn't bear to hear my inborn instinct
so like a wheeling old man, that came up to me
and tête-à-tête thought aloud: 'Childhood sweetheart.
They're both doomed to need looking after.'

'Walk away' instinct repeated to me,
taking my arm like a wise old professor,
and we walked through the virginal, impenetrable reeds
among the hot trees, lilac and passion.

'Walk before you run' it kept repeating,
and a new sun looked down from the zenith
as though a native of the planet
was being taught to walk again in a new plan.

All of this was blinding light to some.
To others it was darkness that no eye could pierce.
The chicken scratched in the dahlia bushes,
crickets and dragonflies ticked like watches.

The tiles swam, and the noonday stared
down at the roofs impassively. And in Marburg
someone, whistling loudly, built a crossbow,
and someone else silently got ready for the Whitsun fair.

The sand was yellow and devoured the clouds.
The time before the storm played on the eyebrows of bushes.
The sky curdled as it fell on some
blood-clotting arnica herb.

That day, like a tragic figure of the provinces
carries a Shakespeare play in his heart, I carried all of you
from the slide in your hair to the tips of your toes,
staggering round the town, rehearsing my lines.

When I fell down before you, embracing
this mist, this ice, this surface
(How beautiful you are!) – this choking whirlwind . . .
What do you mean? Think again! Lost cause, rejected.

Martin Luther lived here; and here the brothers Grimm.
Sharp-clawed roofs. Trees. Gravestones.
All of this reminds and draws one to them.
All is alive. And all these are also similes.

No, I will not go there tomorrow. A refusal is
fuller than parting. All is clear. We're quits.
The bustle at the railway station has nothing to do with us.
Ancient gravestones, tell what will happen to me?

The mist puts away all the travelling bags,
and places a moon in each window.
Sadness glides over the books like a passenger
and settles down with a book on the sofa.

Why am I such a coward? I know sleeplessness
as well as a school book. We are bound together.
Why am I as scared of ordinary thoughts appearing
as of a sleepwalker approaching?

You see, the nights sit down to play chess
with me on the moonlit parquet floor.
The windows are wide open and you can smell the acacias,
and passion grows grey in the corner and witnesses it all.

The poplar is the king. And I am playing sleeplessness.
The queen is the nightingale, and I am drawn to the nightingale.
Night is winning, the pieces are scattered.
I will recognise the white morning's face.

From Marburg Boris went to join his family in Italy, as we have
seen. They had been in Bavaria; Sasha had paid Boris a visit and
was stopped from getting in the way of his work only by a waiter
who cleverly diverted him to early-morning billiards. Boris
travelled by way of Basle and Milan, descending from the Alps as
from the clouds, and visited Venice and Florence, but Rome was
too far. Venice and Florence are more than enough for a young
man of twenty-two to take in. I like to think of him, guidebook in
hand, sopping up monument after monument, to the fury of his
cousin Olga. But what came of it all in his writing was indirect and
largely in prose. There is no necessary and direct correlation of a
poet's experience with his output, however satisfying the experience may be to him. Painting and architecture had little
obvious effect on him in his early twenties, either because they
were his father's kingdom, and one that futurism was rendering
insecure, or because he had found no new, daring and elegant way
of expressing them. Yet nothing passed him by: he is visually very
conscious for a poet, he had a painter's mind in his verses on the
river-boat if not exactly a painter's limited wishes. However that
may be, he was forced back on his parents at Marina di Pisa by lack
of money. The chief thing he got from Italian art was 'a sensation of
the tangible unity of our culture. . . . Italy crystallised for me what
we breathe in unconsciously from the cradle.'

By this he intended not only that consciousness of Europe which
was central to him all his life, but that curious, always unexpected

succession from known to unknown like a chain of inventive equations which we call artistic tradition. It was in this light that he was, but more importantly was not, a futurist. In 1914 when he joined Centrifuge with Bobrov and Aseev, the opposing 'cubist-futurist' wing of the futurist movement, which was called Hylaea, including Mayakovsky and Kruchenykh and David Burliak, whose sense of European tradition was by no means something binding by logic or in any way similar to a mathematical progression. How long ago they seem now, those educated and destructive boys, naming their magazines and their movements from mathematics and in Greek. I take the name Centrifuge to be a statement of an ideal or a sort of motto about what artistic tradition and innovation mean, but like most such statements it is impressively obscure. Pasternak contributed manifestos to the infighting of the day, but they are best dealt with among his prose, since they have little in common with the reality of his marvellous verses.

There were girls as well as boys among his circle. Aseev married Oksana (or Xenia) Siniakov, one of three sisters who ran a futurist salon in Moscow and at Kharkov; the other two were Maria and Zinaida. With them Boris saw a good deal of Kruchenykh, who was a former art teacher from a school; he had a quality of pedantic extremism or radicalism about language which I have always found pleasing and amusing, as I am sure Pasternak did. They were lifelong friends, and when Kruchenykh was a forgotten man, and his causes looked like fantastical creatures of a lost world, he used to be seen in the late 1940s whenever Pasternak gave a public reading. Zinaida Siniakov married a Mamontov: it was in their house that Pasternak used to meet Mayakovsky, cooking meat patties and reciting his verses in the first winter of the war. 'By then I was accustomed to seeing in him the greatest poet of our generation.' The patties were cooked on the first primus stove that Boris had ever seen, which must have added considerably to their wonder.

At this time Mayakovsky became close to the Brik family, who belong essentially to Petersburg, not Moscow. Osip Brik was only two years older than Boris, the son of a coral merchant and a woman addicted to the works of Herzen. He met his Lili in 1905 and married her in 1912. Lili was then twenty-one; her sister Elsa, who was sixteen, grew up to marry a Frenchman of no significance called Triolet, and then the French poet Aragon. She had the most beautiful and penetrating eyes – small wonder that Aragon wrote a collection called *Les Yeux d'Elsa*. Aragon was a more or less faithful communist, but the connection across Europe is fascinating because it helps to place Mayakovsky's and therefore Pasternak's world, or what that world would have been had Europe remained undivided. One ought to note, however, that he hated the idea of exile, and that even his father held a Soviet passport to his dying day. Osip Brik published and befriended Mayakovsky and Lili fell steeply and perhaps deeply in love with him, but they were not faithful lovers and the affair ended in tragedy. It is interesting but need not be underlined that both Mayakovsky and Pasternak were capable of falling for both partners of a wedded couple, in Pasternak's case the Neuhaus family later in life, but neither was in a formal or any normal sense homosexual. They were just extremely uninhibited in their affections, alarmed though they both often were by the consequences.

In principle, Boris was still living with or around his family. In spring 1913 he graduated. He went on summer holidays with them to a flat at Molodyi, a manor house on the Kursk road lapped in quiet neglect which they loved. The park around it had converging avenues that smelt of lime trees in flower; the tall proportions of its rooms recalled Catherine the Great, who used it on her journeys south. The Cossacks of the retreating army had used it to shoot at Napoleon's vanguard. 'Deep in the park where it merged with the cemetery their graves still stood, neglected and overgrown.' Experience filtered indirectly into poetry: Venice at night through the tinkling of a guitar and the tingling of a constellation. 'I needed to get the whole of Venice into one poem and the Brest station into another.' Sasha observes the importance of the true sentence in his *Essay in Autobiography*. 'Art did not invent the metaphor of its own accord, but found it in nature and reverently reproduced it.' So Venice reflected in circles and figures of sight, 'like a rush dipped in tea'. The density of Boris's early poems arises from their being packed with accurate observations. The deeper experience of life, the meaning of the poems, is in something implied, something that scarcely exists in the text except as a powerful undercurrent, a scarcely conscious undertone in the reader's mind. These are profoundly personal poems and that is how they communicate so immediately and so profoundly.

After the idyllic summer of 1913, writing his poems and imbibing Tyutchev, he sealed his emergence as a poet with the five poems in *Lyrika*, in its first issue as an almanac. Literary politics more or less absorbed him that next winter: in retrospect he speaks with irony of the marching and counter-marching and the discipline. The confrontation with Mayakovsky in the Arbat café as a new member of Centrifuge led as we have seen to a warm friendship. Mayakovsky's star was ascendant over him for about two years, after which, he says, he determined to drop the showiness, or straining for effects that he noticed in Mayakovsky. In the summer of 1914 he deserted his family to work as a tutor to the son of a Lithuanian poet called Baltrushaïtis, who was forty-one to his twenty-four. The estate was at Aleksin on the river Oka. Baltrushaïtis was a friend of other poets of his own age like Ivanov and K. Balmont, and a well-known translator of Ibsen, Strindberg and Oscar Wilde. He had connections with figures of the progressive theatre, including Gordon Craig, whose extraordinary *Hamlet* had recently stunned Russia after being three years in preparation, and Meyerhold.

This opens a new perspective for Pasternak, both as a translator and as a new recruit to the theatre. Not much that we value resulted immediately, but the subject deserves attention because it recurs in Pasternak's life. He was the greatest of all Shakespeare's translators into any language, bold, free and precise, with an intuitive understanding few critics have had, and an energy of intelligence that has not been applied to Shakespeare since Dr Johnson. He made his living under Stalin by working himself to rags at the translation of poetry from a wide range of languages. His conversations with the actor Gladkov reveal his fascination with the theatre. He came to admire Meyerhold greatly. And his last, unfinished work, *The Blind Beauty*, was a play. I have not read the Russian text of the *The Blind Beauty* and I could find almost no one in Moscow to say a good word for it – it is a costume drama and not the kind of thing they find exciting – but it seems to me a wonderful beginning which he would have improved greatly in revision and even in rehearsal. Its only strong supporter was Lev Ozerov, a poet who was a close friend of Pasternak's and acted as his secretary. It is about to have its first performance.

There are two further reasons to be interested in Baltrushaïtis and his influence. When the revolution finally broke out in Russia, Pasternak's immediate reaction was to begin writing a verse play about the French revolution, bits of which have survived. They are not well known but their quality is extraordinary. The second reason is that he translated not only Kleist's *The Broken Jug* for the Moscow Chamber Theatre for Baltrushaïtis, but also Swinburne's *Chastelard*. His version is lost, but the Swinburne original is a terribly dank play. The mind boggles at what Pasternak can have made of it. We know he did plenty of research, because the few bits and pieces he quotes that seem to come from it are not in Swinburne at all; he must have had another source. It is as if his father had suddenly become the lamest of Pre-Raphaelites. As for Baltrushaïtis, he was sphinx-like in expression, as befitted a disciple of Strindberg, and spent the summer of 1914 writing poems about the soul and spiritual views of the fate of individuals.

It must be stressed that the Russian theatre in 1914 was like a tree exploding into blossom. It had been tried and found wanting by its inability to make the most of Chekhov, but experiment was now raging. In 1914 Balmont was translating from Sanskrit while Pasternak tackled Kleist. The motionless dialogue of Maeterlinck in which everything is implied but little is said and nothing happens was a bad moment, but it had passed. Meyerhold, who was the life and soul of the present generation, had an interest in pantomime and *commedia dell'arte*. He once adapted almost negligently while he had flu a play called *The Kings of the Air and the Lady from the Box*, a sensational melodrama of circus life based on a short story about four devils by a Danish writer called Herman Bang. Meyerhold wrote it for a bet, but in the same year (1909) he translated a Kabuki play from the German. The posturings of the absurder futurists were a small part of this extremely rich dramatic life. Had it continued it would have been a world in which Boris Pasternak could have flourished, as Blok flourished, though not without furious rows with Meyerhold. In other directions it is rather hard to see how Pasternak could have made a living. Tutoring was not for ever, and both his employers as tutor were in a way his patrons as a poet. In the first two summers of the war he seldom visited Molodyi or his family. He stayed as long as possible in Moscow, eating and drinking only bread and milk and working day and night, or more night than day, at poetry.

Poets do live like that at times in their twenties, but he either ruined his health or was being ruined by his deteriorating health.

The habit of insomnia, which we first hear of in Berlin the night after his proposal to Ida, and again the night before he left Marburg for Italy, almost as precipitately persuaded by a friendly waiter who looked him up a train, is mentioned in poems. One hardly knows how seriously to take that. Early in the 1914 war it had become a habit. No doubt insomnia has advantages for a poet, obvious ones to a young poet, but Boris was going to suffer for it to the point of nervous breakdown. Pasternak's insomnia was not precisely a self-inflicted wound, but it does look as if it arose from a situation which is clear to us, and which nothing cured, not even marriage.

The summer of 1914 had been one of drought, with a total eclipse of the sun. At the end of it war broke out. Incredible as it may sound now, the Russians were fearful that the French could not survive without them, and their amazing manoeuvres in the forests in which they got lost that autumn were intended to draw off the German armies from the French frontier. The course of the war was like the course of a Greek tragedy: it began with trumpet calls, continued with rumblings and roarings and ended as the audience foresees from the opening line. Boris Pasternak had been to Moscow and been exempted when Russia was mobilised in July: at that time he was still with the Baltrushaïtis family on the Oka. By the outbreak of war he had become tutor to a boy called Walter Philipp, the son of Moritz Philipp, whose house was looted by an anti-German mob. The same kind of thing happened in England of course, but in this case it meant that Pasternak lost his manuscripts and his books. The raid was planned like a pogrom, with police connivance.

'I well remember an evening soon after that, when the sound of an army band playing polkas and marches came wafting towards us over the river, shrouded in a mist which clung to the reeds. Then a small steam tug with three barges came into sight round the bend. They had no doubt seen the estate up on the hillside and had decided to moor their boat for the night. The tug turned round to face upstream and towed the barges to our bank. There were soldiers on board – a large detachment of a grenadier regiment. They disembarked and lit their campfires at the foot of the hill. We invited the officers up to the house to dine and spend the night with

us. They set off again in the morning – a tiny incident from the
advanced mobilisation scheme which was being put into effect.
War had begun.'

He was with Walter Philipp for about a year, and it was during
that year, in the intervals of tutoring, that he first got to know the
Urals, the Kama river and the river-boat of his poem. One winter
he was at Vsevolodo-Vilvo in the north of the province named
after Perm, where Chekov once went. The next winter he was in
the Tikhiye mountains, at the Ushkov chemical factories on the
Kama, working in an office. For a time he was in charge of the
papers dealing with conscription. 'I exempted whole districts, men
attached to the factories and men engaged in defence work.' As the
war went on it became clear to him that as a Jew he himself would
be extremely unwelcome in the army, certainly unacceptable as an
officer, and as an educated Jew all the more suspect. The army was
of course crawling with communists and doubtless the Russians
were right to be worried, but it does look like the famous stupidity
of the officer corps to have fussed so much about Jews. The English
army of the day rolled its eye at Jews socially, but appears to have
accepted Jews as officers. Boris Pasternak was warned by his friend
Shestov who was on leave for God's sake at all costs to stay out of
the war. Shestov was killed soon after that.

The group called Lyrika had formally ceased to exist, according
to Boris Pasternak's own record of events, but admittedly
precision about time is not the strongest aspect of his memoirs.
Later in the year his early collection *Twin in the Clouds* was printed
by Lyrika, with a pleasant introduction by Aseev, who had moved
with him to Centrifuge. About the same time Centrifuge printed
three fresh poems by Pasternak in their collection *Rukonog*. *Twin in
the Clouds* is a very rare book, and I have never seen a copy, though
there is no mystery about its contents. No doubt in the five-
volume edition of Pasternak's poems that we are told to expect
from Moscow it will all be reproduced. Certainly the third of it that
the poet selected for his *Collected Poems* makes a strong, fresh
impression. We must assume that without the war and the
revolution it would as a collection have made him well known
among poets. The book was a new footprint, a sign in heaven to
the young, a new poet. Eliot was noticed in Bertrand Russell's
Harvard seminar because he remarked that Heraclitus reminded

him of Villon. In Pasternak's circle, such a remark would have been normal.

> Where like incinerated pears
> from skies full of branches the rooks
> tumble into puddles and
> drop desolation in deep eyes.

In December 1915 he published some poetry in a collection edited by Osip Brik which included a manifesto by Mayakovsky. His own early manifestos need not detain us for long. What are called his 'Early prose fragments' were written before he went to Marburg, when he was still absorbed by philosophy and very interested in the art of music. They seem to be no more than an attempt to clear his head. He tries out the minutiae of observation, and throws some light, though not much, on the prose he was soon to produce. These writings came to light among his Moscow philosophy notes. 'The Black Goblet' was at least a published essay, written probably in 1914 and published by Bobrov in 1916 in a Centrifuge collection. The title refers to the post-office stencil on packages, remembered no doubt from his father's studio, meaning 'Handle With Care'. He applies it to art: 'The art of impressionism – the art of the thrifty handling of space and time – is the art of packing . . . the absolution of the lyrical.' His language is so over-clever in this piece as to be all but solipsistic: he does not feel the urgency of communicating a view; his essay is a brilliant, self-loving display.

His paper 'Some Propositions' is so much clearer and more mature. It was written much later, perhaps in early 1918. It appeared only in the first issue of the *Moscow Contemporary* of 1922, but it harks back to unfinished earlier business. His futurism is on the whole looser and more amusing, less self-regarding than 'The Black Goblet'. He begins by observing that he can talk easily and freely about mysticism or painting or the theatre, but literature inhibits him. 'A book is a cubic piece of burning, smoking conscience. . . . A book is like a woodgrouse at its mating-call, deafened with itself, spellbound . . . Like the rustling of a forest . . . suddenly it begins to speak with all treetops at once.' What is a miracle, he wonders. It turns out to be Mary Stuart and her lovely little verses which he never forgot (they are not from Swinburne):

Car mon pis et mon mieux
Sont les plus déserts lieux.

The miracle is also Swinburne, he says, with October raving outside, finishing *Chastelard*, 'in which the quiet plaint of Mary's five stanzas swelled into the uncanny booming of five tragic acts'. Uncanny booming is the right word for them. How did the Elabuga (Urals) blizzard know Scots, or how could she and her English poet tell him so lucidly in Russian what was bothering them? The unity of these lives in art is the real miracle. Further ominous October noises suggest this piece was written, or probably only touched up, after October 1917. The rest of Pasternak's essay makes excellent sense. 'By its inborn faculty of hearing, poetry seeks out the melody of nature amid the noise of the dictionary . . . picks it out like a tune and improvises on the theme. . . . Poetry stumbles across nature. The real world . . . has once succeeded and goes on being endlessly successful. It is not something you are disappointed in next morning. . . . It is natural to strive for purity. And so we approach closely to the pure essence of poetry. It is disturbing, like the ominous turning of ten windmills at the edge of a bare field in a black and hungry year.'

His own development as a poet has been disguised by the 1917 revolution, which quickened his pulses of course, but masked his regular and magisterial improvement, because it created an artificial divide between his second book, *Above the Barricades*, which appeared late in 1917, and his third, *My Sister Life: Summer 1917*, which was written between the Tsar's abdication early in that year and the October revolution. A second book is always a new chance for any poet and almost always involves an intensification as well as a criticism of the first. It was *Above the Barricades* that contained 'Marburg' as its endpiece, a fuller and more successful statement than is 'Venice' and his 'Railway Station' in the first collection. He was the laureate of steam and snow and starlight, but Petersburg conquers new territory and flexes new muscles, just as Marburg does. As for the snow, it is not surprising that in the Urals it intensifies.

The Urals are not, as western readers afflicted by a proverbial east wind imagine, an immensely high range of mountains, but they are cold and remote from Moscow. The peasant novelist Rye-shetnikov (1841–71), on whom Kropotkin offers some amazing information in his history of Russian literature and whom Turgenev admires for his truth, records the Urals as a region of semi-Russified semi-savages, most of them unable to count up to five. The Urals were to the Muscovites almost the edge of the known world. Beyond them lay Siberia, on this side of them lay the great Russian river systems. The northern Urals nowhere rise above 860 metres, the southern nowhere above 1077 metres, and the central Urals, which concern us, nowhere above 600 metres. The new road from Perm to Ekaterinburg, a recent imperial foundation of some luxury with a dam and an ironworks and the end of the communications system, never climbed above 380 metres. The iron mining of the region, which is first heard of when it was carried on by Finns, had been exploited by Russians since the eighteenth century: Ryeshetnikov wrote the gloomiest of his novels about it. It is doubtful how deeply the recent Russian industrial and educational revolution had penetrated the Urals by 1917. The law enforcing universal primary schooling was passed in 1908, but it was not carried out until the late twenties. Boris Pasternak feels all his life that he has only to mention the Urals, or in *Zhivago* the Urals as they once were, and their remoteness and coldness will be understood, but the poet himself appears to have enjoyed them greatly. All the same, the coldness in his poetry intensified.

Stars frozen a week ago in midflight
plucked down out of the air and the thin smoke:
the gang of skaters reel head over heels
and their rink tings against the glass of night.

Slower and slower skater, slowly by,
cut your ice-curve and bend away
figure by figure, constellations
cut deep in the Norwegian sky.

Air's shackled, iron fetters froze,
O skaters it is all the same
that earthly night has ivory eyes
snaking along like dominoes.

Numb as a dog's tongue, moon freezes
tight on cage-bars of iron, mouth
filled brimfull like a forger's mouth,
lava-pouring, breath-taking ice.

   Somewhere in the third stanza I get lost; the fourth is complex
but not hard to unravel. It is the image of an animal's tongue frozen
to what it licked. But the fetters and the iron bars have special
meanings, and so perhaps have the mysterious lines of skaters. The
poem therefore is not just a metaphor about reflected light that has
got out of hand, it is not as purely aesthetic as it looks, and its final
stanza is frankly horrible. It is far worse than the rain in his prose
*Suboctave Story* which 'ranted and choked itself in the throat of the
foliage'. This is a fair sample of the Pasternak of the war years. He
never forgot the deep grief of the Russian people at the outbreak of
that war, and he used what authority he attained to exempt as many
people as possible from it. The Urals are 'hands clawing the night',
and the people there are 'Asians on skis with garlands for the pines'.
   The Urals towered, hands that claw the night, in the dark,
without midwife or sign of life,

         they screamed in their childbed, fainted away
         and blind with agony gave birth to light.

         The masses and bronzes of the mountains
         at one touch avalanched in thunder down.
         The train panted along, shyly somewhere
         the ghost of the fir trees went to ground.

   This book as it was first issued was heavily censored by the old
tsarist censorship. The cut lines and phrases were restored later, but
the small, original paper pamphlet, which Lev Ozerov possesses
(though I do not believe any library in England has it), shows entire
stanzas as lines of black dashes. Nothing could make it clearer that
Boris was still writing in the Tsar's world. Still, it was not only
tsarist oppression or incompetence that brought about the
revolution. Russia was still shaken by her humiliating defeat in
Japan, still mutinous with the widespread influence of Tolstoy, and
as the war went on sapped by the Bolsheviks, who had a monopoly
of proposing an alternative to the disastrous war. Why did the same

The 1905 revolution: the soldiers are about to shoot at a demonstration at the Winter Palace on January 9th.

The 1917 revolution: troops brought into Petersburg by the Kerensky Government shooting at a peace demonstration in July.

Youthful allies. Boris Pasternak and his junior by a few years Mayakovsky, not long after the Russian revolution. They are already famous poets, but their paths are diverging.

BELOW The event is nothing: a photo-opportunity for writers to meet the Russian lady parachute champion in 1934. Left to right: J L Bloch, Ehrenburg, Boris Pasternak, Paul Yashvili, N Tikhonov and I Selvinksy. Yashvili and Pasternak met in 1930; Boris had been to Georgia twice since then, and he and Tikhonov were just finishing a book of Georgian poems in translation. In 1937 Yashvili died by suicide. This absurd group is therefore a rare photograph of Boris happy with one of his best friends.

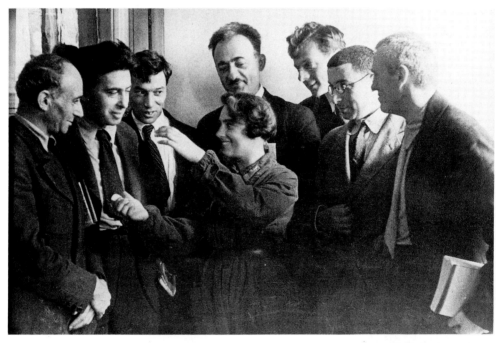

The house in the writers' colony in the woods of the old Samarin estate at Peredilkino. In this house, Boris Pasternak wrote *Zhivago*, in the big bow window on the first floor the side of which is visible to the left. In this house he died.

not happen in western countries? The Russians had more serious revolutionaries, hardened by a hundred years of Siberia and floggings and hanging, and they remembered 1906. The poet passed two and a half years in the Urals in winter and tutoring in summer. Centrifuge were his publishers: he wrote a few poems in their 1916 anthology and they printed *Above the Barricades*. Some of his papers got lost: the poetry of his 1916–17 winter notebook has not been recovered, though its material was recycled from memory, and his version of the awful *Chastelard* got lost by a printer. News of the first revolution of 1917 reached the Urals only in March.

It was not the pressure of war on the economy that caused the trouble. Industrial growth continued at a rapid rate, until in 1916 Russian factories were producing more munitions than the French and twice as many as the British. In that year they made 20,000 light cannon, all their own howitzers and 75 per cent of their heavy artillery. The artillery reserve at the revolution was big enough for three years of successful civil war. But politics were not so rosy: by 1915 almost every one of the numerous parties in parliament was in opposition. The Tsar in that same year assumed command of the army. By 1917 the combined forces of military defeat, extreme war-weariness and constantly diminishing food supplies, partic-ularly in Moscow and Petersburg, had brought people to the end of their patience, and the soldiers joined the people and the Tsar was deposed. The war should have ended then and there, but incredibly and most unfortunately a provisional government was formed which insisted on redeeming Russian honour at whatever cost. Even in January 1917, Lenin had not foreseen the revolution: it was the Tsar himself, with an idiocy that in anyone else one would scarcely credit, who had brought it on, like someone losing a game of chess as fast as possible. The riots and demonstrations had begun in late February. 'The problem was', wrote the politician Shulgin, 'that in this immense city it was impossible to find even a few hundred people who sympathised with the ruler.'

On 28 February a committee of the Duma or parliament set itself up in one room of its palace while a Soviet was already in session in another. Nicholas abdicated on 2 March only because a general assured him that was the only way to go on fighting the Germans. To say that the resulting situation was uneasy is to put it too mildly. But it is important from our point of view to distinguish

clearly between February and October, because in the time
between Boris Pasternak wrote like a man inspired. No one
foresaw the future very precisely, and those months were not a
period of stability or a lull before the storm, they were a process
and a desperate struggle, so that the end came almost as a relief even
to those who cannot have relished it. The most important pressure
on Lenin's side was that the war should end. The 'provisional
government' had no programme and no confidence: it was a
chicken running round the farmyard with the fox already over the
wall. Lenin had arrived on 3 April. Stalin had been in the city three
weeks and in control of *Pravda*, but it had not yet occurred to him
that the strongest Bolshevik card was immediate peace.

When news of the February revolution reached the Urals, Boris
set off, racing towards Moscow. He never forgot that thrilling
winter journey: it became mythical in his memory. He recorded it
in his essay in autobiography, later in *People and Situations*, and in
fiction in *Without Love*, which is the earliest written record, and in
some ways the most truthful. In the account he wrote at the end of
his life it seems clear to me that he was in some slight degree
involved in revolutionary organisation, like the character in
*Without Love*: 'I had to go to the Izhevsky factory to find a
remarkable man called Zbarsky, an engineer recently sent there to
take charge; there I was to put myself at his disposal and work
under him from then onwards.' They travelled fast, in a covered
sledge drawn by three horses, night and day. 'Wrapped in three
long coats and buried deep in hay, I rolled about on the bottom of
the sledge like a heavy sack. . . . I dozed, nodded off, slept and
woke again. . . . I could see the road through the forest and the
stars of the frosty night. Mountainous snowdrifts made huge
bumps on the narrow path. . . . The white shroud of the snow
reflected the twinkling of the stars.' In each version the description
gains in precision, it becomes sharper and harder. 'The waggon
caught the lower branches of the overhanging pines, scattering
their snow'; 'the top of the covered sledge often hit the lower
branches of overhanging fir trees, shook the hoar frost off them,
rustled past.' The forest posting station where they changed
drivers was like something in a story about robbers. 'Later the next
day, there in the far distance were factory chimneys, the boundless
snowy desert of the great frozen river and the railway line.'

Zbarsky was a Social Revolutionary who happened to be an old family friend; Boris Pasternak may have been treated as a potential recruit. To judge from his short story, *Without Love*, one of the best and more direct of his early works of fiction, he was a close but innocent witness. He wrote the story in 1918, when in retrospect it had much more than its physical vividness. Goltsev, a lyrical, dreamy character, feels reality more closely than Kovalevsky, a somewhat sinister political activist who lives in a world of practical revolutionary ideas. *Without Love* was intended to be a chapter from a longer work: it was printed in an obscure socialist journal of 1918 and lay there unnoticed until after the poet's death; but the way in which it announces one of the deepest themes of *Zhivago* is now obvious. It is a perfect fictional vignette of the provincial town, the urgent departures, the special drunken and speed-drunk world of the Tatar coachmen, and the journey itself as they skirt the crowded early-morning road. 'Legs rose and fell, trampling the still lit stars.' The drama of some compromising documents that get left behind, which serves as the thin skeleton of the piece, may really be fact. Such things must have happened often enough in March 1917.

In the year 1917, before he turned to *Without Love*, Boris Pasternak wrote three dramatic fragments, and published them in *Banner of Labour (Znamya Truda)* in the early summer. One of these fragments is in prose; it appears to be intended to read like a nineteenth-century classic, but the result is more like Bernard Shaw. 'They were transporting some convicts,' says the agitator. A little later, 'When I start talking about the countryside, my hands get irresistibly attracted to the window-panes. I start squashing flies,' says the policeman. The dialogue has implications, but it was surely not intended to stand alone. It seems to be a wood-shaving from Pasternak's workshop, at a time when he began more works than one man was ever likely to finish. But the other two fragments go together and they are in verse.

A verse drama of a kind did exist in Russia, less self-consciously than it did in England, but one may fairly claim that nothing in Russian tradition serves to explain these verses. Ostrovsky had written historical dramas in verse back in the 1860s, and there was symbolist dramatic verse, but here is a new voice, very strong indeed and very crisp. It may reflect the influence of Racine; Ben Jonson has been suggested; an appreciation of Shakespeare and of German verse may well underlie it. It has nothing to do with

Swinburne. The truth is that this voice so suddenly heard and so suddenly extinguished is as original as it is impressive. Why did Pasternak never finish his novel or either of his plays? I suppose that he was unable to make up his mind about those crucial issues that must underlie the full working out of a plot, or he was unable to screw himself up to the necessary courage and clear-mindedness. Yet for the brief moment of his dramatic verse fragments, in May and June 1917, he was very clear-minded indeed. He did not return to dramatic form until the Second World War, in a still-unpublished play called *The Here and Now*, which contained some things that later went into *Zhivago*. The process of clarification and concretisation seems to me the same here, only incomplete. It took him a lifetime to write *Zhivago*; *Without Love* is only a brief astounding hint of his powers, as these verse fragments are.

St Just is the protagonist of one scene, and Robespierre of another, though in that also St Just has an important speech. We are in early July 1794 and then in late July of that year. The missing play is about revolution and its morality and consequences, no less. Thunder offstage while St Just meditates on the future, when all our light will wane and insanity will swallow God and light and reason. Men crawl like crabs or lurk like tigers, reason alone can shatter life's black glass. Action is like a flash of ecstasy.

> Is it so often
> Paris lime trees applaud the thunderburst,
> and clouds rave and heaven's unsealed eyes
> blink at the lightning glare as the rain falls?
> Storms are unusual. Sleep and silence . . .

The language is almost naïvely dramatic – at any rate in Russian. I find it powerfully effective, and pointed at moments like Victor Hugo's plays with romantic flourishes that are almost Edwardian in feeling. 'What lance can probe that ulcer?' 'My duty . . .' St Just is closer to Pasha Antipov in *Zhivago* than any other of the prose figures that foreshadow him. 'I love the smokeless flame of men intoxicated by the glow of flaring nerves . . .' The unusual observation of minutiae is rampant in this play. In translation its verse often seems overburdened, and yet in Russian it runs clearly enough. 'The stubble's dusty and the sunbeams gleam / As taut as the drumskins of regiments.' Insomnia is one theme; heavy, thunderous weather is another. Boris Pasternak was not the only writer to think of the French revolution in 1917, but he is surely the most ominous. The violence of reason which is going to look like unreason is a paradox that contained dynamite in May 1917. Does he seek to warn, and did he abandon his play when warning was too late?

The second scene has guns wheeled into position offstage instead of innocent summer thunderstorms; it takes place three weeks later, the night before the 'tenth Thermidor', 28 July, when Robespierre and St Just will be executed, because the Terror has begun to feed on its creators. The verse is tense, playing with exact ear on metrical stress and counter-stress; but the characters are understandably so nervous that their speech patterns become staccato, and thereby harder to reproduce without loss. 'Give me your kerchief.' 'My kerchief?' 'Yes, I need you.' 'Dai Platok.' 'Platok?' 'Nu da.' But Robespierre's monologue is eloquent in a more conventional way.

> That idiot Danton could never grasp
> what I intended. He never dreamed
> what barricades of ideas I built up,
> what castles of the intellect and reason,
> he never knew the mutiny of dreams
> or the thrill of pure concept in revolt . . .
> . . . What is the matter, Robespierre?
> The traitorous confusion of my mind!
> That maddens me. I try to think and cannot.
> Cold sweat, dry fog and mist are all I make.

St Just's reply is as eloquent but more admirable.

> Your words are natural. When you compare
> me to a gnawing mouse, your thoughts to rats,
> it's true: your thoughts go scurrying like rats
> inside a blazing house, they sense the fire
> and prick their snouts up at the flames, snuffle
> hot air: not only your brain boils
> but all the kingdoms of the world within
> throb to the scuttling of those rats, those thoughts
> all tainted with the nasty fumes of death.

> We are not alone. All men have known this;
> they endure the numbness of their final hour.
> But some who overcame that hellish din,
> that brazen roar, smiled and laid down their heads
> triumphantly under the guillotines,
> and those brief days that passed before their death
> make up the story of our commonwealth.

However the rest of this play would have gone, it was a tragedy. Robespierre is full of schemes, St Just is dreamier and more in tune with the weather and with eternity. He is the theorist of the Terror, and a distinctly tragic theorist. His views of the future in the first and second fragment are separated by only twenty-one days, but they do appear to be distinct. In the summer of 1917 there had been no terror, but revolution was on everyone's mind. We are told that Boris Pasternak's fragments fitted well into the general style of the magazine, which printed several excellent poets, mostly of a symbolist tendency. My impression is that he dislikes Robespierre but has a soft spot for St Just, and a tragic understanding of his tragic understanding of revolution. The play is not about Lenin, and on close inspection it turns out to be less directly relevant than first appeared. Yet the lime trees of the boulevards applauding the thunderclap are like the lime trees of the Moscow boulevards. The invasion of human history by a great drench of reason, a prolonged electric storm of reason, is what Russia suffered in 1917. The most extraordinary thing about both fragments is their power to impress directly, their power as poetry. As poetry of revolution, I do not think they were equalled until the poetry of Robert Lowell.

This is a useful place to introduce that great man, because in *Imitations* (1962) he published some Pasternak translations which are exactly right in tone, though they are not always correct in other ways. But as poetic translations they are the best by far that have ever been done of Pasternak, and the liberties they take are only those that Pasternak allowed himself. One is 'Spring', a poem dated to 1916, the year before the revolution. I have reserved it to treat here because the liberation of its mood and language, at least as Lowell catches it, goes with Pasternak's personal sense of progressive liberation in all the various writings we have observed in this chapter.

Now the small buds are pronged
to the boughs like candle-butts.
Steaming April! The adolescent park
simmers.

Like a lassoed buffalo, the forest
is noosed in the ropes of shrill feathered throats –
a wrestler, all gratuitous muscle,
caught in the pipes of the grand organ.

The shadows of the young leaves are gummy.
A wet bench streams in the garden.
Poetry is like a pump
with a suction-pad that drinks and drains up

the clouds. They ruffle in hoop-skirts,
talk to the valleys –
all night I squeeze out verses,
my page is hollow and white with thirst.

Orthodox translations do not much modify this impressionist masterpiece. April in the original is alight, but steaming works better. In the original, the park reeks of puberty and the woods are even more blatant – bolder than Lowell in fact – but steaming and simmering carry the meaning effectively, and he was right to get rid of the woods in the first stanza and to simplify whatever it is that happens in the second. But Pasternak's sponge is alive and has suckers, it is a Greek sponge, and his bench is green-mottled, so, although Lowell is pleasing, Pasternak's third stanza is better and wetter. In the fourth stanza the Lowell is the more obviously exciting, or conveys in his own direct terms the same electric charge of the original. Pasternak is still talking in terms of his Greek sponge, but Lowell has had to abandon his pump. None the less, his version is a brilliant success, and so are the parts of it or related poems that follow, for which I refer the reader to *Imitations*.

In Moscow, Boris was not living at home, more likely because of girls than because of poetry or secret political activity: he was round the corner on Lebiazhii Lane, then in Gagarin Street. Later he settled in an eyrie overlooking the Arbat. But in the summer of 1917 he was in the country with his family at Molodyi with its park and the graves of the dead Cossacks. There he set to work on what was probably the most famous book of poems he ever wrote, *My Sister Life*. What appears to have happened is that he had a new girl who demanded the dedication of a book, but the old book was unsuitable, so he simply wrote a new one on what must have been a proof copy of the old, on its fly-leaves and blank spaces. I spoke to someone who had seen this manuscript. It was not published for years, but long before its formal publication it became extremely well known because written copies circulated and it was heard at readings. It had nothing to do with Russian history but everything to do with being in love.

The surmises of critics that the lost 1916–17 notebook would have showed a smooth transition to *My Sister Life* seem to me ill founded for a number of reasons that I have already implied. The same critics think he was sentimental to praise Aseev for making music out of nothing and crazy to admire shaggy Mayakovsky; but those men were like forces of nature, and that is what he liked. Anyway one should not call Mayakovsky shaggy; he was shaggy only on the inside of his skull. The title, *My Sister Life*, conveys a force of nature. It comes from St Francis of Assisi, whose biographical myth under the title *Little Flowers of St Francis* was the rage of Edwardian Europe and was brought out in Russia by Centrifuge in 1913. What he said of his own poems of this time was that 'In 1917 and 1918 I wrote down only what by character of language or turn of phrase appeared to break from me entirely of its own accord, spontaneous and indivisible, surprisingly beyond dispute.' That happy state comes seldom to self-critical poets, but it does come at times to those who have mastered their native tongue and forged their personal language. It came to Yeats, the most hesitant of writers. It is not the same as improvisation. *My Sister Life* was his credo in a way, and as a credo it deeply impressed his generation and the next. He never went back on it.

Lenin's ruthless leadership dominated the year 1917. When the war was over old Ludendorff wrote that 'In April and May of 1917, despite our victories on the Aisne and in Champagne, it was only the Russian revolution that saved us.' One of the first and boldest of Lenin's touches was of course his journey to Russia through Germany. The next was his declaration of 4 April, reversing the views of *Pravda* and of Stalin and others, by taking a stronger line with other parties and with the provisional government. His proposals were concrete and utopian: the end of the war, fraternisation, and the nationalisation of land, a trump card. He was received with smiles as a crazy old theorist out of touch, but contrary to expectation his proposals turned out to be exactly what people wanted: every one of them was a winner.

The other parties, and the Bolsheviks inside Russia, wanted a preordained historical process to take place, but Lenin saw realities and opportunities for power where no one else noticed them. In June the Minister of War Kerensky contrived to launch a successful offensive, but it was counter-productive because it created a panic in the Petersburg garrison, who had no wish to be cannon-fodder. Lenin did not feel he could act at once because the morale of the front-line soldiers was not yet entirely rotted, but he knew that autumn would be his moment. In August the army tried and failed to take Petersburg. Supplies dwindled, factories shut, the currency collapsed. In September the Bolsheviks had a majority in the Petersburg Soviet, and in October they took over. Lenin's most difficult problem was the resistance of the Central Committee of his party to his strategy as week by week it emerged. The moment before the end, the Foreign Minister Tereshchenko had a conversation with the American ambassador. 'I expect a Bolshevik action tonight.' 'If you can crush it I hope it happens.' 'I think we could, but I hope it happens anyway. I'm tired of this uncertainty and tension.' Meanwhile Chaliapin went on singing as Don Carlos at the Opera, and everything was discussed in the newspapers. Lenin's people took over slowly but surely in the course of a few days in which no one was sure what was going on, not even Lenin until the end.

In Moscow things were even less clear; the relief and excitement that greeted the first of Lenin's decrees are well recorded in *Dr Zhivago*. Those decrees are to be seen in the Krasnya Presnya Museum of the 1905 revolution. They are plain, small handbills about a foot long, simply headed 'DEKRET'. The articles announced are very brief and the sentences are numbered. 'Banking is declared a monopoly of the State. All private banks, offices and syndicates are hereby absorbed into the State Bank. . . . The interest on small accounts will be honoured.' 'All titles and ranks are abolished.' The prose style recalls a handwritten note signed by Napoleon, about three inches by two, in the archives on Corfu. 'Tous les fiefs et droits quelconques sont abolis dans cet isle. Napoléon.' Lenin's style of government was extremely invigorating and dramatic, whatever else may be said of it. At Moscow there was gunfire; a gunner hit the clock-tower of the Kremlin and knocked the clock out of action, but its chimes were restored to play the 'Internationale'. Sasha Pasternak recalls a noise like hammering, as if 'all Moscow beyond the river took it into its head to rebuild itself from its foundations'. At Petersburg the slowness of events was largely due to the reluctance of each side to shoot at the other, but at Moscow there seem to have been fewer inhibitions. At dawn there were scenes of street-fighting and flying bullets. Later the Pasternaks found a dozen bullets embedded in walls inside their rooms, and the outer plaster was pockmarked.

That was only the beginning of the Moscow rising. The telephone was soon cut and there was no news for a week. The shooting went on, Boris came home and the family took refuge in a couple of back rooms overlooking a yard. Tsarist artillery fired shrapnel from the Arbat, including a shell that failed to explode, which remained stuck in the yard wall until 1936. Another hit the guest-room tap. The family took shelter in someone else's flat on the lower floor. Sasha and his father poked their noses out into the yard. 'We found ourselves in the midst of a frenzied bee-swarm, the air rang with objects buzzing to and fro . . . metal squealing through the air, the jarring whine of steel, a thin, sustained ringing . . . frightened birds in flight.' There were casualties in the flats; the fighting lasted many days. When Boris Pasternak's critics forty years later claim that he left the actual October revolution a blank, and failed to embody its heroic myths in *Dr Zhivago*, one should remember this. Moscow and Petersburg had different experiences; it is against a Moscow background that one must feel Zhivago's excitement at Lenin's early decrees.

No lamp burned. Sasha records that 'Occasionally they glowed red and dim of their own accord, to flicker for a moment and go out. Water in the taps was equally uncertain. There was no paraffin.' Candles were hoarded for extreme emergency, and life in one's lair was as monotonous as life in the air-raid shelters of the Second World War, except that it went on like that for much, much longer. 'Bedlam surrounded us. No one spoke any longer. . . . And then suddenly everything stopped. The air drained clear, and a terrifying silence fell.' Boris and Sasha crept up to their own flat and Boris opened the piano. Sasha begged and implored him not to play, not to attract fire. He slammed the instrument shut with a crooked smile. At that moment the last tank trundled down the street, firing this way and that from the merest ostentation. In a few minutes the telephone rang. Josephine and Lydia Pasternak had been trapped with a cousin by the firing, and they were hysterically glad to hear that their family was alive. Days later there were still outbreaks of shooting, disorganised and wholly unlike the regular volleys of 1905, but frightening enough. That was when Sasha was left in an abandoned tram between the university and the Kremlin, and deserted it himself, preferring the icy nuzzling of the snow. 'At home they were waiting for me with even greater anxiety than before. From then on, the anxiety of waiting got its teeth deep into every citizen, never to let us go.' That is the end of Sasha's book.

The Bolshevik leadership slipped into Moscow in 1918 with deliberate secrecy, because they were still uncertain of the support of the railway workers. Stalin tore down a ministerial requisition notice from a grand house in Moscow and guarded it for his smaller ministry with Lapp sharpshooters, but the Council of Ministers pushed him out. Lenin had austere tastes: for the rest of his life he lived in modest quarters in the Kremlin, but a door of his office led directly into a telephone exchange, the nerve centre of the revolution, and he commanded a private library of ten or twenty thousand books.

Moscow was once again the governing city of Russia; the usurpation of beautiful Petersburg was over. Moscow herself is by coincidence the heroine of Pasternak's lifework.

# 4

# Consequences

When the Minister of Education Lunacharsky first arranged for the government to meet the writers, only Mayakovsky and a couple of his friends turned up. Mayakovsky was furious that his own branch of the futurists was not immediately accepted as the official and exclusive expression of the revolution. The idiotic situation was mirrored in several directions. If Mayakovsky or whoever it might be was personally in revolution against the bourgeois world and its values, then the new state should accept the extravagances of the new art as its natural expression. So movements proliferated, some of them in the wildest mutual contradiction. Lenin was mostly too busy to care, though the acid comments that he did let drop would have been warning enough for less fervent artists than those ego-intoxicated sectaries who loomed so large at the time. Meanwhile a working-class writers' movement arose with some obvious claim to inherit the fruits of victory, but Lenin and Trotsky viewed it with doubtful eyes. How could there be a working-class culture, since by the time it becomes a culture it will cease to be working-class? This embarrassing question has never really been answered except pessimistically; one must remember that Lenin's mother was a German schoolmistress.

Yet against all physical likelihood the early years of the revolution saw an explosion of new life in all the arts: not because the revolution itself was an intellectual event, but because of the new-found sense of freedom and daring, the removal of tsarist censorship, and the excitement of the young. The new movements in the arts, and even the new individual styles, had their origins before 1917, but the revolution offered them a national and a world stage. And they were intensely dramatic. Constructivist monuments and the modernist decoration of railway trains must have been as amazing to live with as they are extraordinary to read about. The one element of modernism the Russians were lucky to

Cartoon of Boris
Pasternak as the sphinx
of Russian poetry, about
1930. The proletarian
poets thought him
insufficiently
downright.

have abolished was one that today we inevitably supply when we
think of them: nostalgia for a golden age that has passed away as
irrevocably as Elizabethan court dances or the sculpture of fifth-
century Athens. It passed away very quickly.

In 1922 Boris Pasternak had a conversation with Trotsky, in
which he was asked why as a writer he 'abstained from social
themes'. The government did vaguely wish to mobilise all talent to
forward the unfinished revolution, though it had little idea how.
Pasternak wrote to Bryusov about this conversation. 'I wish I had
told him *My Sister Life* was revolutionary in the best sense of the
word. That the phase of the revolution closest to the heart and to
poetry – the *morning* of revolution, and its outburst, when it returns
man to the *nature* of man and looks at the state with the eyes of

*natural* right . . . are expressed by this book in its very spirit.' He harked back to that moment more than once. In 1925 he wrote to Mandelstam about *Spektorsky*, a kind of verse novel he was then writing. 'This is a return to the old poetic rails of a train which was derailed and lying at the bottom of an embankment for six years. . . . Everything is rusty, broken, unscrewed, covered with encrusted layers of superficial insensitivity, deafness and dull routine. It's disgusting – but at least my work is far removed from the present day, just as it was at the time of our first literary efforts, our joyful labours – do you remember? That is the charm of it. It reminds me of forgotten things, gives new life to powers which seemed exhausted. The illusion of an amazing epoch vanishes. The apocalyptic style (the end of an age, of a revolution, of youth, the collapse of Europe) sinks back between its banks and gets shallower until it ceases to flow. . . . And so I return to unfinished business.'

Life was terrible: war led to famine, civil war (in which the revolution was extremely hard pressed) and typhoid. It was lucky that Sasha Pasternak as a young architect knew exactly which bits of the roof-beams one could cut away and saw up for fuel without causing the house to collapse, as a number in Moscow did in the winter of 1918–19. Intellectually, Russian life was freer than it ever had been or was going to be, always providing the writers did not meddle with power. Even the top anti-Bolshevik generals had their memoirs published in Moscow, once the civil war was over. The Parnassian poet and adventurer Gumilyev (1886–1921) was shot for conspiracy and treason, but not because he was married to the aristocratic Akhmatova in 1910 (divorced 1918) or because he was crazy about Théophile Gautier. He was a man of action, a traveller in Africa, who enlisted as a private soldier in 1914 and was twice decorated. He wrote his best poetry in his thirties, worked hard at translation as Gorky advised, and taught younger poets. Mandelstam published *Tristia* in 1922, Akhmatova her *1921 A.D.* in 1923. Zamyatin, the advanced novelist and designer of ice-breakers, and Shklovsky, the military engineer and linguistic theorist, were typical of the times as much by their eccentricity and loneliness as by their mechanical skills. Middle-class skills continued even though middle-class lives and incomes had altered. Sasha Pasternak designed Lenin's first mausoleum. The problems for poets were only the usual poet's problems of how to make a living and how to become famous and where to live.

From Surtsev Vrazhek Street, where he rented rooms over-looking the Arbat from 'a bearded newspaperman, extremely absent-minded and kindly', who in turn thought him 'eccentric and unsociable', Boris went to work at the Commissariat for Education as an analyst of foreign news, working in the library. Meanwhile Blok worked in the same ministry, and Tsvetayeva very gloomily at another. Boris's minister Lunacharsky was his father Leonid's friend, a resource and refuge to a number of intellectuals and particularly well disposed to the Pasternak family. Sasha lived on at Volkhonka Street until the thirties. There was nothing to eat or to burn, and superfluous possessions were swiftly sold. Leonid worked on with freezing fingers all winter in a sealed room. In spring when Sasha and Boris went to open it they found an abandoned cup of tea with its disc of yellow ice. 'We were ice-locked music', 'We were the music in tea-cups', 'the slush-slobbered backstairs'. Sasha is surely right to associate these phrases from his brother's poem 'The Sublime Malady' with that winter (1918–19), which they spent together at Volkhonka.

Boris became brilliant at conjuring fire and conserving wood; he was also writing poetry of genuine greatness and newness that electrified Mandelstam and Tsvetayeva and every other poet who heard it. Manuscript copies exist in handwriting not his, like the copies of the young Tennyson's poems made at Cambridge by his friends. In the winter of 1918–19 Tsvetayeva met him on the way to sell his books. Boris wrote at the end of 1918 and in January of the Kremlin as a ship torn from its moorings in a roaring sea, of the temptation to suicide in the past year and the terrifying new year: 'Take me shattered as I am, and tackle my re-education.' He was translating with incredible energy and industry for an ambitious scheme sponsored by Gorky to bring literature to the people and to keep writers alive. Boris had a low-grade ration book at that time. In the year that ended in June 1920, he reckoned that he translated 12,000 lines of verse: about a thousand a month, about fifty a day. Most writers have worked that hard for a week or weeks, but very few for a year. If it was true as he said that he had to give up creative work (one must insert a 'more or less') in the spring of 1918, then his creative power in 1917 is utterly astounding; but the truth probably is that he worked in a fever at every moment that he could.

> Life my sister in flood today breaking
> in waves on all our heads in the spring rains,
> people are grumbling in their cheap watch chains
> and like snakes in the grass politely sting. . . .

> . . . They wink, they blink, and yet sweetly somewhere
> my love like a mirage and others sleep
> while the heart splashes along carriage footboards
> scattering bright windows over the steppe.

The tone of urgency, of an energy which is just controlled but might easily break out into fever, is in the core of these verses and many others from this time. He read them aloud when he had to, but not as the poised dramatic poems they are, as he read them later: as a young man, he was shy of public performance and stuttered and forgot lines and read badly. But their quality communicates immediately. Take this, for example, on Pushkin's famous poem 'The Prophet', with an interesting allusion to Dante as well as Pushkin in the last line. The poem enacts the control of creative fever and insomniac power.

> Stars were racing, waves washed a headland,
> salt was blinded, tears slowly dried:
> but the mind raced, bedrooms darkly sighed.
> And the Sphinx listened to the desert sand.

> Candles swam. Colossus's blood chilled:
> over his lips and spreading all the while
> hung the blue shadow of the Sahara's smile,
> and the night waned and the tide turned and spilled.

> Out from Morocco touches of sea-breeze.
> Simooms blew. Archangel snored in snow.
> Candles swam. The rough draft drying now:
> *The Prophet*. Dawn broke over the Ganges.

He was not unwilling to write poems about poetry, or philosophy, or any other subject. But the root of his verse was a superhuman, perfectly human hymn to life itself, as both Tsvetayeva and Mandelstam saw. 'A moment's pause, a spring. With Pasternak even sleep is on the move,' Tsvetayeva wrote. And Mandelstam said that the experience of reading him was 'to clear the throat, strengthen the breath, renew the lungs. Such verse must be a cure for tuberculosis. We have no other poetry so healthy in these days. This is fermented mare's milk after American tinned milk. . . . He has opened up a new Russian verse structure adequate to the maturity and virility attained by the language.' It was not only that he could be rhapsodic, though the longing for that underlines much of the hunger so thwarted by most poetry. 'Thoughts whipped to a white froth / Of woodpeckers, clouds, heat, firtrees and pinecones.' Nor is it only his technical mastery, which makes him to this day an example to young poets and a fertile source of unexpected lessons, but it is what he has to say, it is his confident sense of the world, that make him admirable seventy years afterwards. He enjoys the paradox that poetry is a simple natural force.

> It is a whistle blowing taut,
> the crash and crush of the spring ice,
> the leaves that night's icing has caught,
> two nightingales in a duel,
> the cradled pods of the sweet peas,
> and what tears of the cosmos fell.

These are famous lines, but perhaps Boris Pasternak is at his best when he is not quite so obviously astonishing. For him all poetry is a *tour de force*, and so is all prose at this time, but it is often his quietest poems, more like Tyutchev's, that haunt the mind. The paradox itself is almost too elegant; it is as light as a sorbet or a well-whipped syllabub, a special taste like the poems of Herrick. The more particular and personal poems are more universal and enter deeper into the world.

> Heartbeat of a boat in the breast of the lake,
> the willow hangs stroking and kissing
> neck, knuckle, rowlock, tickling.
> Could it have happened? There was no mistake.

This could be used for a beguiling song
and it would mean lilac reduced to ash,
richness of camomile, dewdrenched and crushed,
lips bartered for a star half the night long.

This is to embrace the universe as strong
Hercules holds, hugs to him, embraces,
this means the fortunes of the centuries
squandered for nightingales and for their song.

This beautiful lyric appears to indicate romantic love at least by
heavy hints, but the consummation remains unclear and cosmic;
the book was written as a collection and certainly dedicated as love
poetry, one might suppose, until one sees it is dedicated to
Lermontov, a poet who was both cosmic and romantic in dashing
verse. The poem about the boat on the lake is also surely a
philosophising lyric. The poet's playfulness with the problems of
epistemology (the nature of experience and truth) is a little more
than play. The nature of time and the eternal present nature of
reality have entered so deeply into his thoughts as almost to
consume them. In case readers pause too long over unnecessary
difficulties one should perhaps add that lilac burns with a delicious
smell, and the smell of trodden camomile, commoner in nature
than in gardens, is better still, and 'half the night long' is added by
me for the sake of a rhyme. Rhyme is relatively easy in Russian,
and Pasternak was a master of sounds including subtle half-
rhymes, which cannot be reproduced in translation; but since
standard translations of his poetry already exist it seemed worth
attempting rhyme of some kind as an essential feature of his verse.

*My Sister Life* is divided into sections and carefully planned. The
first poem is a section of its own and a tribute to Lermontov's
'Demon'. The mctre is not Lermontov's, but the dash and the
Byronic lightness are his. The next section is 'Isn't it time for the
birds to sing?' about rooms, gardens, orchards, girls and mirrors in
which gardens wrestle and shake their fists. 'The Book of the
Steppe' follows, with a girl and a train and a search, then
'Entertainment for the Beloved', including the boat poem, an
extravaganza on 'the ear-splitting pea' of a policeman's whistle,
and an ominous 'English Lesson' about Desdemona and Ophelia,
who 'entered with faint hearts / The pool of the universe / and

quenched their bodies with other worlds.' 'Lectures in Philosophy' begins with splendidly unexpected definitions of poetry, of the soul and of art. 'It falls like a ripe pear into the storm / With a single clinging leaf.' That is the soul, and art 'rips open its shirt, / exposes the hairy chest of Beethoven'. Gardens and creation itself are somehow the eruptions of accumulated human passion. In the rest of the book we seem to follow a story of an affair which we cannot quite follow, as in *The Waste Land*. Near the end is a section dedicated to Helen, who turns out to be Helen of Troy. Here and there throughout the book come short flashes of light on his sense of what was happening in Russia in 1917: 'the surf of Europe's wavering right / proud of itself on our asphalt', an emergence from the catacombs.

The sixty or so poems that resisted the pattern of *My Sister Life* were gathered in *Theme and Variations*, written at more or less the same time but published in Berlin in 1923. The theme is Pushkin, surely the greatest of all nineteenth-century poets in any language, who has the distinction of inventing the Russian short story and the Russian novel (he was Tolstoy's formal inspiration) as well as Russian verse, which at a stroke became in his hands a pure, strong, flexible and modern medium capable of infinite resonances and still unexhausted delights. Boris Pasternak can never have written a poem of more grandeur and simplicity than his 'Prophet' in *Theme and Variations*, which can be dated to 1918. His despairing poems of the terrible winter of 1918–19 were a short separate cycle called *Illness*. They were not published at the time, but nor of course were any other books of his verse in the awful conditions of the civil war and the epidemics that went with it.

> In all the world is no sorrow
> that is not medicined with snow.

His translations and prose ran into worse difficulties than his verse. His translation of Ben Jonson's *The Alchemist* was probably intended for performance, but it was not printed until 1933. His Swinburne's *Chastelard* was lost, and his Goethe's *Secrets* was lambasted by Blok as editor, who called it 'cumbersome, contrived, stilted, fussy and untalented'. Pasternak agreed with what he described as 'this contemptuous and devastating comment', and meekly revised his version, which was printed in 1922. By spring

1918 he had set his heart on writing a long novel, of which he sought a vague model in Balzac. He told Tsvetayeva of this project, which after all is a normal development for a young poet. He called it 'a long novel with love and a heroine'. I am sorry we cannot read it, because one would like to confirm that by 1918 he knew a lot about women. But the manuscript got lost, all but the first chapter, which came out as a short story called *The Childhood of Lyuvers*. He also wrote his *Letters from Tula* (a provincial railway town a few miles from Tolstoy's house) in 1918. All these came out in 1922, and it was on the grounds of these 1922 prose publications that Zamyatin in an essay written much later, and yet long before *Zhivago*, hailed him as the most promising prose writer in Russia of the entire *nouvelle vague*. Zamyatin's opinion should make us pause: it is a thrilling and a highly unexpected compliment. Nor was it just the intuition of an eccentric genius. Fedin, who helped to condemn *Zhivago*, wrote in *Novy Mir* in 1936 that 'we prose writers are as proud of him as a prose writer as you poets are as a poet'. V. S. Pritchett, a critic equal to Zamyatin and light-years beyond Fedin, wrote that the key to Pasternak is his prose; his idiom 'puts poetic and popular speech side by side . . . one of the few writers in prose to create a language close to the voice of our aural, visual and scientific culture.'

The first of Boris Pasternak's prose exercises to survive was written as early as 1915. It is called *The Apelles Mark*, and directly reflects on juvenile notes (the name of the character 'Relinquimini') and the Italian holiday after Marburg. But it has little significance beyond its cleverness and its German colouring. It is a young man's story about Heine in love, such as might appear in an undergraduate magazine and be noticed for its brilliance. Heine is challenged to a literary contest, but transfers it to life and seduces his rival's mistress. The game is played out like super-chess, and one notes that in 1915 a Jewish poet still appealed. The lovers are 'as excited as children playing the siege of Troy in the back yard'. But *The Apelles Mark* is no more than a clever exercise, something less than a detective novel though more densely and intensely written. It was printed long afterwards. *Suboctave Story* was written about eighteen months later, but rediscovered and printed only after the poet's death. Once again it suggests Marburg, but though it is more gripping it is less clever. Had Pasternak written nothing but stories like these, he would at least have become a Russian equivalent of M. R. James. As it is they are the merest fallout, but fallout rather of his interesting and wide-ranging talent than of the genius which was already apparent in his poetry.

*Suboctave Story* has a German setting and reveals German influences: Hoffmann and Kleist have been mentioned, though the prose style does not look to me like Kleist. A provincial organist in a fit of inspired improvisation has somehow crushed his son to death by an unlikely accident with the organ's mechanism. He flees and later returns but he is recognised and expelled again. The tale as Boris tells it is full of resonances from what we know of his life, but it tells us nothing new, except perhaps that he like other writers could feed his experience of life quite ruthlessly into fiction, remoulding it as he saw fit. There is a town fair with nicely sinister undertones, and a character who 'could have forecast everything that happened'. One feels a foreigner in the homely German community, as Pasternak had done. This story is the merest experiment with certain aspects of fiction, yet it is memorable and frightening, perhaps disturbing. *The Childhood of Lyuvers* is masterly by comparison, because it enters so delicately into the psychology of the young girl. To judge from what transpired in later life, sibling rivalry and the intimate love that goes with it were rampant in the rather crowded Pasternak household. Sasha was as bright-eyed as a monkey, and never forgot his younger-brother attitude to Boris. Josephine married a cousin; her sister was a psychiatrist and married one. Their sisterly friendship was not without rivalry, and for many years Josephine felt her brother's reputation was inflated at her father's expense, while Lydia felt her own talents as a poet were overshadowed by Boris. Yet the moving story of *The Childhood of Lyuvers* must to some degree be based on theirs.

Lyuvers is born and brought up in Perm in the Urals. 'The white she-bear in her nursery was like an enormous chrysanthemum shedding petals.' On all his stories he lavishes 'poetic' phrases, but in this one they have the simplicity, not just the complexity, of his verse. The story is complicated, but it was due for development in a long novel. There are wonderful sweets and still more wonderful stones: 'like drops of almond milk, others like splashes of blue watercolour, others like a solidified tear of cheese. Some were blind or somnolent or dreamy, others had a gay sparkle, like the frozen juice of blood-oranges. You did not like to touch them.' Trains depart, lights are thrilling, the idea of Asia is intoxicating.

The events are genuinely dramatic, one rushes from page to page, and, most satisfying of all, the whole elaborate construction winds back into the young girl just becoming aware, just beginning to grow up. Lara in *Zhivago* contains a good deal of Lyuvers as an adult. She is passive and feminine, her brother is active and boyish; one becomes extremely fond of her and feels protective. The grown-ups are rather deadly, rather false. It is a great pity that the novel is lost. Akhmatova noticed later in life a quality of eternal childhood in Pasternak. My own view has been for a long time that genius is only a mysterious survival of the powers of childhood, with adult powers that for some reason have not destroyed them: that fits Boris Pasternak, and this chapter illustrates it.

Of course he was not writing in a vacuum, even though he constantly refers to his experience before the revolution. The saddest event to him of the few years under Lenin in which he was writing but not publishing much was the death of Blok, a victim of poverty and the weather, but also of a deep personal disappointment and despair. Desperate attempts were made to save him by sending him abroad, but they were too late. Mayakovsky and Pasternak tried to defend him publicly, but they were not successful. 'The Twelve' was a famous poem, written swiftly in a mood of manic exaltation that had not lasted. It was obvious to anyone with literary common sense, which neither Pasternak nor Mayakovsky, nor of course Gorky and Lunacharsky lacked, that Blok was a great poet, the greatest survivor from the symbolist movement and from the Russian past, but Blok was hounded by a rabble of revolutionary idiots. He was unable to keep himself warm, he was very ill, and appeared vulnerably old, though when he died in 1921 he was only forty-one, just ten years older than Pasternak, and thirteen older than Mayakovsky. His greatest poetry was written between 1907 and 1916, between the ages of twenty-seven and thirty-six; he could not have survived long except in exile.

In 1905 Blok carried a red flag. In 1908 he gave a courageous, incendiary oration about Bakunin. In 1914, when Mayakovsky's enlistment was disallowed 'for lack of loyalty', Blok was one of those who appeared in print with the futurists in *The Rifleman*. Still, the Briks preferred the bread of Mayakovsky to 'Balmont's tasty éclairs, Blok's sugar candy, and the new lilac-tasting ice cream'. Lunacharsky was excited by Mayakovsky, but had the hard task of quieting him on committees. Lenin rather disapproved of him. Blok's view was that 'the intelligentsia can and should co-operate . . . it has always been revolutionary. Its rage with the Bolsheviks is superficial. Reconciliation is coming.' That was in January 1918: his poem 'The Twelve' appeared in March. He wrote an essay on Catiline that year, which compares interestingly with Pasternak's dramatic fragment on Robespierre. In that year May Day was Russian Good Friday; Moscow was full of futurist exhibitions, and an old lady observing a large picture of a fish's eye lamented that 'Now they want us to worship the devil'. Mayakovsky revelled in fame, films, the theatre, but according to a Tsvetayeva letter of 1921 he protected Akhmatova. Lunacharsky in a review denied his central importance and admitted Akhmatova's role: 'the hermit Akhmatova . . . can represent old Russia.' Blok's decline was swift.

In 1918 he was writing 'On the last days of imperial power', but early in 1920 a mysterious, incurable disease began to consume him. 'We saw his deep sadness,' wrote Chukovsky, 'but we did not realise it was the sadness of a dying man.' When he read some poems aloud at the Press Club, he was followed by some young ass, one of the numerous imitation Mayakovskys, who said, 'Where's the dynamics? These are a dead man's poems, written by a corpse.' 'It's true,' murmured Blok. Whenever he was asked what made him stop writing, he answered, 'All sounds have stopped. Can't you hear there are no longer any sounds.' In 1921 he gave a speech about Pushkin, in which he attacked the mob. 'I close my eyes so as not to see those apes,' he said to Chukovsky. To Mayakovsky he was friendly, and even in private Mayakovsky admitted just how inimitably good a poet he was. One day Blok was due to give three readings. Pasternak and Mayakovsky met at the first, at the Polytechnic, and found that an attack of booing and catcalls had been planned for the second, at the Press Club. They went on together to prevent it, but fatally they walked, and by the time they arrived it was over and Blok had left. 'They did not shrink from telling him he had outlived his time and was inwardly dead.' A few months later he died. Mayakovsky met him once in the early days of the revolution, a thin, stooping figure in a soldier's coat, warming himself at a street fire near the Winter Palace. 'Do you like it?' he asked. 'It's pretty,' he answered. Then he added, 'They've burnt my library in the country.'

The elder Pasternaks went abroad with their daughters as soon as travel was permitted, to Germany, as a temporary halting place which became permanent until they ended up in England during the Second World War. All that sad, rather noble story of Leonid's and Rosa's later lives and their deaths belongs to the very nature of exile. In 1920 there was economic crisis in Russia, and Boris took on some responsibility for his family. He wrote a petition that summer to his ministry, complaining of the drudgery of translation at the rate of 12,000 lines a year, which drove him from the province of art and even of craft, and subjected him to 'an impossible professional slavery which given the inevitable social inertia cannot be removed'. The ironies and sarcasms of this petition are fine, but its substance is less reliable. Writers can and do learn from translation even on a Herculean scale, as Boris Pasternak could and did, but slowly, at the slow speed of life, because one can learn only what one is ready for, find only what one is looking for. Boris Pasternak's *cri de coeur* was not just about hard work but about money.

His mother had a serious heart condition and Leonid had trouble with his eyes. Lunacharsky seems to have arranged their passports, which of course were simply an excuse to get out of an intolerable situation. In the triumph of Malevich and his constructivist friends, Leonid's generation of artists were victims. Even Chagall lost his job at Vitebsk. Yet Leonid was actually loyal to his country, drew and admired Lenin in Russia (and Gorky in Berlin), planned a Soviet exhibition, and was close friends with the Soviet ambassador in Berlin. He moved to England only under the shadow of Hitler, to settle after the death of his wife in August 1939 in Oxford, in an enclosure of early Victorian buildings and overgrowing gardens, not too far from the painting collection of the Ashmolean Museum. His diaries die out into sad Tolstoyan jottings, but in his last days he liked and trusted Churchill, and spoke of peace and progress. He died at the end of May 1945. His daughter Josephine wrote later that 'When Mother died it was as if harmony had abandoned the world. When Father died it seemed as if truth had left it.'

Somewhere along the line there are persistent rumours of a certain alienation from Boris, or even a rejection of him. It is not apparent in any letters that I have seen, though it might be thought to be implied in the poet's failure to visit his parents in the mid-thirties, but as we shall see there are other interpretations of that. We are told, in what sounds like a quotation from Boris exasperated, that he applied 'every year' for permission to visit his parents but never got it. In what correspondence we do know they exchanged, Leonid sounds elderly and somewhat petulant, attempting to rein in his son from a distance when he was nearing forty. His pride in Boris hardly appears, though he must by then have felt it. I was told in Russia that the trouble was Boris's 'abandonment' of Judaism, but Leonid was not Orthodox, and, although that may well lie at the bottom of whatever estrangement took place, it cannot have been a clear, formal quarrel.

In the autumn of 1921 Boris met an extremely suitable Jewish girl, an artist from Petrograd called Zhenya (Evgenia) Louré, and in spring 1922 he married her. In August they left by ship for Berlin, where they stayed nine months. The passport excuse was health, but it looks to me as if they might have moved into that state of suspense which in his family's case transformed gradually into perpetual exile. Zhenya was well educated, spoke French perfectly, and looked like a Ghirlandaio. 'One wanted to bathe in her face.' Boris found life in Berlin far less interesting than that of Moscow, and Germany reduced and sad. Berlin at that time was full of Russians. Many of the aristocracy and officers of old Russia were driving taxi-cabs or working as waiters; an incident is recorded where Babel got up and left a restaurant because his companions were deliberately teasing these people. Berlin in the twenties was lively enough in a cosmopolitan way; English homosexual intellectuals adored it, but Boris spoke for the rest of his life about the bad effect, the vacuum effect of exile on writers.

It is important all the same that with the massive emigration of a hundred thousand Russians to Berlin alone there came the most enterprising publishers. Berlin had no paper famine like Moscow's, and books published in Berlin were in the early twenties still sold in Moscow. Grzhebin was a publisher with a mania for producing new books and authors. In 1922 he produced *My Sister Life*. The publishing house Helikon produced *Theme and Variations* in 1923. In the autumn of 1922 Mayakovsky signed a contract in Berlin for his *Selected Poems*. The Russian area of Berlin consisted of upper-class Charlottenburg, and some drearier outer suburbs. Boris Pasternak frequented their cafés and *Weinstuben*: in Moscow writers' cafés flowered and faded almost overnight, the

Pittoresk, the Bom, the Futurists, the Imagists, the Stall of Pegasus, the Domino, and the Smithy, which specialised in proletarian writers, and Pasternak had rather feebly trudged the circuit; in Berlin it was the Café Leon, the Prager Diele, and the Café Landgraf, where the Russians met on Fridays. The Landgraf was described by Ehrenburg as a sort of Noah's Ark where clean and unclean beasts might consort. The Russians called that the House of Arts, and Yesenin, Tsvetayeva, Mayakovsky, Beliy and Pasternak read there. So did Severianin, a performer of ghastly slickness known as an 'ego-futurist', who chanted his verses to a stringed instrument rather like the 'mandolute' that T. S. Eliot encountered in Bloomsbury about the same time. Poor Severianin was popular for his *Thunder-Seething Cup* (1913) and for his able middle-brow performances, but he lacked fire. He went into exile, where he lived long enough to welcome the Russian invasion of Estonia in verse. He died in 1941.

Shklovsky knew Pasternak in Berlin, and writes about him in *Zoo, or Letters not about Love* (1923). He is an important witness, and deserves a few line of explanation, which I base on an important article by Henry Gifford (*Grand Street*, autumn 1988). He was three years younger than Boris Pasternak but lived to be ninety-one; the youngest son of a poor schoolmaster with Jewish blood, he looked like a cucumber, lectured on futurism at twenty in 1913 at the Stray Dog café, and founded formalism in 1914 with a pamphlet. As a theorist he had an influence on the clichés of criticism equivalent to Eliot's. In the 1914 war he conceived an enthusiasm for machinery, particularly armoured cars; in the civil war, as a demolition expert he blew himself up but survived. In 1920 he taught literary theory at Gorky's Translators' Studio, and poetic theory to the 'Serapion Brothers' with Zemyatin. In Berlin in 1922 he felt as uneasy as Boris Pasternak: 'like a cow on ice . . . we're like people on a ship. . . . We are going nowhere. . . . Germany is rusting away, and so are we.' In 1922 some intellectuals were expelled from Russia, but publication began again there; the result in Berlin was turmoil, and the end of the truce between factions that the House of Arts had represented. 'The whole wind of poetry', wrote Shklovsky, 'was in the Soviet land, and Mayakovsky was the sail.' He returned to Russia and survived there all his life, publishing his memoirs, *Once Upon a Time*, in 1964. When he was blown up in 1920 his last thought was who could now write *Plot as a Manifestation of Style*, and his first thought on coming to was how extremely red blood is against the greenness of grass.

Shklovsky liked Pasternak's trick, so difficult for foreign critics, of 'hurling a dense throng of words this way and that, while the most important thing remained unsaid'. Tsvetayeva and Pasternak had met five or six times in Russia, and respected each other in a low key, but in 1922 he read her *Versts* and she read his *My Sister Life*, and a passionate poetic form of *amitié amoureuse* at long range developed instantly. She said he was like an Arab riding across deserts, and like the Arab's horse. Shklovsky found that irresistible. 'He is always straining in some direction, but without hysteria. He pulls like a strong and fiery horse, he trots but he wants to gallop, he throws his feet far forward.' There was something horselike about his long neck and chin extended in welcome, a special gesture of his which Zoe Afanaseyevna caught in bronze at the end of his life. 'Pasternak was feeling the propulsion of history. He feels movement; his poems are remarkable for their propulsion: the lines bend, they do not align themselves like steel bars, they collide like the cars of a suddenly braked train. Good poems. A happy man. He will never be embittered. He will surely be happy and cherished to the end of his life.' It was a sense of propulsion that Germany lacked: even Brecht lacked it in those days, and the Russian colony was 'an enclave of waiters and singers within a conquered nation'.

Boris and Zhenya visited Marburg but were disappointed. 'Germany was cold and starving, deceived about nothing and deceiving no one, her hand stretched out to the age like a beggar (a gesture not her own at all) and the whole country on crutches.' It took him a bottle of brandy a day and a dose of Charles Dickens to forget about it. Tsvetayeva was in Prague, where she heard too late that Boris was going home, but he had the rooted instinct that a writer can exist only in the country of his own language, so home he went. Naturally such an instinctive feeling, which in spite of all exceptions represents a painful truth, is entangled with other deep feelings, such as patriotism, the roots of oneself in childhood, and in those days in Russia maybe even hope. When the time came for the crisis over the Nobel prize, and exile was a serious threat, he begged the regime to let him stay. He was a Russian, he felt like a Russian, not like a member of the international Jewish intelligentsia, to whom Berlin in the twenties was central. And as

Shklovsky, who was never an orthodox Bolshevik, observed, 'There wasn't a man alive who didn't experience periods of belief in the revolution. For whole minutes, you would believe in the Bolsheviks.'

At the time, Pasternak tried to sum up his feelings in a longish, coherent poem called 'The Sublime Malady', which I shall discuss. Later, in 1957 near the end of his life, he sent 'A New Year's Message' to his western readers, which André Sinyavsky quotes in his biographical introduction to the *Collected Poems* of 1965, a just and sober assessment and the most searching essay on Pasternak I have come across, better even than Gifford, Hingley, Max Hayward and Maurice Bowra. 'And there is one more thing that you have to thank us for. However great the difference between us, our Revolution set the tone for you as well: it filled the present century with meaning and content. It is not only we (our young people) that are different: even the son of one of your bankers is not what his father and grandfather were. . . . It's us you have to thank for this new man, who is present even in your ancient society, us you have to thank for the fact that he is more alive, more subtle and more gifted than his pompous and turgid ancestors, for this child of the age was delivered in the maternity hospital called Russia. Should we not therefore peaceably wish each other a happy New Year?' Whenever it was possible, and at times when it seems to us scarcely conceivable, he was always deeply and instinctively optimistic about his country. The strange misted future of peace and happiness that he foresees one may say mystically at the end of *Zhivago* is oddly close to the Russia of 1989, so it is open to one to think that his instinct was sound. Yet part of it was surely that very deep, scarcely conscious need to identify with one's country which sometimes occurs in Jewish families in the long process of their assimilation. Readers must judge for themselves.

The most difficult thing about 'The Sublime Malady', or 'The Noble Illness or Fever' is its title. Its hero is undoubtedly Lenin, whom he observed in action, perhaps on the same occasion as his father, who drew Lenin speaking before he left Russia. The poem mentions the Ninth Party Congress in Moscow in September 1920 as a confused occasion, and as if it were before Lenin's arrival, but seems to focus on the Tenth, which was in March 1921. At that time, after the Kronstadt revolt, Lenin was in a masterful mood; 'a number of circumstances', says the resolution on the unity of the party, 'are intensifying the hesitancy of the petty-bourgeois population of the country.' The poem was written later, but this particular resolution makes sense of it. Lenin's speech at the end marks a later stage, but the fact that the poem was written in retrospect over politically active years and events which are alluded to rather than charted is the likeliest explanation of its apparent contradictions. The poem treats politics in terms of moral attitudes and moral attitudes very metaphorically, until the brilliant climax of Lenin's speech.

Sinyavsky groups 'The Sublime Malady' with Pasternak's 'strenuous attempts at the epic genure (1923–30)', which it certainly at least prefigures and towards which it leads, but most of it is a series of lyric metaphors without any discernible narrative skeleton. Its definition of its own title is like the definitions of poetry and the soul in *My Sister Life*. 'The shifting riddle glitters,' it begins. The poet is ashamed that in an age of shadows 'the sublime malady escapes censure. And still goes by the name of song.' The malady is not exactly poetry, but something the matter with poetry, perhaps inaction. The first stanza well expresses that: the siege goes on, years go by, messengers are believed or not believed,

> they falter, they go blind – the days go by –
> And the walls of the fort fall apart.
> February passes and we await October.

This part of the poem reminds one of Shklovsky on Kerensky's rhetoric like burning alcohol which will neither consume nor ignite the wood on which it burns so purely. Connoisseurs of Pasternak as the poet of railways will be pleased to come across a railway station glistening 'like a pipe organ in the reflective ice.' Then

> We were the music of ice . . .
> I am a guest and all over the world
> this is the sublime malady . . .
> We were the music of teacups . . .
> We were the music of thought
> And sought to sweep the stairs.

Whether Sasha is right or wrong about the application of these lines to the winter when they burnt the rafters, they do seem to deal with bourgeois intellectuals ripe for conversion or mobilisation, but if you ask what is their offence the answer remains extremely obscure. Does the title mean 'The Disease of High-Mindedness'?

The Ninth Party Congress is more concrete. 'The Karelian question stared / From every poster.' That sounds almost like Lenin on the national question in 1917, but the same question continued lively into the twenties, and the Moscow edition confirms that in this poem Pasternak principally intends 1921. The story of the Congress is like the moral in a fairy-tale, suddenly revealed at the end; it is about 'the fever of genius', which levels out trivialities. Like a musical movement, there follows an eruption of the forces of reaction from the sea –

> again the frigate went broadside –
> The pullman cars and hooded
> two-headed eagles brooded
> in that black field where earth
> and the Tsar's railway train
> heaved with the smell of March.

The Tsar's train was a relic that survived; indeed it toured Russia in 1945. Now the poem is almost over, and one may suspect that once it might have ended about here, but suddenly 'I remember his turn of phrase', which struck like a white flame or the whiplash of a thunderbolt. He grew on to the platform, he entered like a black ball of storm into a stuffy room. To roars of applause he spoke. 'WE ARE HERE TO REMEMBER THE MONUMENTS OF THE FALLEN. I SPEAK OF TRANSITORY THINGS.' So when Lenin finally utters he sounds like the Gettysburg oration. The poet ponders on Lenin's right to speak in the first person, and grants it. The last words of the poem are these:

> From the lines of generations
> someone steps out in front.
> A genius bears promises of spring,
> terror revenges his exit.

The poem was first printed in 1924 in Mayakovsky's magazine *LEF*, which was also the title of a movement to which Pasternak belonged for a time. That was the year of Lenin's death, on 23

January. It was reprinted in *Novy Mir* in 1928, dated 1923–8, with massive alterations. If it was not an attempt to please the government, it was at least an attempt to placate Mayakovsky, who was vehemently propagandist, even though he sometimes thought Pasternak's attempts at populist or propagandist poetry misconceived. Maybe all such attempts are misconceived, but Pasternak's are remarkable and must take their place in his long development, in which, to put it mildly, Lenin was as important as Scriabin. It is a resolution drafted by Lenin in October 1920 that declares: 'All educational work . . . in the field of art in particular should be imbued with the spirit of the class struggle . . . for the overthrow of the bourgeoisie, the abolition of classes, and the elimination of all forms of exploitation of man by man.' Pasternak made a serious effort to defend and to expound the revolution, in poetry of great originality. But one should note that the resolution I have quoted is really intended to repress 'proletarian' groups who were entering cultural politics, and to tell the proletariat to go on imitating, as they had always done, the better achievements of the bourgeoisie.

Mayakovsky went further; the best pages of Boris Pasternak's various autobiographical works read like a quarrelsome love affair with Mayakovsky, and constitute the most discerning criticism of him ever written. Boris wrote for *LEF*, he belonged to LEF, his 'May Day' came out in its second issue in 1923, yet in *People and Situations*, the last of his memoirs, he says: 'People have exaggerated the closeness of our friendship. . . . I never did understand his enthusiasm for propaganda. . . . Even more incomprehensible to me was the magazine *LEF*. . . . I could understand neither its contributors nor its ideology.' He was far closer to Yesenin, who wrote 'with stunning freshness retained from childhood' about his native forests, but hanged himself just after Christmas in 1925 at the age of thirty, cast off as a lover, sad about the revolution, and decayed by serious alcoholism. Pasternak had a passionate relationship with Yesenin; when they met, which was seldom, they drew blood or wept together. With LEF on the other hand his quarrel was public and less intimate. As he wrote in *People and Situations*, he really preferred young Tretyakov to Mayakovsky, because he followed Plato in disapproving of art altogether; Tretyakov followed Mayakovsky as editor and wound up the magazine. Pasternak wrote in his letter of resignation, 'I consider

LEF's existence, now as before, to be a logical puzzle. The key to it has ceased to interest me.' As the critic Lezhnyev had written a month earlier, 'LEF is lying across the road and blocking traffic.' All this is not entirely a story of attitudinising, because behind literary polemics lay the politics of the new state, which was slow to take action against writers but did so in the end. Pasternak's poetry after 1922 must inevitably be seen first against the ghost and later against the reality of state interference and the exclusive patronage of the state. The fearsome doctrine of 'social realism' was not invented until 1932, when it was suddenly introduced without discussion as a dogma. Lenin liked satire but only tolerated Mayakovsky, and Trotsky questioned Pasternak about his old abstinence from social themes: special literary pressures did exist even in the twenties, even apart from the pressures of everyday life.

And the idiotic wars of writers between themselves did mimic real social conflicts in the new state. In 1921 Chukovsky lectured on Mayakovsky and Akhmatova (together), saying, 'I love them both.' In the same year Lenin protested that 'these futurists' should be printed only at the rate of not more than two a year in 1500 copies only. He called Mayakovsky's poem '150 Million' a most interesting piece of work, 'a new brand of communism, hooligan communism'. Mayakovsky meanwhile was swiftly outflanked and overtaken on the left. At a Conference of Proletarian Writers in 1925, Demyan Byedny refused to speak after him, on the grounds that proletarian writers had nothing to learn. One cannot help liking Mayakovsky. 'I am so tall, bear-pawed, loathsome. Today also sulking.' 'Fame, like the beard on a dead man, will grow on me after death. While I am alive I shave it. Pushkin had a long one. They've been combing it for a hundred years.' When in the end he killed himself, in April 1930, anxious about his future and disappointed in love, the pistol he used was an old film prop. Boris Pasternak was stricken with grief. When he had first read Mayakovsky some poems from *My Sister Life* the reaction was 'ten times what I ever hoped to hear from anyone'.

When Boris and Zhenya came home to Moscow in March 1923, she was already pregnant with their eldest son and first baby, another Zhenya (Yevgeny), who was born in September and is still alive. He had a nanny to whom he was extremely devoted, a lady from the high aristocracy: such people could be trusted, and were longing for work, but it is pleasing to know the arrangement worked so well. The little boy was particularly close to her because when he was six or seven years old his parents separated. I have heard Boris Pasternak's first wife variously described, but never without affection by anyone who knew her. She was beautiful and perhaps languorous; she had blue eyes and Jewish blood. Between 1919 and 1923 Boris had done little of his personal work, though the effect was not apparent to other people, because of the long queue of earlier writings awaiting the printer as soon as printing began. He seems to have moved towards civic themes as early as 1922, with a poem of quite un-Bolshevik gloom and horrified Tolstoyan feeling called 'Famine', about the terrible conditions on the lower Volga. He wrote in it that his ink was corrupted and his verbs needed rinsing in carbolic. In 1923 there was 'May Day', and then 'The Sublime Malady', first as fragments but finally as a complete poem long after Lenin's death. The exception to this scheme of development is his delightful children's poetry written for his son Zhenya. As one might expect of Boris Pasternak, the verse is fragile but perfect, and it summons up the reality of its subject and the psychology of his intended audience at the same time. Russia has some good children's poetry, by Marshak among others, but one of Pasternak's two children's poems is better than any I can discover.

Of course this poetry is a consequence of personal life, but also of the relief in publication, as Lenin's New Economic Policy took hold, and with the end of the civil war. There is now no doubt at all that Lenin made deliberate use of terror as an instrument of government. Terror is a servant that swiftly becomes a master; as an instrument it was inherited from the Tsars, but it was already beginning to grow with the gigantism of the revolution itself. That does not seem to have affected Boris Pasternak at this time. The point was that the civil war was over, and the sense of relief was exquisite: civil war is more traumatic than any other kind, and the nations who have lived through them do not ever risk another. Among Boris's closer acquaintance Samarin, whom Boris remembered as an arrogant and aristocratic pre-war under-graduate, had returned from Siberia after some nasty adventures on both sides of the lines: he came back chastened and humble like a man with a religious conversion, and died of typhoid. Khlebnikov had returned from the south emaciated and ill, and soon died.

Neither the thinnest Japanese shadows
nor the euphonious daughters of India
utter so funereal a sound
as after-dinner speeches at the last supper.
Just before death your life flashes by,
it flashes fast and with a difference.

It is always a pleasure to translate Khlebnikov, but his poems melt in the hand like snowflakes. That is a deliberate technique. He almost falls into light verse, which may well be a besetting sin of futurism or a *memento mori* that haunts it. Khlebnikov's play with sound patterns is childlike as well as poetic. This poses an interesting problem about Pasternak in his children's verse. We do not need to believe with Socrates that the arts of tragedy and comedy are one and the same, or to abolish the distinction of serious and light poetry, though we surely ought to view suspiciously the way that distinctions like that of poetry and verse mirror some kind of class distinction. Pasternak's generation had rejected the pretensions of poetry and abolished its Victorian airs and graces, in art as in life. It was therefore easy for a futurist like Mayakovsky to turn to satire and humour in public performance while not quitting the ground of the irrational won for poetry by futurism. The futurist Petersburg magazine, in which Pasternak had published a poem in 1915, was called *Baraban Futuristov*, 'The Futurists' Tiddly-om-pom'. Pasternak's tiny handful of children's verse is crisp, and sensually intense, and uses futurist techniques almost automatically.

Comic and children's verse have a certain association with resistance in Russian as in English. Many children now adult delighted in Chukovsky's wicked Cockchafer, which ate people and had huge moustaches thought to resemble Stalin's. But Pasternak's efforts are innocent. 'Carousel' was printed in Leningrad in 1925. The poet is courteously uncomplicated except in a very few phrases. He takes a classic form of stanza and fills it with comic surprises, full rhymes and half-rhymes. The same association of trochaic tetrameters with humour has been exploited in English, but I find this very delicate poem untranslatable. It begins on a fine summer's morning, the maple leaves are rustling, no one is too lazy to get up; they stuff apples and a cottage loaf and sandwiches into a bag, and take a tram. It seems a queer picnic, it falls below the Edwardian standards of Rat in *The Wind in the Willows*, but Russian picnics have remained extremely informal; what they were like before 1914 who knows. The child in the poem does not feel at all deprived. The gang changes trams. They are going to open country, which Moscow will long ago have swallowed. In the distance 'carousel by river gleams'. The effect is magical. The fields are carpeted with scented dodder-grass, a kind of grass not found wild in England now, very shivery (hence its name) and scented like bean-flowers. They sprinkle themselves about in it waist-high, run head over heels down a ravine, and beyond that on a plateau come to games and flags where 'wooden horses gallop with no dust'.

> Black-maned, long-tailed, they lift in air and drop,
> each circle slower, slower, slower, stop.

Whirlwinds are hidden in the columned roof, bars open wide on the circle, the carousel bends with weight, the canvas is stiff with tension, as if the horses bounded factory-fresh to the kicks of children 'and clicked more chic than croquet balls'. In the glade by the machine the crowd are cracking melon-seeds. A man with an accordion has a jester's hat with bells; he shakes his fringe of trinkets like rain rattling on a bath-house roof, with a drum-rattle and a wooden leg. He is a horse in a three-arch harness (for a troika), he beats his bones, he moves from foot to foot.

> The curled manes of the horse lace
> into the bottomless daylight:
> the cars and festooned horses chase
> and sink into the rustling grove,
> and the pond rushes left and right
> to hold them in his arms with love.
> Steeply we turn, meet and go round
> over the grove, over the pond
> the grove, the pond have vanished round
> the columned roof, the hollow ground,
> each circle slower, slower, stop,
> and slower, slower, slower, stop.

The more of the poem one dares to translate the more liberties one is forced to take with it; it slows down the carousel and ceases to dazzle. The original perfectly conveys the experience of going very fast indeed, to the point of surrealism in the stanza following the wandering jester, who is a lineal descendant of Shakespeare's Feste, and come to that of Molière. But it cuts as crisply. In performance (he used to read it to his son) it must have been unbeatable. His other children's poem is called 'Menagerie' or 'Bestiary'. Mandelstam and Khlebnikov both used the same title, but not for children's poetry. Pasternak's version was printed in 1929, and one must assume it was written for an older child. Once again there is not a cloud in the zoo sky. The bears chat to the children and there are a lot of queer birds. The elephants are the main characters. They are like haystacks; they stand densely with tusks above ceiling height. They fling up chaff, their chains rattle, their trunks wreathe on the ground with a snuffling sound. We see only a third of the animals: with a last look at the eagle's claw we are off to the roar of the tram, and of pumas. This poem may be thought no more than an elegant trifle, but it moves and is alive, and there are few poems to match it in our language.

His stray prose continued to appear: *Letters from Tula* and *The Childhood of Lyuvers* in 1922, *Aerial Ways* in 1924, and a volume of prose including all these with *The Apelles Mark* in 1925. By 1927 he was at work on his first autobiography, *Safe Conduct*, which as he said later was rebarbatively stylish like the rest of his early prose. About that he exaggerated and we must distinguish. But his poems were becoming fragmentary, and being published in fragments before they were finished: the fragmentation still shows in the finished products, as we shall see. It was a strange time. Old Beliy wrote that 'In its most difficult days Russia became a garden of nightingales. Poets sprang up as never before. People barely had the strength to live but they were all singing.' Shklovsky wrote in his diary, 'Art must move organically, like the heart in the human breast, but they want to regulate it like a train.' That was more or less what Pasternak had said to Trotsky, silencing that blather-skate, to his own later regret. Khlebnikov had written:

> When horses are dying they whinny,
> when grasses are dying they wither,
> when the sun is dying it will wane,
> when peoples are dying they sing songs.

As early as 1920 Zemyatin had written the brilliant novel *We*, on which Huxley's and Orwell's visions of the totalitarian state are based. But Zemyatin was privileged as the designer of the first Soviet icebreaker, the *Lenin* (he had worked in British naval dockyards during the war), and easily escaped into exile. Bulgakov, the best of the other Russian novelists, had a novel adapted for the theatre which Stalin saw sixteen times; he suffered persecution, but he died a natural death in Moscow. Babel fell silent and was arrested in the end, having coolly attempted to observe the eye of the storm by sitting in the office of the chief of police, just watching. He is said to have been kicked to death in prison; whatever happened, he died. Boris Pasternak came to find poetry a blocked road, not because he was incapable of going on writing it, but because of the dangers and difficulty of publication. When at last he turned to the full and devastating expression of himself in fiction, in *Dr Zhivago*, that was an act of extraordinary courage and of moral and creative daring. His earlier prose may foreshadow it here and there, but does not obviously or directly lead towards it.

*Letters from Tula* dates from 1918. It deals with truth and falsity in human beings, and circles round a memory of Tolstoy, but it is a thin sketch. *Aerial Ways* is dated 1924, but it still in several places aspires to the condition of a poem. It is the tale of a lost child. ' "Where, oh where," came the continual cry from the hare lip of the half-witted herd girl; and following a cow, dragging one leg, brandishing a wild bit of a branch as though it were lightning, she came out of a dustcloud at the end of the garden where the thickets began: deadly nightshade and bricks and twisted wire and evil-smelling shadows.' This lacks the long, breathing rhythms of fully embodied fiction, it is almost panting with excitement, almost self-parody, a self-expression turned inside out like Baudelaire's 'Fanfarlo', and as with that youthful and fragmentary work there is no sense in seeking the source of his style, only its cause, which lies among the hothouse quarrels and conversations about writing of pre-war Moscow. This is a tragic and a dreamlike story, a collage of vignettes. Suddenly fifteen years pass, there is gunfire from the sea and the railway, and the thought of Lenin and 'a few other minds of the same greatness' arrive like a train along 'aerial ways'. Revolutionary soldiers enter, and the hero sees that 'the child might be concealed under any of the names he knew from the documents'. The tale ends gloomily on its eighteenth page. If it were less melodramatic, you could regard it as the sketch for a powerful novel. Seen in retrospect from *Zhivago* it has fascinating details, but essentially it is only a series of scenes, it does not make enough sense of reality.

With *Povest (A Tale)*, or, in George Reavey's fine English translation, *The Last Summer*, we are surely close to the beginning of Pasternak as a serious novelist, even though the story is quite short, a very thin Penguin of only seventy pages, and has little to boast of in the way of plot. V. S. Pritchett liked it because 'it puts poetic and popular speech side by side', and there has been a tendency to call it a halfway house between *The Childhood of Lyuvers* and *Zhivago*. But although it was published only in 1934 it seemed to have been written in or before 1924, when Boris Pasternak had started work on his verse novel, *Spektorsky*, to which he later compared it. It was illustrated with *pointilliste* drawings of admirable rationality, and a portrait of the artist more convincing than most of his photographs and less romantic, somehow better characterised than his father's charcoal sketch of 1923. In English it has a passionate and most interesting introduction by George Reavey (1959), and an informative and well-balanced one by Lydia Pasternak (1960). Its epigraph reads: '. . . *that last summer when life still appeared to pay heed to individuals, and when it was easier and more natural to love than to hate.*' I am not sure who wrote that (Gorky?) but it does not sound like a fervent revolutionary. Whatever he felt about the revolution, Boris Pasternak was haunted at this time by a deep nostalgia for the days of his youth.

The scene is set as before in Perm in the Urals, a town to which he was pleased to notice in later life that Chekhov had once penetrated. Should one imagine Boris as one of those revolutionary idealist student tutors in Chekhov plays? Yes, but with the difference that things were more serious after 1905, and his tutorship must be set against the background of the world war. Serezha visits his sister early in 1916. 'For the past ten years the scattered fragments of this tale have kept coming into my mind, and in the early days of the Revolution some portions of it found their way into print.' Ten years from 1924 maybe? But what bits got into print? The journey to Moscow in March of 1917? The childhood of Lyuvers? What of the lost novel? A mystery remains, yet it may have no foundation except in art: 'as to the fates, I shall leave them as I found them in those years in the snow under the trees.' To say as he does that no difference of opinion exists between this version and his latter verse novel *Spektorsky*, which had mystified and infuriated a number of critics, is to explain the obscure by the more obscure: for some reason the obfuscation of this fiction is important to him. Yet his setting of the scene is exact, almost Tolstoyan, and the poetic phrases are not intrusive: metaphor does not take over from narrative or common sense.

Admittedly there are more feelings than events, but the old-fashioned telephone down which one screams and the primitive machinery keep the opening lively. Chekhov is mentioned, so is women's higher education: the period touches are lovingly drawn in. Yet not much happens. Serezha is a writer, recently graduated but quite well known at least to Petersburg editors. He is a tutor in the Fresteln family, in a grand two-storey mansion where husband and wife have quarrelled and live on separate floors. The lady had a companion under sentence to leave, an intellectual Dane who begins her first speech to Serezha, which is in German, with the formidable assertion that she knows Chekhov and Dostoevsky and has been in Russia only five months. Serezha counters with Ibsen, but does he not know that the Frestelns are Jews? So is Serezha, who fails to say so, but he does say her views of women are pure Tolstoy. In thirty-six pages, the situation has become fraught. Later the Dane bangs away at Chopin upstairs on the grand piano, 'whole trays of smashed and broken harmonies slid downstairs.' At twilight they try English, but their conversation is always the same labyrinth.

Serezha gets interested in money, and has an adventure with a woman. 'More pungently than all pungencies, it smelled here of the signal pungency of Christianity.' The woman would have preferred a young doctor: 'Listen, you aren't a Tartar, are you? Well, you must come. . . . You won't lose the address?' Somewhere at that time a book is being written about her eyes and heels, called *The Childhood of a Woman*. But the town is different and the name is not Russian. This I assume to be *The Childhood of Lyuvers*, yet this woman, Sashka, sounds very unlike her. As a writer of fiction, Pasternak is shuffling an old pack of autobiographical cards; his fiction is a game of patience that still never quite comes out. 'Though the day had barely begun, tangled threads of sultry heat, as nightmarish as crumbs in the beard of a corpse, hung

already in the turmoil of the limetrees. And Serezha felt feverish.'
Even the lime trees have been used before.

He wants to redeem the bad women of Tverskie-Yamskie with
money. His mind dwells on the Dane, but he goes about his work
as a tutor, and just imagines a story. Then he finds himself in the
Dane's bedroom, with the consequence that words and tears flow,
both in some profusion. As a study in late adolescence, the whole
story is a *tour de force*, but it is hard to keep track of the women, who
appear to be mostly in the mind. The main event apart from his
mixed and disturbed feelings is that Serezha writes his story,
though we are warned at once that he never finished it: we have just
read it, but 'There was much on his mind that was never recorded
on paper.' Enter Mrs Fresteln, wet through and furious, having
almost broken her umbrella. Tutoring is over on the next day.
Serezha walks all night in a Moscow street where he knows the
Danish woman has friends, and she takes him in. A long train
journey follows, with a missed connection. He suddenly understands happiness, and wakes, and it was all a dream. The reader
must forgive me if I have missed some fulcrum on which this long
short story turns. I am sure that the end is obfuscation, and that the
passionate fantasies about the women are close to confessional. The
story becomes less intellectual and more psychologically impassioned as it goes on, but only about the hero himself. Mrs
Fresteln is nicely furious and well drawn, but he does not care
enough about them all to keep up the startling and most promising
realism of his opening ten pages. He seems to have intended a book
about women, but seeing them through the eyes of his heated hero
is a mistake, so that what he produced was just an interesting story
about a young writer in a turmoil. Even so, when the writer
actually starts to write, the turmoil ceases and his processes are as
cool as a cucumber's.

His letter to the Petersburg editor does ring true of Boris
Pasternak. 'I intend to marry and am in desperate need of money.
The story which I told you about I am now rewriting as a play. The
play will be in verse.' Nothing came of that, alas. Serezha in real life
would have given Lenin or Gorky a fit, but Pasternak keeps an
option open by setting this story safely in the past, a year before the
end of the revolution.

When all is said and done about these years, what one wants to
know about Boris Pasternak is what happened to his lyric poetry,

since neither prose nor civic nor epic poetry can quite have absorbed that pure and intense impetus of *My Sister Life* and *Theme and Variations*. His economic circumstances do not really explain where it went, though overwork may do, but then why the other writing? The unhappy political situation is not an adequate extinguisher for that fluttering lyric candle. It appears to me that he sang as a bird sings, and that the birdsong natural to him mingled with philosophy and thought to become poetry. It went on in the daily expression of his love for Zhenya Lourié, of which we have just one example, from the spring of 1924 when she went with her child to Taitsy near Petersburg for a holiday, and he wrote her a letter that survives. It is not poetry, though many poets have said or written such things, it is just pure love, and that is where his vein of lyric poetry went. His life story is essentially a love story.

'Hullo, hullo, my happiness, my wave washing over my eyes. Stand proudly, laugh and cry, show off, pay no attention to me, but don't ever leave me. Turn away like a goddess, and like a goddess watch over me. Turn away as you lie beside me, undressed by a man with your ring on his hand, undressed as the hand of your happiest imagining would undress you, as a hot summer night would, as a memory would. Turn away undressed by me, because the unfathomable turns away, you are the sublime, higher than high, better than best. Lie with your eyes shut, don't look at me, ignore my existence while I worship you and kiss you. Always, eternally be with me, my cold sky, my dreaming nerve, sleepless vein of forest and field in blossom. When we came together we went up onto a high place where all is visible, where one cannot be alone, my joy, my joy, my joy, my joy!'

# 5

# The Epic Temptation

The lives of a few poets seem to have a clear, almost linear development. Others spend all their lives going in circles around their essential, their unwritten poem and secret inspiration. In Pasternak's life many things were happening at once. His antennae were like the most curious snail's after a downpour; he found his work and his nourishment in several directions, and it would be a mistake to dismiss his longer poems, *Spektorsky* and *Lieutenant Schmidt* and *1905*, as false starts, since they were experiments but not failures, and it is only in retrospect that we see him stumbling like a blind man towards his great novel. We can more reasonably dismiss his volume of philosophic essays, *The Quintessence*, which anyway is lost, because, although philosophy was always close to his heart and entered into his conversation at times to the end of his life, he did outgrow the need to work on his theories.

The temptation (let us call it) to write a kind of epic verse seems to correspond with a kind of intellectual love affair with Maxim Gorky, who at this time was in one of the less positive phases of his own ebbing and flowing affair with Soviet Russia. I assume the poet met Gorky in Berlin in 1922, where Gorky had his portrait done by Leonid Pasternak. Lenin was thrillingly ruthless in Pasternak's eyes, he had let loose a devastating storm like a natural force, he was not a possible father-figure. But Gorky was the supremely respected writer of the older generation, Babel's and everyone else's mentor and Tolstoy's friend; he had his place by name in the first version of the 'The Sublime Malady', and I believe Boris Pasternak ached to please him. He was quite equally excited by the idea of pleasing Rilke, who here re-enters this story, as a great European artist and friend of artists of his father's generation. Pasternak was also entranced by Tsvetayeva, into a kind of mayfly dance of mutual admiration.

Gorky, with Zemyatin and Chukovsky, edited a journal of the

early twenties called *Russian Contemporary* (an old liberal title from the last generation), which was by no means a hard-line communist organ; in 1924 it printed verse by Pasternak and Aseev, but it is interesting to observe that Pasternak took no part in Aseev's anthology of the period, *Flight* (1923), a socially conscious collection of verse about aeroplanes in which Mandelstam fails to shine, and not one of the contributors is even as good as Blok was in 1912.

> Propellor sings like singing strings –
> in unfathomable height
> the copper on the motor shines
> and half lost from sound and sight
> propellor sings and sings and sings.

A little later, Gorky in Sorrento thought *The Childhood of Lyuvers* brilliant, and wrote an introduction for an American edition of it in 1926–7, never published alas. He urged Pasternak to write more prose. In 1927 Boris was concerned to try and entice Tsvetayeva back to Russia, and wrote to Gorky about her immense talent and her entangled fate. Gorky made a cautious assessment of her political and literary position, and did nothing – very wisely, as things turned out, though Boris wrote to him sharply about it at the time. Their letters were exchanged through Tsvetayeva's sister Anastasia, the dedicatee of 'The Sublime Malady'.

In 1926 and 1927 the bookshops were full of patriotic epics, of which Boris Pasternak's *1905* was only one: Bagritsky's *Lay of Opanas* on civil war in the Ukraine, Aseev's *Twenty-Six* on some Soviet martyrs executed in 1918, the same poet's *Proskakov*, and Mayakovsky's *Good!* Pasternak's *1905* is in some ways a transitional work, but it is better than the others; it beautifully fills the strange limits of the genre, and it transforms and extends those limits, as we shall see. If anyone wants to recapture some sense of what the genre itself was like in its brief period of flourishing, they would do better to look at C. Day Lewis's *Flight to Australia* (1935) or *The Nabara* (1938), which is about the Spanish Civil War; both poems are more naïvely and vulnerably hopeful than Pasternak's. In 1927 he wrote to Gorky: 'I don't know what would be left of the Revolution for me, or what would have become of its *truth*, if Russian history didn't have you. But for you in the flesh and you fully individual – and as a vast generalized personification except for you – the lies and shallowness of it are immediately obvious. . . . Having breathed its inevitable falsity for ten years, like everyone else, I had gradually come to think about liberation. For that purpose, one had to choose the revolutionary theme in a historical perspective, a chapter among chapters, an event among other events.' Mayakovsky and the friendlier wing of the pro-letarian critics were pleased and welcomed a recruit, but they were mistaken. His letter to Gorky, like his dedications to him, sounds that note of intransigent individuality which had silenced Trotsky and which was now central to Pasternak. Indeed, it was the core of his life.

In 1925 he began to publish *Spektorsky*, and to work on *1905*. Since his work overlapped, it will be as well to give a clear account before plunging into details. His correspondence with his cousin Olga Freidenberg began again at this time. In 1924 Lenin died and Pasternak produced fragments of 'The Sublime Malady', and in 1925 three of the nine parts of *Spektorsky*. In that year he also began work on *Lieutenant Schmidt* and on *1905*. In 1926 his wife and son went abroad; he began his excited and exalted correspondence with Rilke and Tsvetayeva, and Rilke died. This episode brought him European fame by word of mouth, as we shall see. *Lieutenant Schmidt* appeared in *Novy Mir*. In 1927 he was still at work on *1905*; he read Tsvetayeva's *Poem of the End*, which moved him as greatly as his own new poems moved her. He sent Gorky *1905*, and started work on an essay which became his first near-miss at a masterpiece of autobiography, *Safe Conduct*. Only in 1928 was 'The Sublime Malady' published complete in *Novy Mir*, with its striking finale about Lenin. In 1930 a fatal visit to friends led to his divorce the next year. It was also in 1930 that Mayakovsky shot himself.

*Spektorsky* is a most curious poem: it occupies thirty-nine pages of the Moscow edition, not counting the notes on its various versions. It is dated 1925–31, and consists of over 330 four-line rhyming stanzas of extraordinary boldness and ingenuity. They are extremely readable but by no means perfectly lucid, as Lunacharsky darkly complained to himself about all of Pasternak's poetry, in some private notes he wrote at the time. Some of the material is undoubtedly autobiographical, about the architectural devastation of the Arts Building gardens at the old Pasternak flat, for example, which Sasha laments in prose, and in characters that seem to echo the poet and Tsvetayeva. He called it a novel in verse, but it is not like other novels. Its early parts are set in 1912 and 1913, but he put it aside to write *Povest* in prose, and critics believe that *Povest* in some way carries on its plot, being set in 1914–16. At least it has a hero of the same name, and shares other characters. But, when *Povest* was already out, Boris added the eighth and ninth parts of his poem, set in 1919. The introduction was written separately and published on its own in 1930. Yet, when all this is said, *Spektorsky* is neither as strange nor as queerly constructed as one might think. In its way it is masterly, however dreamlike, and has no French or English equivalent.

Sergei Spektorsky's name appears to be based on *spektr*, the word for the spectrum, as in spectral analysis: I take it to mean that he and the events of the poem are to be seen from many angles or reveal unsuspected component colours. He works in a ministry compiling references to Lenin, when he comes across references to Maria Ilyina, an émigrée poet based partly on Marina Tsvetayeva, and then the goose-chase begins. Spektorsky was a private tutor in the Urals, with a bad leg. He is a passive spectator of life, an antihero.

> I do not think much of my hero
> I might have jibbed at one so doomed
> except I want to show the cage
> of rays in which he dimly loomed.

Boris claimed in 1931 that in *Spektorsky* he had shown 'the crisis in the world as we see it, with a generalized, composite picture of this age, a natural history of its lifestyle'. He claimed further to have said more in *Spektorsky* about the 1917 revolution, and said it better, than in his *1905*. That seems a fair claim, since *1905* was about 1905; but it has little to do with the poem.

Boris was seconded to read foreign papers on Lenin, but he discovered twenties fashions and Conrad and Proust and 'Ilyina'. Two-thirds of this bit of poem is rain and the weather. In Moscow space sleeps in love with space and the town dreams picking at raisins of song. Boris was poor, his son was born, he had to leave his own childishness for a time, and his mandate was at least broad: day by day he took his paperknife and forced the Bosphorus. It was December 1924, December ground into the window-glass, it was cold as a coin's impression on a warm, shaky swelling. The library was untroubled, snow fluttered and through the crêpe of troubles he glimpsed the glory of Ilyina, who gained the world's attention. (That role of course was his own, not Tsvetayeva's.) Was she English or Russian, people argued. So Boris wrote about Spektorsky, her friend, in blind obedience to the object under the lens. He sees him through the hazy twinkling of a cellar lamp, where prose runs wrong, as news of an unknown masterpiece raises the hackles of our hair.

A futurist epic verse novel is a terrifying idea, but it seems to me that, even when it is translated and cast into semi-prose, the poem conveys a little of its always unexpected power. Perhaps it is what happens when a futurist reaches maturity. I like the dark being alien, drizzle alien, splashing from pipes on to gutters and hats, as alien as the miller in Pushkin.

> Earth, water, freewill like woodspirits
> burst through the coats and hangers in the hall
> lips searching for lips searching
> beyond the nude nymph alcohol.

To those who have followed this book so far, 'Thunderclaps dying in railway stations' will be less surprising than these brilliant and extremely Russian lines. They are Russian in their brilliance in that they could not, for example, have been written by Baudelaire or Rimbaud, still less Eliot. The story suddenly goes back by a year (the prose story also is deeply enmeshed in flashbacks). Frost crackled and the sun's disc flung itself in hot punch, hardly awake. Life and Spektorsky's girl Olga and the winter itself are not as beautiful as when the hard lock turns under the ice. We are in a forgotten house, the base for a circle of friends from all over Moscow. Like a modern and more concentrated Byron, Pasternak gives us the feeling of mandarins, quadrilles and indoor fireworks, but poetry at the same time is under an ominous condemnation. 'I see no way to forget myself. We are condemned dumb and without trial, the drink-carrier is eternally sober.' Some passionate and surprising love poetry follows, fully sexual and yet (or therefore) somehow impersonal. In later versions he cut out the most explicit erotic lines. They depart on skis. The spectrum has broken down, and that is why the barometer dances.

In part three we have a new girl, Natasha, his sister, and a long journey, with stern words against sleeping by daylight. In part four a morning dawns hotter than the summer; Natasha reproves him, young as he is, for being cut off from his generation. (The malady in this poem, the antiheroism of its hero, is obscurer than that of 'The Sublime Malady', and yet each casts light on the other.) Natasha is a revolutionary, and reproves her brother for dragging his feet politically. It turns out to be May Day. The scene ends in beer and argument, palm branches and the steam of bortsch. Nature with all its body thirsts for change, dark hurls itself at the capitals of columns, the maple plays on the windows, the wind whips up the foam of the birch trees. The fifth part retreats into a labyrinth of obscure images: the soul spent in the smoke of mutinies, taps rumbling like arteries; something rows smooth and wordless towards him, as if a scream is coming, as if people are careless of their skins, and take the shackles from their neighbour and fling them on the piano keys. The effect of all this is of a great poem disjointed, perhaps of a great disjointed poetry. In part six we get a saner but somewhat unrelated line of narrative, in which he meets Ilyina in Moscow mourning for her father. This is where he introduces the dead building and the chaos of public works.

> They met to birdsong and rainclusters,
> cherryblossom, thunder overhead
> wherever life and the two of them
> cannot now be separated.

The poet like his hero keeps falling into the soup of life, and into love poetry: that surely is the deep, intimate theme of his lifework. It is quite important, though I am sure absent from his confessional intention, that it does not seem to matter who the girl is, or that one girl fades into another. They are Virgilian visions or they are literary devices that have strayed from symbolist novels or from Blok; and yet they are intensely real. They swear to be sensible, but of course they forget, and the past turns their life upside-down, as it does in *Zhivago*.

> A grey, dense, hungry, hot city:
> they let them go, coffee was made
> as always in catastrophe,
> dawn broke in shade by ominous shade.

They were separated somehow. Scarcely touching the piano he plaited the gold thread of improvisations. Damp morning hunched and slept, handfuls of wind flung at the window. The atmosphere crumbled on to the pages of her new notebook. She furrowed the page with a fountain of blots. Part seven is an undistinguished narrative, except for a series of four fine stanzas on the city of Moscow itself, Boris Pasternak's true love or guiding star. In part eight six years suddenly pass, and Moscow is the war's goodbye to war. Poetry, do not go for expanse (Mayakovsky), keep your precision, that of private truth: do not mess with punctuation or measuring the grains in bread (acmeism?) do not hold your breath in innocence of bronze (Yesenin?) but ask the reader does the picture live, is the character real? Part nine has a fine satiric passage about furniture and union warehousemen. 'Night falls, super-numerary Lycurguses close down the warehouse.' The poem moves into an equally satiric drawing of the party woman.

> Do you remember Christmas dinners?
> She showed some frivolous interest,
> and laughed and pulled out her revolver.
> In that gesture all was expressed.

> . . . I dreamed, bell rang, I ran to open,
> ran back, and I was frozen cold,
> and only then did I remember,
> while I slept their tracks went cold.

The poem ends in obfuscation like the prose story, and as it fades into dream one can scarcely tell who is who, but perhaps that is not important. It conveys a very sharp image of other days remembered, not through the magnifying glass of revolution, but through the opaque medium of one man's mind, one poet's individual style. Perhaps it is really intended as a mixture of Conrad and Proust in verse. It is certainly original, and to an amazing degree a success, but I have never known a poem so hard to expound. Still, a reader finds places to perch in it, and taken as a whole it is the *tour de force* Russians have always thought it was. It has many facets, but it is not exclusively, maybe not at all, the piece of anti-Soviet propaganda that Ronald Hingley, by far its most helpful English critic, has seen it as. I find it a deeply exciting poem, but I do not claim to understand it; I am left longing for a spirited translation of all its 1220 lines.

*Spektorsky* established Boris Pasternak as a public Soviet poet. In April 1926 Mayakovsky and the Briks moved by requisition into a small Moscow flat in the Taganka, a poor area where most of the houses have now been demolished, not far from his present museum, once his workroom. They proudly bought a nameplate 'like people have'. Mayakovsky lectured on Pasternak about this time, hailing him as a great poet, though their relations continued stormy; he and the Briks explained Pasternak's poetry as 'the application of dynamic syntax to a revolutionary task', a formulation superficially attractive but deeply fatuous. Meanwhile Pasternak's international reputation was made by the freak chance of an appearance in French, in a magazine edited by Valéry. Its patroness was also a patroness of Rilke, who noticed the poems and was moved by them. We know from Rilke's letters that he thought of Russia at this time as a long-lost spiritual home, and the memory of his visits there, and of his personal acquaintance with Boris as a boy, undoubtedly played some part in his curiosity. He was most dubious of the revolution, and his ideal Russia was more or less exactly Yesenin's, primitive, religious and sempiternal. Still, to the Pasternak family his was a potent name.

*Commerce* was a Paris quarterly, and Boris Pasternak had two poems in Cahier 6 for winter 1925, translated by Hélène Iswolsky, who had a connecton with this review, probably through its patroness, and produced further translations from Russian in another number. It was not widely read (no such literary review ever is), but it was highly distinguished and influential. Joyce and Rilke had already appeared in it, and Saint-John Persse translated Eliot in its pages, as 'adaptation de St-J. Persse'. 'The Hollow Men' was first printed there. Eliot's version of *Anabase*, which was notably free in its first edition, must have been a return compliment. It is also possible that he was influenced by some of the right-wing flavour of *Commerce*, which in Cahier 4 printed some Ungaretti with a dedication to Mussolini, but the postal relations of Russia with the rest of the world were so queer that Boris Pasternak was entirely innocent of any such political tincture. The three editors were Valéry, Léon-Paul Fargue and Valery-Larbaud. The Pasternak issue included Hugo von Hofmannsthal, Ortega y Gasset, Teste's 'Log-Book' and Iswolsky's version of Mandelstam.

The first poem is 'Nuit accablante', 'Dumnaya Noch' from *My Sister Life* ('A Sultry Night'). The translation retains the Russian stanza form, but without rhymes. As a poem in French it appears to me a little neurotic but very sharp, and as if it were born in French. The second poem is 'Départ', which is 'Putting out to Sea' in the Penguin translation, dated Gulf of Finland. Where did she get that? Probably not *Moscow Poets* of 1924, but Gorky's *Russian Contemporary* of the same year. Its definitive text dates from 1929. The translation has the same unrhymed stanzas, but the heart of the poem is perfectly conveyed, and one can see what appealed in it: not just the unexpected metaphors, but the profound and sad sense of exile.

> Et le flot qui s'élargit
> Ceuille encore les baies,
> Longe les bois, et gronde,
> Et inonde furieusement le bord.
>
> Visible encore, encore visible
> Est la terre. La voie – non sans taches,
> Est déjà insolite
> Et insondable comme le malheur.
>
> Par un virement terrible,
> – Changement brusque du regard,
> Les mâts entrent dans les portes
> De la mer grande ouverte.
>
> La voici. Et, telle un présage
> De l'inconnu qui gronde doucement,
> Une mouette, lancée comme un gobelet
> Tombe lourdement dans l'abîme.

It is extremely likely that Eliot read this translation, and not impossible that some faint echo of its 'Jaillissement jaillissement, jaillissement sans échos' may be picked up in his 'Marina'; or is it only the sea's voice in both? The Mandelstam that follows the Pasternak is his 'New Year's Poem' for 1924, eight-line stanzas here reduced to four-line ones: it is a substantial piece, which must have seemed the very voice of modern Russia, where Boris

Pasternak was presented as a beautiful, sad, wandering ghost, a Hamlet with a touch of Baudelaire. Still, he appealed in this disguise to Rilke, and at about the same time the best Russian critic, the exiled Prince D. Sviatopolk-Mirsky, heard of him and his reputation among poets, from Tsvetayeva in Paris, and began to acknowledge him in print as the most promising young poet of the age in his language, and a poet on the threshold of greatness.

Mirsky had an unhappy history; he somehow converted himself in exile to his own kind of Marxism. Part of this process is to be discerned in the chapters on real history with which he interleaved his *History of Russian Literature*, now unfortunately reprinted without them. But he believed in forces, not in individuals, and when he returned to Russia under Stalin wrote a complete history of the country in which personalities played no part. This was not well received, and he vanished and perished. In the days of his exile he was a close friend of Maurice Baring, whose *Oxford Book of Russian Verse* represents Mirsky's taste as much as Baring's. He used to work in the London Library. I have not discovered whether Pasternak came to know him, but it appears very likely.

In 1924 Boris moved from a hellish flat in Yamskaya to a better one where the neighbours 'don't even wear beards or smell bad, and that at a time when the pure swinishness of our species is unadulterated and its character unchanged. To my sinful and still swinish eye, our new apartment is the Lyceum, the Stoa Poikile, the Propylaeum.' That was in a private letter to his cousin Olga at what we had better begin calling Leningrad. Boris was still very badly off and not well organised, however famous he might be becoming. They would reprint his stories if he added a new one, but he was unable to write it. He sold another medal. Someone rediscovered his forgotten version of Jonson's *The Alchemist* and he was paid for it.

His life sounds rickety to the same extent and in the same way as that of any Bohemian writer in the west, and yet it was worse. He lost his room to someone else's housemaid who had typhoid, then to three sick students, 'one of whom looked like a deep sea diver, with his head swathed in towels and his face hidden by bandages because eczema covered his whole body'. The Pasternaks had to get through this room, which now stank of carbolic, animal humanity and cheap tobacco, to get to their kitchen and running water. Even so early, in October 1924, we encounter the sentence

'Yesterday, while making enquiries about a fellow innocently sent into exile, I found myself in a Kremlin apartment where there was diphtheria.' He was doing piecework at foreign journals in the Foreign Ministry, which is where he read about Proust and also Satie, but the moment he had even a little money he set to work to translate *Hamlet*, 'a task I had been putting off for years'. But then, 'before Horatio had time to doubt the reality of the ghost', both his two contracts, for the prose collection and for *The Alchemist*, were annulled. He then owed 120 roubles to his child's nanny, quite apart from her salary. All these invaluable details come from his correspondence with Olga.

Boris began to correspond with Tsvetayeva in 1922, over her volume *Versts*, issued the year before. In the summer of 1925 he wrote to her expressing his personal difficulties and his doubts about lyrical poetry in those times. She was delighted at his 'first really *human* letter, the others were spiritual'. In December 1925, Leonid Pasternak in Berlin wrote to congratulate Rilke on his fiftieth birthday, which the papers had mentioned; in March he got a reply from Switzerland. 'Last year in Paris I met old Russian friends and found new ones, and the youthful fame of your son Boris reached us from more than one direction.' Rilke had been delighted with some poems by him in an anthology of Ehrenburg's, who in those days was also a poet. The Paris friends had included Izvolskaya, and as a postscript in his letter to Leonid, which is chiefly about being moved by being rememberd by old friends, Rilke adds that he has just seen the publication in *Commerce*, and how impressed he is by it. A comedy of errors follows, because Switzerland still had no postal union with revolutionary Russia.

Leonid writes to Boris a slightly doddery letter in which he promises to send extracts from Rilke's letter 'next time'. He seems to believe Boris was translated by Valéry. Boris writes to Tsvetayeva, still in March 1926, in the seventh heaven of exaltation over a typescript of her *Poem of the End*; as well he might be. The poem is about the end of a love affair, and one cannot help wondering whether it struck some personal chord in him by 1926. It turns out later that Rilke had invited Tsvetayeva to stay, but it seems clear that although correspondence with Rilke through her in Paris was Boris's idea she was a jealous woman, and aimed to interpose herself as the medium of any friendship between Boris and the great man. Meanwhile he is writing furiously to his sister Josephine about not being sent Rilke's letter about him, which she now has. He is terrified, not without justice, at how his father may have boasted about him to Rilke. He begs to be sent Tsvetayeva's works from Paris. It turns out he is not being sent the whole of Rilke's letter because it contains anti-Soviet phrases, and what he was sent had at first failed to arrive. In April he gets his copy of Rilke's remarks, and writes off at once: 'Great, most beloved poet! . . .' His letter was exaggerated but perfectly sincere and very moving.

'I am indebted to you for the fundamental cast of my character, the nature of my intellectual being. They are your creations. . . . The passionate joy I feel at being able to make confession to you as a poet is as uncommon with me as what I would feel when confronting Aeschylus or Pushkin, if that were conceivable. . . . The magical coincidence that I should come to your notice was a staggering event for me. The news of it was like an electric short circuit of the soul. . . . I rushed to the window. It was snowing, people were walking outside. I could take nothing in, I was crying. . . . For hours I was unable to talk.' He then tells Rilke his thoughts about poetry and reality and 'the special refraction of the general light of European intimacy' (*Spektorsky?*) and the excitement of Tsvetayeva. No old poet would be wholly displeased to get such a letter from a young poet. To Tsvetayeva he writes about leaving Russia and living with her and about stopping on for just one year, for the sake of his poetry. It is hard to discern how far he intended that seriously; his letters to her are like an intimate journal, but the thoughts are even more fleeting.

His father imagines a slight and reproves Boris for referring to him without the correct respectful intimacy, merely as L.O. He is even more disconcerted that Boris has proposed Rilke should sign a book for Tsvetayeva. 'Can it be that among poets the exchange of books between total strangers is the accepted practice?' Leonid writes at the same time to Rilke in a clinic: 'How delighted I was to read the description of your solitary life among the beauties of nature . . . the greatest blessing an artist can know on this earth . . . pursuing your beloved art among your beloved roses.' Meanwhile Boris now wants to join Tsvetayeva in Paris in order to visit Rilke together. Or he will settle down to work. 'Tomorrow I will be a different person. I will take the bull by the horns and work.' He shows his known tendency to love her husband (a member of the underworld of intelligence and counter-intelligence, perhaps an assassin) as well as her. Tsvetayeva suspects Boris loves Elsa Triolet. He replies with transparent naïvety, 'There are thousands of women I would *have* to love if I let myself go.' It took Rilke about three months of poetry and fine feeling to get fed up with Tsvetayeva and to see through her devices. His last letter to her, on 19 August, is one of rebuke, and when she replied, and later when she sent him a postcard, there was no answer, although he was writing letters in those weeks, which were the last of his life.

Perhaps the most unexhausted value of all these letters is the light they constantly throw on *Lieutenant Schmidt*. In May 'I will write to you as soon as I finish *Schmidt*. It will be three weeks or so.' He speaks of the sense of freedom in 1917, and refers to *Schmidt* to illustrate it, some gloomy lines into which, as he says, his poem wearily sinks. 'Out of their cages aeons idle, beasts roam the Colosseum floor. . . .' At the same time he discusses the details of language in the 'Potemkin' section of *1905*. *Lieutenant Schmidt* and 'Potemkin' are of course inseparable, and the poem is conceived as a part of *1905*, but in fact it has an independent existence. The subject was a rich and popular one: the famous film, Eisenstein's *Battleship Potemkin*, is almost exactly contemporary, but there is no influence either way. Pasternak thought of furnishing his poem with technical footnotes. In May he was working all day long and all night at *Schmidt*, and writing letters only to tear them up. He sent Tsvetayeva a dedication with an acrostic of her name.

That was printed in *Novy Mir*, but never again. The reason appears to be that he cancelled it. He wrote *Schmidt* with subtlety and irony, which even Mayakovsky and Tsvetayeva failed to see. She constantly complained that he laboured to make his hero unideal. Schmidt had been her personal hero since 1905, and she was unable to accept Boris Pasternak's extreme realism and Tolstoyan accuracy. Her nagging resulted in the poem being cut (temporarily) by half: she is recorded by her friend Kruchyonykh as having written that the poem was a waste of time, just one intellectual buttering up another. Before the 1926 publication the poet had forgotten which bits he had cut and which not. It was certainly not a case of one intellectual praising another, but *Schmidt* was a serious attempt, though less strange and less powerful than *Spektorsky*, at narrative verse on an epic subject.

Their exalted mutual admiration did not dissolve in a literary difference: what have survived of their letters contain many sentences of criticism of verse which are worth reading and rereading, like the best of Eliot's correspondence or of Pound's. But they grew cooler: neither of them wanted a drama like a railway smash; she deliberately cooled him down. In summer his wife went abroad and he wrote to Tsvetayeva, when she left in July: 'I must tell you something about Zhenya. I miss her terribly. Basically I love her more than anything on earth. When she is absent I always see her in my mind's eye as she was before we got married. . . . The spiritual essence of our union parted company with its transient, everyday play-forms. It was vitally important for us to recapture and reinstate that essence. I saw no success in our efforts. The dark shadow of our powerlessness fell across the years, spoiling both our lives. So writing about her to you I must often have made things look worse than they were.'

To speak as objectively as possible about *Schmidt* as it now stands, it consists of thirty-two pages of verse, mostly in regular stanzas, just twice the length of the whole of *1905*, and concentrating on a single fascinating and heroic episode. Schmidt was a daring, strikingly handsome young man, capable of simple and thrilling sentences which were almost poetry already, and of actions in the same spirit. He led a mutiny, captured the cruiser *Ochakov* in harbour at Sevastopol, and sent the Tsar a telegram: 'I assume command of the fleet, Schmidt.' A fleet of ten mutinous ships put out to sea, but they were swiftly overcome, Schmidt jumped overboard and he was captured in the water. In prison he had no writing materials but wrote sayings in candle-grease on the stone floor, which were widely reported, including the famous one, 'Soon the whole people will awake.' Boris Pasternak's poem is like a long lament, steady-eyed, but full of a real grief.

> In vain in days of chaos
> men seek to be happy,
> some judge and some repent,
> some go to Calvary.

> Like you I have my share
> in these times of tempest:
> I accept your verdict
> without anger or protest.

I know you will not tremble
to kill me at your ease,
O martyrs of dogma,
victims of centuries.

My love for Russia's a coat
threadbare its thirtieth year,
I do not pray or hope
for mercy anywhere.

These were the days you knew
these memorable days,
I was plucked out of them
by the storms in the skies.

Terrible to have missed
my land's rebellion,
now I have no regrets
for the road I have gone.

I know I shall be tied
on to a wooden post:
it stands between two ages,
to be chosen is my boast.

No one need ever say again that Pasternak was incapable of simplicity, or of popular, heroic verse. If this poem were any better it would not be as good. I have quoted his version of Schmidt's final speech to his judges. Its last verse is one with which the poet passionately identifies. It was his fate also when the time came to stand his ordeal at the frontier-post of two ages of the world. That is quite correct for 1905, but would not have done for 1917. Think how differently Brecht would have written Schmidt's last speech. But Pasternak's loyalty to 1905 was unswerving. It was the revolution of his youth, and whatever he felt about later history he kept its pure flame alight: not revolution or a new world, but only the pure flame that he had felt when he was fifteen. It burned for the dead almost more than for the future. We shall see that the same is true of his strange attempt at a fuller, wider statement in the poem *1905*. *Schmidt* is dated March 1926 to March 1927, and *1905* July

1925 to February 1926, but he began work on both in 1925, and he was still at work on *1905* until the autumn of 1927 when it was published; he sent it to Gorky, whom he called 'the greatest expression and justification of this epoch', in September of that year. The two poems must be regarded as complementary, neither as an extension of the other; one is more concentrated on its single story, the other has a wider range.

Just because it ranges widely over events, *1905* is very interesting. After an introduction its first part is 'The Fathers', about the forerunners of the revolution. The terrorist ancestry of one of his heroines interested him in part nine of *Spektorsky*. The second is 'Childhood', as if his autobiography was already taking shape in his mind. Then come 'Peasants and Workers', 'Mutiny at Sea', 'Students', which returns to an autobiographical theme and contains an elegiac piece of great beauty, and finally 'Moscow in December', which describes the end of the revolution, the fires and the aftermath. Some of this material has already become mythical twenty years later, and the disjointed air the poem has today may be due to the simple fact that many of his first readers remembered what he was talking about. If you were twenty in 1905 you were in your early forties when *1905* came out. Boris Pasternak was thirty-seven.

Take Baumann's funeral, for example, which is vividly treated in the section 'Students'. Baumann was a Leninist Bolshevik of twenty-two who was murdered by the paramilitary Black Hundred, and buried two days later. This funeral was on 2 November. We have an excellent report of his funeral by Maurice Baring, who was in Moscow as a journalist.

This afternoon I went to see Baumann's funeral procession, which I witnessed from many parts of the town. It was one of the most impressive sights I have ever seen. A hundred thousand men took part in it. The whole of the Intelligentsia (the professional and middle class) was in the streets or at the windows. The windows and balconies were crowded with people. The order was perfect. There was not a hitch nor a scuffle. The men walking in the procession consisted of students, doctors, workmen, people in various kinds of uniform. There were ambulances, with doctors dressed in white in them, in case there should be casualties. The men bore great

red banners, and the coffin was covered in a scarlet pall. As they
marched they sang in a low chant the *Marseillaise, Viechny
Pamiot,* and the *Funeral March of the Fighters for Freedom.* The last
tune is the most impressive.

From a musician's point of view it is, I am told, a shockingly
bad tune; but then as Du Maurier said, one should never listen to
musicians on the subject of music any more than one should
listen to wine merchants on the subject of wine. But it is the tune
which to my mind is exactly fitting for the Russian revolution,
with its dogged melancholy and invincible passion, as fitting as
the *Marseillaise* (which by the way the Russians sing in parts and
slowly) is totally unfitting. The *Funeral March* has nothing
defiant in it; but it is one of those tunes which, when sung by a
multitude, make one's flesh creep; it is commonplace if you will;
and it expresses – as it were by accident – the commonplaceness
of all that is determined and unflinching, mingled with an accent
of weary pathos. As it grew dark torches were brought out,
lighting up the red banners and the scarlet coffin of the unknown
veterinary surgeon, who in a second, by a strange freak of
chance, had become a hero, or rather a symbol, an emblem and a
banner, and who was being carried to his last resting-place with
a simplicity which eclipsed the pomp of all royal funerals, and to
the sound of a low song of tired but indefatigable sadness
stronger and more formidable than the paeans which celebrate
the triumphs and the pageants of kings.

The impression left on my mind by this funeral is deep. As I
saw these hundred thousand men march past so quietly, so
simply, in their bourgeois clothes, singing in careless, almost
conventional fashion, I seemed nevertheless to hear the
'trampling of unnumerable armies', and to feel the breath of the

> Courage never to submit or yield,
> And what is else not to be overcome.

Nowadays they speak of three hundred thousand, but perhaps
they count the bystanders. Baring was not writing in retrospect; he
did not really see what 1905 would lead to. The same week he went
to a Gorky play at the Arts' Theatre and wrote about that. But his
intuitive sense of occasion was remarkable, and what he wrote at
the time still summons up the reality. Boris Pasternak is perfectly

conscious of what happened between 1905 and 1927, and for him to summon up the old demonstration and the funeral is an act of deliberate commemoration like the laying of a wreath. It is what he owes to the past, to his own past and his memories.

> Baumann!
> Funeral march
> and thronged disturbance of your name,
> as they march
> as they bow to banners
> balconies high to thread
> roads lined with heads.
> And all the while
> surging below
> uncovered heads:
> 'A victim you fall
> in a battle ill-starred.'

The song is the same. The words are anonymous, but the tune was an old, familiar soldiers' song, probably composed by some long-forgotten military bandmaster. The song became widely known after the execution of Perovskaya and others for the assassination of Tsar Alexander II in 1881; Shostakovich uses it in the third movement of his Eleventh Symphony. Boris Pasternak is looking down from the balcony in Minitskaya on the flags towering to his level above a river of bare heads. This memory is collapsed into the time he saw a demonstration ambushed, and suffered the results at street level, and a memory of the wounded being rushed inside the Arts Building on some third occasion. 'Gaping doors. A sigh point-blank. From the sulphates and the paints.' His recollection or imagination of the fighting is terribly real, wherever it comes from, and it is probably the scenes of violence mingled with solemnity that have made *1905* such a popular poem. 'Hot pitch in puddles, the frozen snow steaming with blood, corpses caught in stiff postures of flight; the rustling pleats of the snowdrifts. All is blank night, and at once: to the four winds eternally tossed.' This is better than Blok's 'Twelve', I believe, and the only poetry ever written about a revolution to be as vividly effective as a film.

It is fascinating to what extent the people in this poem are

victims, moving if they move as slowly as a sad ballet. Boris
Pasternak's evocation of Bloody Sunday at Petersburg, at which he
was certainly not present, is a brilliant example of the same
technique. In representing crowds, both in what he puts in and
what he leaves out, he appears to me to have a lot in common with
Eisenstein, though I am anxious not to push that analogy too far.
The influence that played on him may have been the special
consciousness of these effects that arose from early films, from
their mingling of the frozen or static or theatrical with ambitious
distances and multitudes. Meyerhold, who became his friend and
who admired him, was also a powerful influence on his imagination with a kind of epic theatre of his own, and with roots like
Pasternak's in pre-war artistic movements. Or maybe it was
simply revolutionary Russia that begot in them all a new curiosity
about the crowd, and a new way of seeing. In Meyerhold
productions, the latest battle news of the civil war interrupted the
action, and an ambulance drove through the stalls.

> Notorious dawn,
> cloudbase of blueberry and cranberry,
> You hear the balconies down to the gates
> you see breath curling from the slops,
> from the balconies down to the gates,
> behind the banners
> the crowds pacing
> into spaces
> charred by winter:
> they march from gates into the frozen snow.
>
> Eight waves of thunder
> and the ninth wave
> as stately as the skyline.
> Hats whisked from heads,
> Lord save thy people.
> To the left a bridge, a ditch,
> to the right churchyard and gate,
> and the railway
> runs ahead.
> They are hemmed in by a wood.
>
> . . . From the Neva eight volleys,
> the ninth as weary as glory.

Inwards from the left of right
storm of horses at the trot.
Now the distance howls:
This score will be settled,
and every joint
is cracked apart
in whatever oath may be
sworn to the Tsar's dynasty.

The speed of the poem never lets up or stumbles; the few phrases
that jolt a foreign reader, like 'Hats whisked from heads' or
'washed away from heads', turn out to be the dramatic wheels on
which the verse runs. The rather breathless staccato stanzas are an
essential part of the always fragmented action and the speed. Of
course they can be delayed by many devices: repetition, or a long
lyrical line about the berries which decode as Bloody Sunday, or a
long image like that of night in the square. They can be fortified by
closures, rhymes and half-rhymes. Pasternak's medium is suitable
for the purposes of this poem alone, just as the medium of *The
Waste Land* or that of the *Four Quartets* can be used once only. He
scarcely embroiders, less so than reporters, but his bareness
belongs to poetry, not prose: it holds in control a powerful
undertow of rhythm, and a more muscular syntactic impetus than
prose commands. The words and lines bite the page, as he always
said that poems should. But the momentum of the entire poem is
that of events, and within that momentum the people are victims.
The enormous popularity of this poem suggests they were not
unwilling to see themselves as he portrayed them. The persistent
popularity and present public revival of Bulgakov present an
analogy of a kind.

The introduction to *1905* consists of seven four-line stanzas,
regularly rhymed.

In October came a winter
on the grotesque of our prose,
like the sweep of curtain-edges
dark clouds drooping down in rows.

The sledging snow is fresh entangled,
keenly biting, strange and new,

day and night modern, unearthly,
Revolution, that is you.

In fact it is 'just like you' or 'wholly expresses you', like the girl's
gun in *Spektorsky*. It would be fair to say the excitement of the
revolution itself, a new life, what he later calls 'second birth', is the
motive of the entire poem. By using the word 'October' he pins his
loyalty to the second revolution of 1917, with which he is what
Trotsky was first to call a fellow-traveller, someone going the
same way, not to be despised or alienated by the government.
Revolution came in from Siberia, he says, like Joan of Arc,
weeping with a basilisk face, and hating mediocrity above all
things.

　　His sermon on the nature and origns of revolution continues in
the first part, 'The Fathers'.

> . . . The evening of havoc,
> of circles and heroes,
> of dynamiters and daguerreotypes,
> the soul on fire,
> troikas on roads
> and factories, rising along the roads.
> Savvas are rising.
> Vikulas are ripening . . .

The factories give this composite picture a Marxist air, though we
know that sedition in the old munitions factories was a personal
memory, and so of course was the exhilarating sledge-ride at night
in winter, along the forest roads and the road that followed the
railway. But Savva and Vikula Morozov are not typical capitalists.
They founded model textile mills in deprived areas, they were
enlightened patrons of the arts, and Savva killed himself, leaving
his whole fortune through Gorky to the Communist Party. So he
means friendly capitalists, fellow travellers really. I think the point
being made is that in 1927 they and their buildings, like those
similar ones still standing in Moscow in 1989, looked extremely
dated and old-fashioned, like the dynamiters and daguerreotypes.
They are followed by the Nationals: the People's Will movement,
which produced the assassin Perovskaya (twenty-eight years old).
The nihilists and torture-cells and student pince-nez of this stanza

are well displayed in the Moscow Museum of the 1905 revolution: the dreamy-eyed youths and the home-made explosive contraptions have an almost homely air. Dostoevsky gets a line, so does Nechaev (1847–82), the international anarchist, but this is only a raising of the hat, so to speak, to the generation of the reader's parents and grandparents, whose stories seemed almost to date from the Stuarts, and to those 'schoolfriends of their mothers' who were in the People's Will movement. The blasts of dynamite have a pleasing period flavour for Boris, and even Stepan Kalturin (1856–82) seems mildy comic. 'Dynamite gives him no sleep.' The climax of this section is rightly given to Port Arthur, and to the telegraph, which must have been as startling in its day as the television news is today. I cannot believe that an orthodox Leninist would allow such heavy weight to the disaster at Port Arthur: neither Lenin nor Marx has been mentioned at all.

> I was fourteen
> Vkhutemas still a sculpting school:
> where Rabfak is
> upstairs
> my father's studio . . .

The acronymic slang name for the Higher Art and Technical Workshops (1925) exists like so many acronymic names in Russia (USSR, for example, and OGPU) because the words of the official title are unbearably long. Vkhutemas at full length is *Vysshie Khudozhestvenno-Technicheskie Masterskie*. Rabfak is Workers' Faculties, where working people could prepare for higher education. This introduction to his childhood has no particular political or social weight: it just seems a long time ago, and his father's world utterly distant. 'Our door, our floor of stone, where the mud clings.' He remembers the news of Port Arthur, the post office staring in the twilight, schoolteachers staring in the daylight, the colours staring from the palette. For Proustian quality, the stanza rivals *Spektorsky*. He goes through the main points of his life: the crowded, indescribable classroom with the shuffle of feet mingling with the chimes of the church next door to the flat; then Scriabin, who enters the house and the poem like the demon king ('Scriabin! Where can I flee / From the steps of my idol and god?'): then Christmas, Petersburg, and in the last line of a stanza, with an

entry like Scriabin's, suddenly Gapon. We have reached Bloody
Sunday, but it must be said these do not read like the memoirs of a
young revolutionary.

Yet the pace increases: that is the strategy of the whole poem.
The year 1905 is its climax, and Pasternak is already pondering
how much of his own life to use in order to set off what happened,
in its gradual emergence. That is one of the clues to *Zhivago*, but
from a strictly formal point of view, and because it has the qualities
of poems, *1905* is possibly a more powerful work. It is time we
admitted that the chief motive of Pasternak criticism in the west has
often been anti-communist, and that therefore this excellent poem
has been neglected. In his autobiography, Pasternak constantly
refined its shape, used other climaxes, and gave himself other,
deeper meanings, but there is a strength in the verse of *1905* and its
whole conception which one would be reluctant to lose.

The third part begins with snow and fire, those ominous and
beautiful symbols. But the trains are still running and the general
strike is confined to the cities: not at all how Maurice Baring
described it – he was stuck for a long time in a labyrinth of railway
strikes and official frustrations, trying to get back to Moscow.
'What sparked off the workers', says Boris, 'was the whiplashes
dealt out to the crowd, even at the funerals of the dead.' But I am
not sure he is right about that: the cavalry whip had been in use for a
very long time; it cannot have failed to produce resentment, but
never before revolution. Baring in another book which I am unable
to trace, perhaps in a private letter, describes a lunch party in a
Moscow palace, after which he walked home. The party was
charming, civilised and very elegant. He was already walking
down the street when an old Grand Duke left in a sledge with
outriders. His Cossacks whipped the crowd left and right, simply
on principle and to clear the road. But it was the year 1905, as
Baring points out, that created Russian politics. 'The railwaymen',
he says, 'had secured from the Tsar what the Barons secured from
King John.' Boris Pasternak's view was far more dramatic, and the
climax of part three, with the outbreak of armed revolution, is a
convincing picture.

Part four is action at sea, as if from a few potshots in an urban
disturbance something like war had broken out. 'Concealed in the
white blaze of the waves, the white spice of acacias, the weeping of
the sea.' Four stanzas of marine poetry a little reminiscent of *Peter*

*Grimes* emphasise the power of a natural force, as the snow and fire did in part three.

> In the galvanised gloom,
> in the cloud-huddle,
> the big ships skulk into harbour,
> the blue-legged lightning
> leapfrogs in water . . .

> . . . The sun set
> and at once
> electricity fired *Potemkin*
> from galley to spar-deck:
> infested with swarming blueflies,
> the meat has gone off.
> Long shadows fall on sea, awake,
> lights grouse till dawn,
> dimmed in the wan daybreak.

The tension tightens as the story unfolds, because it focuses more and more clearly stanza by stanza. When action comes it is violent, and the bullet noise 'Trakh-takh-takh' is a small part of it. This passage presents the first full-scale hand-to-hand fighting of the entire poem, and here the crowd are by no means Tolstoyan victims. The position of this part in the scheme of the whole poem is crucial. Conversation is very swift, scarcely intelligible, and description is equally selective, but it sets off the hero Matushenko, 'By the boilers towers / Over the grating / Giant of shadows / Matushenko.'

> Now the day's
> passed into dusk,
> smoke-clouds veil the haze,
> sailor to sailor shouts through loud-hailer,
> Anchors aweigh!
> And the voice of the cloud is still,
> *Potemkin* towards Odessa sails,
> on her stern peak
> the burning blob
> of an orange blaze.

The moment of victory, of what the people might do if it had a mind, is framed and distanced by the sea, and over almost before one spots it. The surrounding sea is a frightening setting. People are shot and thrown into it, and 'For the rest, each a shot, and to sea.' But every reader knows how the story ended. The ship was easily enough recaptured and the heroes became victims in their turn. Yet I find this curiously abbreviated picture of victorious mutiny oddly moving, like the painting of a ship, almost like an icon. Its violence is disturbing. Baumann follows, and Baumann's funeral merges into violence and the ambushed demonstration. The climax is December, the fires that are slow to go out, and the names of Colonel Mien and Riemann, officers of a Guards regiment that overran Krasnaya Presnya and massacred numerous unarmed workmen. The regiment, Semyonovsky Guards, was summoned from Petersburg as the forces in Moscow were too few or not reliable. It arrived by the Brest railway at what is now the Kiev Station, the closest.

> It was morning.
> An expanse
> stretched for the escaping ones.
> Presnya flat on her back,
> in weak folds of storm-crumpled birches:
> with the wailing shawls of women
> washed away the cavalry,
> yielded to superior force
> and laid on sheets her Browning guns.

If I have dwelt at comparatively great length on these longer poems, and in particular on *1905*, it is because they are comparatively unknown in the west, but also because of their unexpected merits both as verse and as narrative, and because *1905* affords us a unique opportunity to look at Pasternak's life and his feelings about revolution in retrospect through his own eyes as a poet, and at the same time uniquely prefigures or announces what is to come, though it will be a long time coming. After these poems, which must have cost him a lot in energy and determination, he was still lively, but he was exhausted. He was like a swimmer who has crossed some enormous river and can only flop down on the further bank. The extension of his lyric powers into narrative and autobiographic verse sharpened his sense that lyric poetry was somehow a muddle, a fudging of the issue, not proper for the age. I do not think he was responding to the party directives about literature at this time, since the party had not yet screwed down the lid on writers. If he did so respond, then he did so obliquely as one might expect of him. Still, it is true that Gorky carried weight in his opinion, and Gorky had the same prose writer's distrust or secret envy of poetry that Arnold Bennett had. He would have preferred a Pasternak who was all prose. And Boris himself liked new beginnings and casting off the old life. His obsession with Resurrection and resurrections, which determined so much of his later work, was already discernible by 1927. In 1928 Stalin came to full power.

A preposterous 'show trial' of a certain Shakhty and some German engineers, which featured a boy of twelve pleading for his father to be executed, and various references to 'corrupt blood', marked his attainment of supremacy; the New Economic Policy of Lenin was now a dead duck, and the sordid rigmarole attendant on the Gulag began to take shape. It is a strange fact that in those early days America was greatly admired, as much by Stalin as by Mayakovsky. 'If only', wrote the idiotic proletarian poet Gastev, 'we can match the hurricane power of Russian revolution with the strong pulse of America, we can do the job as steadily as a chronometer', which does not seem the likely outcome. In 1930 Stalin turned on the peasants like an attack of bubonic plague. But a biography of Pasternak must to some extent be the history of his consciousness, which is best charted through his letters and his writings; I will therefore take for granted the known story of Stalin and his regime, referring to it in detail only when it is relevant. All personal relations with foreigners were by this time monitored, and within the Soviet Union the wildest disinformation prevailed: we must take that much for granted.

Boris Pasternak kept himself busy. 'I am rarely at home and then only for short stretches,' he wrote to Olga. 'I love my fast, mechanised, machine-like day. . . . I hope to be able to do some real work in the future. God grant these hopes aren't an illusion. Until then I must confess my day is spent in continuous pleasure, for I must repeat that I am entranced by the dense mesh of simple, rush-rush trifles that fill the hours. At any rate, this senseless fever is more like the former fever of spirit that made me a poet than the enforced idleness of the past two or three years, after I discovered individualism was a heresy and idealism was banned. But enough of this nonsense.' He forwards a hundred roubles to her from his father. She had got her doctorate in 1924, but she was by no means well paid. He tried without success to lure her to Moscow, to call on Lunacharsky together about employment.

In 1927 he did try to write what he knew was needed but everyone was evading, a prose history of his own generation, which he called *A Novel about Patrick*. Only fragments of it have survived. His family life was difficult, crowded and expensive. His wife had passed through art school and needed a studio. The little boy Zhenya had a tutor (Elizabeth Stetsenko) and there was now a maid. Boris felt the conditions of his existence were essentially normal, but they did not appear so to others. 'I am the son of an artist. I saw art and famous people from childhood. I am used to treating the lofty and exceptional as a vital norm, like nature. Socially, it has been among my everyday household business since birth. I don't distinguish it from the everyday with craftsman's scaffolding, or see it between big quotation marks, as most people see it.' That is part of his charm and interest.

When his wife and child got back from abroad, from a long holiday of which she spent a month making new friends by a lake in the Tyrolean Alps, Boris travelled part of the way to meet their train, because that was the only way he could get to spend two hours alone with them. It was 'a typical Moscow ruse', and the two hours were like an oasis to him. Meanwhile her mother had been terribly ill with a tumour on the spine and creeping paralysis; the doctors removed five of her vertebrae. She then got a severe fever and blood-poisoning. Boris and his wife began to feel considerable discord. He arrived in Leningrad to see Olga, plainly on the edge of being in love again. 'I saw at once', she wrote later, 'that he brought his old feelings with him, and far from feeling the same I felt revulsion. We went for long walks together. Trouble with Zhenya had begun by this time, and made him feel more drawn to me than ever.' She asked for a copy of *1905*, and he gave it to her nicely inscribed, by hiding it under her papers. 'It is hard to convey how vividly he had expressed his love for me in that single gesture of hiding his feelings among my papers.'

In 1928 he wrote to her, 'I was sick a good deal this winter and accomplished little. I have now come to a critical point in two or three works that I have yet to finish. They deal with the past decade, its events, its significance, etc. – not seen objectively as in *1905*, but personally and subjectively, recounting what all of us saw and lived. I cannot take a single step forward in life or work if I fail to give myself a full report on this stretch of time. To avoid facing this by working on something else . . . would rob all future experience of its value. . . . As you know, terror has resumed, without the moral grounds or justifications that we found for it earlier. . . . Terrible confusion reigns; we are caught up and spun round in waves that have absolutely no relationship to time. We are dazed. Last autumn I didn't expect this, so my mood was less gloomy then.'

He spoke of his task as one likely to bring him trouble and 'maybe much worse', yet it seemed to him to lie in the natural course of his duty and the fulfilment of his destiny, rather than being an act of daring defiance. 'And who knows? It might work. I prefer to believe it will.' What he was planning and the way he thought of it would not be purged until *Zhivago*, twenty years later. How he lived through those twenty years is the most painful part of this book. *Zhivago* might after all never have been written. But the story of the twenty years is constantly enlivened by the things he did manage to write and to do. In May 1928 his heart was set on the south.

# 6

## The Waves

*Schmidt* and *1905*, which were printed in book form together, are patriotic poems, but only marginally relevant to the concerns of the Russian government, and *Spektorsky* is splendidly entangled, intransigently personal and more obscure, being longer than all the lyrics of *My Sister Life* or *Theme and Variations*. It has an enticing element of autobiography in its composition. *Safe Conduct* was written to go with *Spektorsky* and the fiction *Povest*, for a projected four-volume collected works, though the publisher's contract remained unsigned and in the air. Boris began it in 1928 as 'a philosophic essay centred on autobiography', in 1929 he was at work on all three undertakings; *Safe Conduct* finally appeared as a serial between 1929 and 1931, and in that year as a book. There was a dangerous clarity about it. An edition of 10,000 sold at once, but it was attacked for 'idealism' almost as quickly, and its second edition, planned for 1933, never appeared at all.

The idea was to write 'something between an article and artistic prose' (what the Germans call *Kunst-Prosa*). It is indeed written in a prose as elaborate as Mandelstam's, but not as sharp or as melodious. It was meant to show, with reference to his own life, how life gets transformed into art, and why. Since I am not deeply in sympathy with this purpose, I must be forgiven for thinking he has not accomplished it. Wordsworth does it in *The Prelude*, because there biography is fuel to send off a poem like some vast rocket that soars across our minds. But 'artistic prose' is a doubtful commodity, giving the impression of the story of a life exhausting itself by simply flailing about in words. Yet it has fascinating pages and surprising insights, and its power as narrative cancels the pretensions of artistic prose. Perhaps it is an attempt to show the poet conceiving the world or his life as poems, but if so the poetical conceptions remain fragmentary, as one might expect: the poems do not in this art-prose form have sufficient definition to make sense of the world. It is an attractive book, but it is like some marvellous film with an irritating director. It would need two geniuses at once to be both the poet producing poems and the prose-writer who observes him. Boris Pasternak managed the same problem much better in *Zhivago*, which gives us the only convincing poet in the history of fiction.

*Safe Conduct* is about a hundred pages. It begins with Rilke, to whom the whole book is dedicated. It deals with sexual awakening, artistic awakening, and at great length, nearly a third of the book, with Marburg. That unforgettable vignette of a pre-1914 university remains vividly in our minds as in his, because it was lost and islanded in a past that already seemed remote in 1929. Boris felt it a matter of conscience not to abandon philosophy, as many young philosophers do, but the subject had moved on as it does for most of us, and his Marburg no longer existed. In 1929 Martin Heidegger had recently taught philosophy at Marburg; in 1923 he moved on to Freiburg in succession to Husserl. Of the old German university towns that have survived, only Marburg and Freiburg have been lucky enough not to become great cities, but the neo-Kantian philosophy of the 1900s is as irrecoverably lost as English Hegelianism. By comparison, his briefer account of Venice might have been written the other day. The other big subject is Mayakovsky; he is treated in a number of sections that show him from different angles, as an amazing phenomenon, a great poet, a dead friend.

Section twelve of part three presents the Terror. It begins: 'The winter twilight, the terror, and the roofs and trees of the Arbat.' The flat where the poet lived belonged to a bearded and genial journalist from Oranenburg, who warmed himself with huge armfuls of old newspapers and bacon rinds. 'When darkness fell, the sentries on duty began enthusiastically firing off their revolvers. Sometimes they fired salvoes, sometimes just an isolated, rare enquiry into the night, loaded with pathetic, irrevocable deadliness.' Since there were so many stray deaths, and no rhythm to the shooting, Boris felt metronomes ought to be stationed out there instead of militia. Sometimes you heard 'a savage wail'. Mayakovsky telephoned on such a night to tell Boris he was named on a poster to appear with Mayakovsky's closest supporters, 'the most faithful of the faithful, including I believe the man who used to break inch-thick planks across his forehead'.

Christopher Barnes says this was a man called Goltsshmit, 'the Futurist of Life', who did a strong-man act and was also bouncer at the Poets' Café, in the winter of 1917–18. With Mayakovsky the book ends; the impression of him has effaced the elaborate compliments to Rilke, though I do not think Boris intended that to happen, because it was Rilke he thought of as the genius of his poetry. Yet it is certainly as Mayakovsky's friend, not as Rilke's disciple, that one thinks of him now. As for the revolution, this section is the closest he gets to it. It is nothing but chaos and bloodshed; he says Mayakovsky did not understand how these two years had changed him; he had not yet shown anyone the new poems that were going to be *My Sister Life*.

The poems he was writing by the last year of his old friend's life, 1929–30, were often about what a poet is, what he must do. At about forty that is a common enough preoccupation of writers. Their first lyric flights are over, they are considering long-term schemes, longer, more ambitious works, and criticising themselves and others. But there is no doubt that the Soviet state sharpened those old and obvious questions considerably. In 1929 Trotsky was exiled, Bukharin was thrown out of the Politburo, there were purges in literary institutions, and fierce attacks on Pilnyak and Zemyatin, who published work abroad. Lunacharsky, the old protector of so many, had to resign from his post as Commissar of Enlightenment. From April 1929 the whole force of Russia was mobilised to carry out the first Five-Year Plan. In Pasternak's poetry the world is transmuted, but there are still heavy hints that all is not tranquil. Even in fine weather when he is writing about lilies of the valley of all innocent things, high noon comes crashing down, exploding into diamonds. Among the sights and scents of a summer night when everything smells of night violets, 'summers and faces and thoughts', what he is thinking about in 1927 is 'all events that can be salvaged from the past'. An apparently innocent and antiquarian military metaphor about a cannon-ball from the days of Peter the Great makes 'Gathering Storm' in the same year more ominous than Boris may have intended.

His poem to Akhmatova is as pure yet as opaque as one might expect, but some of its lines are frightening: the city with its 'faint eclogues of pavement and kerbstone' sounds an anxious place, and

. . . one can't leave town,
the customer's deadline must be met:
Dawn glows and sews by the light of a lamp,
her back unbending, her eyes wet.

And what is the pillar of salt, in which five years ago, that is in
1923, 'you transfixed your fear of looking behind'? The poem 'To a
Friend' (1931) is more openly about its time than the others. It
belongs with a small class of poems by Pasternak which are almost
verse journalism, and which openly and as it were nonchalantly
deal with his situation in the terms used by the newspapers that
everyone read, which all his poems to some degree presuppose. He
has achieved a style in which every nuance is conscious: he knows
exactly what he is saying and the nuance of every line and word.
'To a Friend' has been well translated by Jon Stallworthy and Peter
France.

Do I not know that knocking on blackness,
Darkness would never have tunnelled to light,
And am I a monster? Is not the happiness
Of millions more than a happy elite?
Do I not measure myself, stage by stage,
Against the Five-Year Plan's rise and fall?
But what can I do with my rib-cage
And the most tongue-tied fountain of all?

When seats are assigned to passion and vision
On the day of the great assembly,
Do not reserve a poet's position:
It is dangerous, if not empty.

In spite of all the feelings of these years, there were things that
Boris Pasternak felt he could hold on to, including some kind of
building up: the construction of a new society, the map which
looks like a children's map for a game of Treasure Island, of the
Five-Year Plan. One is to be seen on the wall of the study in
Gorky's house in Moscow. In 1932 he published a new and
thrilling volume of lyric verse called *Second Birth*. There was really
something regenerated about his poetry then: his statements were
full and masterly and remain unequalled by any socialist or leftist
poet anywhere, because he understands so much and yet at the same

time remains transparently innocent. The only poet I can think of who has a little in common with him is Cesar Vallejo, but Boris Pasternak in 'The Waves', the main sequence of *Second Birth*, is a more accomplished poet. Eluard has false notes, Brecht is more uneven than he intends to be; it is curious that Pasternak should be the sole surviving monument to what was best in his unpalatable age.

Yet there are many sources of rebirth, and the most important ones may be personal. In the disturbed period of Stalin's first years of absolute power and the renewed terror, Boris Pasternak separated from his wife and child and remarried. Anyone who has passed through such a crisis or been close to another passing through it will know how it combines the qualities of a slow, wasting disease and an obsessive mental disturbance. Boris Pasternak, of whom many friends have said that he had a happy and fortunate temperament, was a man designed by nature to suffer the most under these circumstances. One of his simpler characteristics was that he could not bear to see women cry; the complications in his life distressed him terribly. He never abandoned those he loved, or even so far as I can see those that they loved, so that in the course of life he accumulated a horde of different people who depended on his affections.

In the summer of 1928 his wife and child went to the Caucasus, but he stayed in the oven heat of Moscow working, in order to pay for their holiday. That November his wife's mother died. Boris wrote in a letter about his wife, 'She has done nothing but weep these last few days and is in a constant state of shock and prostration. She is frightened and embittered by the swiftness with which nature and tradition (decay and funeral rites) sweep off the path of life that which was life and which *gave* life. . . . For the first time in my life I saw how the Jews bury their dead and it was terrible.' Then there was trouble over an old, dismissed but beloved servant of her family's, who had trailed her way from job to job, lost everything, including all her money and her papers, and was mad. Things were bad in general. He heard from Paris there was no bread in Leningrad, and wrote a frantic letter to his aunt and cousin, offering to help. Meanwhile he was in debt. When Olga called on him in 1929 his wife was in the Crimea. 'He had toothache. He was snubbed by the countless occupants of Uncle Leonid's enormous flat. They got their meals on fifteen kerosene stoves in the kitchen, queued up for the lavatory, overran the corridor, the entrance hall, the bathroom.' Boris's little boy had mumps and a serious fever. 'His eyes were enormous, and I developed an entirely new feeling for him.' The situation about flats was terrifying; the government favoured subdivision at this time, but wheels were busy within wheels. Cousin Olga and her mother lost their flat, their peace of mind and their few possessions, after a process of persecution that involved eleven court cases and twenty-two official surveys. Boris had his toothache cured by an operation that took an hour and a half, for the removal of a cyst that was eating away his jaw-bone. In the letter describing this ordeal, his narrative powers reach a peak. In 1930 he writes that 'my own work has become caught and held in the past, and I am powerless to budge it. I took no part in the creation of the present and bear it no love. It is no great revelation to say that every man reaches his limit at some time. . . . I have no future, I don't know what awaits me.' He had no paper either; he was reduced to writing on forms from the Architectural Institute that Sasha gave him.

From 1929 Boris and Zhenya Pasternak's close friends knew they were likely to separate. Part of the trouble was her Judaism and her insistence on 'Jewish values'. She even went to a party official to complain of his lack of a sense of family, and he was sent for and told off; he meekly accepted this and promised to mend his ways. His meekness and courtesy were deceiving to her, because she did not grasp the contempt he probably felt for her amateurish, art-school kind of painting, and to the last moment of their marriage she imagined that to him she was irreplaceable. When the break-up came, he continued to visit once a week, and at least by 1946 he was lunching happily in the country with wife, ex-wife and all of everyone's children. He fell deeply in love with the wife of a musical friend. They had spent a holiday together (badly needed by Boris) at Irpen near Kiev in the summer of 1930. She was not only musical but Orthodox and not a Jewess. Her name was Zinaida, her husband's was Gendrik Neigauz, the Russianised form of Heinrich Neuhaus; he and Boris were already extremely affectionate and close friends, and although Boris said later that 'at one stage he could have killed me' they remained almost closer than friends.

Irpen was a communal holiday with Mr and Mrs Neuhaus and Mr and Mrs Valentin Asmus. They remained close and loyal friends for the rest of their lives. Asmus was the philosopher who spoke the funeral oration when Boris was buried at Peredelkino, and Irina Asmus still lives there in her old house. In a tall wooden room with big windows where a formidable astral telescope stands by the desk, she showed me the Pasternak manuscripts she has, including the much-revised final manuscript of his translation of *Hamlet*, and a translation of some Verlaine he had slipped into it. At the time of Irpen he wrote her a lyric about 'The memory of people, summer, / Freedom and escape, / Hot conifers, grey stocks' – a poem that gives an accurate flash of real life. His memory could not be in better, calmer or more loving hands than in those of the ladies of Peredelkino. They make one understand what he meant by hope for Russia. They are as educated as the wives of western professors or ambassadors, but they have lived through more, and they are serious intellectuals. The astral telescope was in good working order.

Lev Ozerov, a particularly sweet, small and mobile-featured poet and teacher of poetry, remembers Zinaida's arrival in Pasternak's life as a pianist with two children. According to Ozerov, letters that are soon to be published show how in very hard days she was his closest friend, and all but his saviour. Lev Ozerov was a violinist in Kiev, and had no doubt during the Irpen holiday that Boris was in love with Zinaida. When they married, her role was to protect him from commotion and to let him work. This may have been the greatest crisis of the poet's life, but it was not the last: he was always remaking himself as a poet, and therefore as a man. Perhaps he wore out Zinaida in the end, or life and Stalin wore her out; after the war, at the time of his mistress Olga Ivinskaya, he even told somebody it was really Heinrich Neuhaus he had been in love with. Certainly they were remembered as very close and loving friends, but certainly he fell deeply in love with Zinaida.

Her memoirs have been dictated to her friend the sculptor Zoe Afanaseyevna. According to Zoe's account, Boris's first marriage was an irretrievable mess, and when he met Zinaida he became mad with passion; he was haunted and obsessed by her, he had to have her. She thinks Boris and Heinrich really were in love, 'like two brothers', already. He was a famous musician, a friend of Scriabin and Richter's teacher. Two hours before any class of his at the Conservatory there was standing-room only; when he arrived, the class was a theatrical performance. Often he made some point by reciting poems, often Pasternak's. It is therefore small wonder that he mesmerised Boris Pasternak. Boris deeply needed something new. He asked people to 'be patient a little, because I will write for some time like a shoemaker.' Zoe Afanaseyevna is a humane woman, she worshipped the poet, and kept notes of seventy meetings with him, some as long as three hours, while she worked at his bust at Peredelkino, at the end of his life. So she is worth listening to, but she does not remember 1930 as Lev Ozerov does, since she came to Moscow only as an army girl at the beginning of the war, and knew Pasternak only at the end of his life.

Boris Pasternak's cousin Olga put it that 'At this time Borya and Zhenya were going through a period of strained relations. Each of them was an artist and each had an artist's egotism.' That seems a facile judgement. 'Zhenya dreamed of Paris and thought that her marriage to Borya would relieve her of all worldly cares. She was deeply disappointed.' That sounds more like it. He was, after all, distinctly high-minded and Tolstoyan, as Olga saw, and the life she offered him was Bohemian: that conflict is common enough and irreconcilable enough even without the pressures of Stalin's Russia. 'He was not to be tempted by a Puccini libretto or convinced that art required a loosening of the reins.' Small wonder, then, that he was so happy in Irpen. 'The summer was divine,' he wrote to her, 'and my work revived in the sun; it has been a long time since I worked so effectively.'

I wish I were sure what he meant by 'I have written my *Bronze Horseman*'. The reference is to Pushkin's magnificent poem about the tyrant and the people. He can hardly mean his *Spektorsky*, which came out in 1931, particularly since he calls it 'humble, unpolished, but a complete thing, and genuine I believe'. Unless he refers to something in 'The Waves', which I also doubt, one must assume that this poem, perhaps the greatest or most important he ever wrote, has perished. Only 'Hamlet', among the *Zhivago* poems, can make up for it. We know he began *Second Birth* in the summer of 1930. In October 1930, still in the same letter, he says, 'The censor has begun chopping away at my new editions, and to make up for past neglect he sinks his fangs with excessive fervour into works of mine not yet published.' These teeth can be seen to be biting in earnest by 1933, when a selected edition of his poems was allowed but a collected edition disallowed, and the reissue of *Safe Conduct* was disallowed.

In December 1930 he is trying to send his wife and son out of the country to his parents (she was treated for tuberculosis in Germany), and in June 1932 he writes in retrospect about the very hard winter 'especially after Zhenya came back. She suffered terribly, poor thing – she above all, but everyone including me was miserable. Insoluble problems with the flat! . . . Do you imagine nothing has come of that "fantasy", that "preposterous dream" etc. which you refused to hear of and cautioned me against as sheer madness? . . . I did return to Zhenya for a few days, but so flagrant a violation of life's dictates was doomed to failure. I nearly went out of my mind. Indeed I was in torment those few months, and it was Zinaida who saved me.' He moved in with Sasha and his Irina, and Zinaida joined him. But Zhenya had his permit for hard currency shops, so Zinaida had tough and laborious marketing to do. Her two boys stayed in the Neuhaus flat, which was now neglected. She had several attacks of flu and in the end, in spring, pneumonia. Boris's son got scarlet fever, and for weeks he moved back with his wife, but with no hope of reconciliation. He had to brush his clothes with disinfectant every day before he saw her. At this stage he at last got a flat from the Writers' Union. It was on Tverskoy Boulevard, and unfinished, so Zinaida had to wash and scrub continually. There was no electricity and the bath was not connected, but even so it was an enormous improvement. At once, in a few days, Zinaida had the windows glazed, curtains hung, mattresses remade, floors polished and so on, mostly with her own hands.

But troubles about flats can lessen or increase according to season; indeed, some kinds of winter affliction are in a way the product of summer expeditions, such as the Irpen holiday. Among the official activities of the capital, one was the translation or the promotion of translation from the languages of all the states of the Soviet Union into Russian. Gorky was for some reason promoting Georgian poetry, and Pasternak was swept up into the enterprise, which led to some of the most delightful friendships of his life. It seems Paolo Yashvili and his wife were befriended by Boris Pasternak in Moscow in the winter of 1929–30. In the situation created by the Irpen holiday, Boris and Zinaida headed straight for the Yashvili house in the Caucasus in late 1930; they met their close friends the Tabidzes at Khodzory near Tbilisi (Tiflis), in those days a provincial capital of enchanting, dusty beauty. The Georgians are an intensely attractive people, combining the innocence and big eyes of the most unspoilt Greeks with a gypsy warmth and fire. Russian poets adore them, because they are so un-Russian, or because they uninhibitedly are what Russians would like to be, or become after midnight. They have the further advantage that they speak Russian, and have a past of their own and a poetry of their own as refreshing and enchanting as everything else about them. No one else naturally knows their language, but Pasternak learnt it in the end (though not at first) rather well, largely by indefatigable translation. In August 1931, when Gorky raised the question of Georgian poetry in *Pravda*, Pasternak was just back from a winter among the Georgians.

It may easily be that this Georgian connection attracted the favourable attention of that great Georgian, Stalin, but like most relationships with Stalin it ended badly. It began in the winter of 1924–5, about a year after Lenin's death. Stalin appears to have summoned Pasternak with Yesenin and Mayakovsky to discuss the translation of Georgian poets. What was said is not recorded; but the story is Ivinskaya's and she is definite about it. She says Boris told her three or four times that Stalin was the most terrible creature he had ever seen, a crab-like dwarf with a yellow, pockmarked face and a bristling moustache. At the same time Ivinskaya claims that Boris thought of Stalin then as a true leader. There I doubt whether she understood him. Certainly his addition to the *Essay in Biography* in memory of Georgian friends who perished under Stalin is a tragic and deadly serious tribute. The published series of his letters to them, of which the translation into English by David Magarshack was rather mishandled (the Italian is a little better), runs from 1931 to the end of his life. Even in 1989, I met the granddaughter of one of his Georgian poets visiting his grave and his surviving friends at Peredelkino. I think it was the extraordinary warmth of these letters that first made me interested in Pasternak's personality, beyond the call of literary admiration.

It was the life as well as the people that enchanted Boris and Zinaida in Georgia. He liked the café life of Tiflis as it used to be (the city is now a modern sprawl), and the fact that you could see what climbed the hill above you and below you from the house. He liked the timbrels and the bagpipes. 'There was nothing to eat, nothing to wear, nothing tangible at all, only ideas.' The writers loved him, and he loved them, particularly Yashvili and Tabidze. It may well be true that they revived his own lyrical high spirits, since it was there that he turned back for a time to his own lyric poetry. The new poems are as full of the Caucasus as Lermontov's, but also very pure, and original in their observations: the swaggering peaks that try to toss away storm-clouds as a horse tosses at its collar, the gorge smoking like a poisonous cauldron, river-mist like a gas attack, and ruined castles like the throats of beheaded men. The streak of dramatic evil in this treatment of a noble landscape derives to some degree from Lermontov, but it goes far beyond even his vividness. Even more important, it was Georgia and the Georgians that made Pasternak a thoroughly professional translator of poetry from this time on. Later, in 1936, he wrote another crop of his own travel lyrics; they are a charming record of roses and apricots and shepherds and waterfalls, which he printed as 'Travel Notes' in *Novy Mir*, but he hated them later, and called them 'silly, bird-like twitterings'. One's mood alters, and he felt badly about the iambic trimeter, but I am not sorry he wrote them.

> We were in Georgia: understand this country
> as inferno multiplied by paradise,
> bare poverty by gentleness, as if
> a hothouse were the stepping stone to ice. . . . (1931)

> O if we had their luck; if out of time
> peering down through the mist, the day we've past,
> our programme could be so substantialised,
> frowning down like a mountain, so steep, so vast,

> . . . there would be no one I could quarrel with,
> and as for my poems I would give them
> not one more hour, I'd live hidden from men,
> my life not a poet's but a poem . . . (1931)

One can go back further. Mandelstam in the early twenties was thrilled first by Georgia, then by Armenia, because they were ancient and Christian, and all but Hellenic. 'The Georgians', he wrote, 'keep wine in long, narrow jars which they bury in the earth.' The idea of all this fermentation and smell in the cool embraces of the earth thrilled Mandelstam as if he had been Keats. Boris Pasternak was more a modern man, as a poet, and less a Hellenomane (except through Annensky). All the same he liked the fermentation and took to the life like a duck to water. Tabidze had been at school with Mayakovsky in Kutaisi, and as a schoolboy published his own translations of Blok, Bryusov and Annensky. In 1929 Tabidze wrote to Beliy that his whole Georgian generation has 'passed through Blok and through you, like a second birth'. Boris must have been deeply excited to find poets still so free-minded, so old-fashioned, so pure and devoted, and so like himself. He thought that in Georgia 'the symbols of popular tradition, with their mysticism and Messianism, were favourable to imaginative life, and made every man a poet, as in Catholic Poland.' And again: 'Tiflis will be to me what Chopin, Scriabin, Marburg, Venice and Rilke have been.' He said the same thing in 1951 to Tabidze's widow Nina, in a catalogue of what he had valued most in life. 'My father's example, love of music and Scriabin, two or three new notes in my own art, night in the Russian countryside, the revolution, Georgia.' He called it his second home.

In 1931 he felt the landscape 'rhyming summer with Lermontov, and Pushkin with geese and the snow'. And it swayed him towards love. Zinaida and Boris did not actually marry until 1934, but 1930–1 was their real honeymoon. Lara says beside Zhivago's coffin, 'They had loved one another because all things around had wished it so, the land beneath them, the sky over their heads, the clouds and the trees.' He translated a bit of Tabidze roughly like this:

> I do not write poems,
> I am written by them:
> as a story is written,
> and with them runs the course of life.
> What is poetry? an avalanche
> that breathes and breathing dies:
> that is poetry. It buries alive.

Tabidze thought he was only a mouthpiece of the spirit, 'the untrimmed stalk of a reed, that sings untouched by lips'. Pasternak identified the 'inward melody' that Tabidze thought was the essential core of poetry with his own method, the immediacy of language that he more or less vowed to observe at the time of *My Sister Life*, when he turned away from the ideal of sheer improvisation, which had reigned over his early poems. The poem must arise phrase by phrase from a linguistic depth, it must be what one might say. I do not think Boris was right to identify Tabidze's simple, Pindaric theory, which after all had few or no consequences, with his own theoretic entanglement. Yet the theory of a poet is only a set of phrases he nourishes in order to be able to write, and at times to be or to appear different from the others. The important point is a rather deep and subtle one about what Boris and the Georgians needed, and what they recognised in each other. In my own view what happened was like a lighted chandelier reflected from mirror to mirror, the meeting of like minds and like innocences, equally hungry. The only exception to that is his translation of the long poem 'The Serpent Eater' by Vozha Pshavela, a poet venerated by all Georgians, a recluse living in the mountains, whom I cannot quite swallow. Russians think particularly highly of this translation.

The earliest Georgian letter printed was written to Titian and Nina Tabidze, in December 1931, reporting some kind of Georgian Poetry Week in Leningrad, after their departure south. They had left their Leningrad friends 'completely enchanted, and they kept recalling the party and yourselves long afterwards'. Paolo Yashvili had been there and Aseev had spoken, but Boris arrived late. All this sounds like a friendly exchange of delegations. He writes to Paolo Yashvili in the summer of 1932. Boris has left several long letters to him unfinished. 'They took the form of researches into the Urals or attempts to tell you what is Georgia.' He is in a country cottage lent by the Urals committee of the Communist Party. From the shore of a lake he can see a forest stretching away for a hundred miles. Everything there, the light on the water, the clouds, graves in the old churchyards, reminds him forcibly of Georgia. 'It is in more senses than one a country that has never known a break in its existence, it has remained down to earth, and has not been carried off into abstraction.' He already knows that a new part of his life will be centred on Georgia, as the last was centred on Mayakovsky, and that his coming work must comprehend that.

The letters are the partial record of a love affair with Georgia but it was not to last him, not to turn out happy, because in the purges of the second half of the thirties Tabidze was executed and Yashvili committed suicide. Boris met and translated other poets, but the moment of promise was unrepeatable. In 1933 he went as a member of the organising committee of the first Congress of Soviet Writers, with Tikhonov, the poet of ballads and a good prose writer. Together they undertook a huge programme of translations, and the first of Pasternak's were published as a book, *Georgian Lyrics* (by *Soviet Writer* in 1935); a joint volume appeared in Tbilisi the same year. In 1945 he produced almost the entire works of the first great modern Georgian, Baratashvili, for his centenary. In an essay intended for a Tbilisi publication in 1946, but printed only in 1966, he writes that 'Baratashvili's tragic conflicts with his environment are so simply and clearly explained by him that they have become a school of the love of peace and of loyalty to society for posterity.'

During those years, the attachment meant many things; it altered with the times and as Boris altered. In 1933, Zinaida will throw him out unless he gets down to serious work. 'But she is not altogether right, because this tendency to form an attachment, of which I am only too conscious as the only definite thing about my character, is so powerful in me that it takes the place of work and seems to be my profession.' In 1934, 'all I want is to free myself from servitude, from my prose.' In 1936, 'Where do I get this verbiage and boredom, this soullessness and stupidity from? . . . I knew that until I was successful in mastering the prose that would set me free and leave me to my own devices, I ought not to think of writing any poetry for a long, long time, for now my mind is not set on poetry, but is far, far away from it.' When his son by Zinaida was born in 1938, he wanted to call him Paul after his dead friend Yashvili, but Zinaida wept at the memory of such grief and bitterness, so the boy was named Leonid, after his grandfather.

But we have strayed too far ahead. When Mayakovsky died in 1930 Pasternak was not only grief-stricken; he was left in the undoubted position of the most famous and the best Russian poet. By his publications in the early thirties he went far to confirm the great hopes that the state had of him. He was loyal to some kind of ideal of the revolution. He was badly upset by a picture he saw of a column of kulaks being driven from their villages, but he shocked Mrs Mandelstam by speaking of the Russian people as having broken through into life, and he in turn was shocked, or she thought so, at her tart response. Somewhere he wrote even of the state itself as having broken through into the procession of the ages. It appears that this was what he or something in him, some part of him, wanted to believe. Now the state was going to take a more vigorous control of literature; the first instrument was the first Congress of Soviet Writers, all-Russian, all writers. That is something we shall need to understand, because it was not simply a thunderbolt from the Kremlin, and it was not aimed at Boris Pasternak's head. He was in a position of danger, because for a frightening moment he was very high in favour, and more was expected of him than he was going to give. At some time in the early thirties he became seriously ill and unable to sleep, because of what he knew or guessed about the fate of the peasants.

Before entering into the analysis of Stalin's policies that will be necessary, I should like to discuss *Second Birth* more fully, because in a way it is his most remarkable collection. Long afterwards, after the *Zhivago* affair, he sent poems from it to his new-found American translator Henry Kamen; I still possess a yellowing page of the versions Kamen produced, cut from a *New Statesman* in the fifties. They are nothing much as English poetry, but interesting and I think moving, like most of Kamen's translations. That was at a time when Pasternak was supposed to hate all his early poems, and to pin all his ambitions on *Zhivago*; it is good to know that 'The Waves', from *Second Birth*, survived his self-censorship. Eliot says somewhere that all poets in their forties need a second birth, in order to go on writing in middle age: but we need not be so banal, for there is a new quality of tranquil mastery in 'The Waves'.

1

It will all happen here, what I have lived
and what I shall live and shall be,
my ambitions and foundations
and the reality I see.

Before my eyes the sea's waves
innumerable that no power can stem,
a great horde roaring in a minor key,
waffles, the surf is toasting them.

They rush to graze the shore like cattle,
herd or horde that the sky has let spill,
hunting them like a wolf-pack and now lies
on its stomach on the far side of the hill.

What I have done runs at me like a pack
and in the full leap of my sad expense
of spirit roll themselves at my feet.
The white crests of experience.

2

Living values will argue out
their struggle here, to their sunset,
the granting of the torrid zone
the riches of the temperate.

One couplet has precedence though
among values in competition,
the enormous shore of Kabulet
for its superhuman vision:

embracing as a poet does
incompatibles in one sight,
Poti at one end wrapped in night
and Batum in the breaking light.

It sees all, it can take away
like a pleasure of fairyland
whatever you take in of it,
the ten enormous miles of strand.

Bare pebbles watching everything
with their eyes always open,
and a sky without spectacles
that pierces like a crystal lens.

3

I want to go home to sadness
in the empty desert of the flat,
go in, drop my coat, collect
myself in the street-light.

I pass in through the weak ribs
of partitions like light passing
as image enters into image,
as one thing cuts another thing.

And if the problem is for life
and the testaments of days just add –
call it the sedentary life,
still, it makes me sad.

Once more the trees and houses smell
of a refrain, of an old chord,
and to left and right outside
winter is playing the landlord.

Before dinner on all the walks
darkness like a passion falls,
and once again the backstreets learn
they are no fools.

Once more I'll hear the heart's muscle's
diminuendo, and find words for you,
for how you creep and smoke and grow,
and how you are built up Moscow.

I will put you on like a straitjacket
against all madness, because you
will learn me like a poem Moscow,
I shall be known by heart in you.

The three parts I have taken to represent this longish work are its
opening, but they have the astonishing rock-pool clarity of the
whole. I have adapted my versions rather freely from a more
accurate but unrhymed version of 'The Waves' by Richard
McKane. The poems are, of course, the purest musings on his
situation as he saw it in the Caucasus. In the first part he engages the
waves, but his own life only in general terms. The second part is a
further attempt to cure himself by landscape, to use the sea almost
as a priest, but the attempt is shown I think as a failure. The slightly
longer third part, in which he wanders in mind back to Moscow

where his flat is empty (still probably the Volkhonka flat with its overcrowding and its insubstantial partitions), and broods in it like a ghost, has a number of echoes of childhood and the Terror, then it ends with a most extraordinary and moving affirmation. 'The way you smoke, the way you grope, the way your great constructions grow,' is how Kamen puts it. For the sake of a rhyme I lost the important final point that the last lines should be 'because you will learn me like a poem, and remember me by heart like a fable'. It happened, of course, just as he predicted. He is not talking about being learnt by heart at school, but about being learnt almost unconsciously, through love, as children remember their favourite stories by heart. Today, when you open a window on a view of Moscow, it is these lines you are likely to remember.

The whole work has much more to offer: an avalanche that is nothing but itself, with no moral though not without a human presence, ends with all the summits of Daghestan rushing to catch a bus 'not to the dagger-clash but the rain-beat', and giant beyond giant, each wickeder and more handsome than the last, 'throttled the exit from the mountain valleys'. But the unity of thought of the first three parts has now been broken, and the unity of the poems has become the Caucasus itself. In another part, the forest runs like a story running on, 'and is conscious of its interest'. It tells a story of a hundred years ago 'of the captivity of things'. This poem is an attempt to understand the life of the mountains and their heroic resistance to the Russians.

> War is not a fool's story,
> it won't be gilded by us,
> Lermontov and Tolstoy showed
> the animal face of victory.

If Pasternak had written these poems and no others, he would still stand very high, for inward and imaginative life, for personal power of language which is political without being rhetorical, because it cuts to the root of politics, and for certain poetic conceptions like the empty flat, Moscow as almost a person, and the forest running on and on like a story. He is Moscow's poet, he was so all his life, and here at last he is Moscow's lover or she is his. Why? Why does he let the curtain slip to show us rawly what he feels like as a poet? He had not done so in his autobiography after all, nor in *Spektorsky*, nor in *Povest*. What has come over him in Georgia? It is simply that he is absent from Moscow, I believe. He inhabits that flat in the poem like a ghost, and the city itself is ghostly until he summons it up. And he is brooding on his own past, on his nature, on who he is. So we owe the revelation of his love for the city, and his consciousness of his own powers, to the crisis of his marriage, which was ended partly by his stubbornness as a poet.

> Over the dish of the Bavarian lakes
> and the bone-marrow of hill-tops heather-clad
> you will see I am no grand writer
> who always has a pretty phrase to add.
>
> Bon voyage. Bon voyage. Our bond
> and honour have no home except the night.
> You will see everything another way
> as a tree-shoot grows straighter in the light.

So much for his former wife Zhenya; to Zinaida he speaks as passionately as a youth of eighteen: 'The scuffling of dreams heard in the spring, the rustle of the news, rustle of truths . . .'

> Lightly to waken, suddenly to see,
> to shake the wordy rubbish from the heart
> and then to live all future days unsoiled:
> that calls for no extraordinary art.

It does call for a consistent degree of integrity, though, which is not a normal human characteristic. In fact this verse may express an impossible ideal; it may even reveal a weakness. It may be that one who believes almost naïvely in a second birth will remain somehow vulnerable. Shaking the wordy rubbish from the heart is not so very easy; indeed, it is usually a lifetime's process, and so it surely was for Boris Pasternak. To visualise him as he was, on the brink of his long struggle with the Soviet state, is to see some shining knight of the Children's Crusade. He was not Quixotic, but he was terribly innocent. I have already quoted his warning: 'Do not make heroes of my generation, we were not: there were times when we were afraid and acted from fear, times when we betrayed.' We shall see that on those scores he has very few black marks against him, but he was no extremist, and would have accomplished much less had he been one. I think he wished he had been less innocent, more knowing – an impossible wish.

> You're here. We are breathing the same air.
> The city's presence like yours here,
> quiet Kiev folded in sultry
> sunbeams outside the window there.
>
> It hasn't slept its sleep out yet,
> struggles unconquered in its dreams,
> tearing the bricks from off its neck,
> a collar sweaty at the seams.
>
> Poplars perspiring in their leaves
> from their last struggling incident
> gather in an exhausted crowd
> on conquered and subdued pavement.
>
> You remind me of the Dnieper's
> green skin of ditches and of creeks,
> the central earth's book of complaints
> open for us to write the weeks:
>
> You being here is like a call
> to sit down hastily at noon
> and read it through from A to Z,
> and write your closeness, write it down.

He is no match for Stalin in this mood, and his life always swings back to the personal love, which for him is always hungry and boyish, as the needle of a compass swings to north. The social demands made on literature at this time seemed to come from RAPP, the Russian Association of Proletarian Writers, to which Mayakovksy once belonged, but the truth was that they originated from the Central Committee of the Communist Party. RAPP arose from the old Proletcult, which began as a workers' education and literary movement before the October revolution of 1917. By the early twenties it had a hundred branches and twenty magazines, such as *The Smithy* and *On Guard*, full of vehement polemics. The young proletarians wanted state money and public recognition; they were full of beans and furious against Ehrenburg, Zemyatin, Akhmatova and anyone obviously middle class. When one group attacked another the party was (fatally but inevitably) called in to decide the matter.

For the moment the trouble was smoothed over: in July 1925 a Politburo resolution told the proletarians to produce the new, but not alienate the fellow travellers. All parties supposed they had won. But the proletarians of what soon became RAPP displayed colossal arrogance. By 1928 there were hints that the Communist Party would respond kindly to them. They spoke of 'cultural revolution . . . a new type of man', and of the 'help' that critics gave to writers. They did like Tolstoy, but they distrusted the French: 'dawn is Schiller,' said their officer Fadeev, but Flaubert, Stendhal, Balzac and Zola were viewed with hostility. They admired a novel called *Cement*. They debated propaganda versus realism, and they hated party interference. One would say they had got a long way out of their depth. In June 1930 the party issued a satiric attack on them for failing to produce great literature. The Central Committee now demanded militancy; it sought at this time to replace all intellectual technicians alien to the state, and foreign 'experts'. In 1931 some views on literature were assembled from fragments and attributed to Lenin; at the same time the first 'Leninist philosophers' appeared.

In April 1932 Stalin dissolved all proletarian organisations in literature, and some of the more enthusiastic RAPP men ended up shot or imprisoned. This was because they were a nuisance; and for no other reason. At the same time Stalin had realised that the Five-Year Plan needed engineers and experts, so they were dusted down and re-employed; 'fellow-travelling' writers were a similar case. In October 1932 the Union of Soviet Writers was founded, to manage not some but all Russian writers. The fellow travellers were rechristened in *Pravda* as socialists, on the grounds that all writers who supported the party programme were socialist and Soviet writers. The article, which was by Iudin, removed the injurious term 'bourgeois' from them. All the same, RAPP had not been wholly evil or idiotic, it was just extremely untalented. As for working-class writers, they had existed since the previous century. RAPP critics were merely condescending to Pasternak, but quite nice about poor old Beliy's novel *Moscow*. When RAPP perished, people said they had no idea whom to blame for the sad state of literature. Prishvin, a writer of nature sketches, remarked that he had no notion why irresponsible persons had got in the habit of calling him a reactionary and a mystic.

Kaganovich revealed two years later, as minister responsible, that Stalin personally had imposed his solution in 1932, and a *Pravda* editorial spoke of the conversion of 'the overwhelming majority of the old technical intelligentsia to the side of Soviet Power', with a similar movement of 'the greatest scholars in the land', and something analogous in literature. There, it noticed that 'the broad cadres of writers' were taking an active part in socialist construction, which had found an expression in their writings. A list of writers was given, one of whom was Tikhonov, but Pasternak was not named. What I think *Pravda* was talking about was the visits now allowed to writers to construction sites all over Russia in order to write about them. It was in that same summer of 1932 that Boris Pasternak, desperate to get out of Moscow because of the accommodation problem created by his broken marriage, went to Sverdlovsk, near Lake Shartash in the Urals, and as we have seen wrote to his Georgian friends.

He hated the construction site. He called it 'herd standardisation and organised mediocrity'. His brother Sasha after all was a brilliant architect and a pupil of Le Corbusier. Maybe Boris was the wrong man to send to any ordinary construction site, maybe any poet would be the wrong man. There is certainly something startling to the outsider about Russian ugliness, which exudes mediocrity like a smell of sweat. At least Boris enjoyed his holiday, and the lake and forest and the gravestones in old country churches; but something far more exciting happened to him. The phrases about mediocrity are by no means the only ones that turn up later in *Zhivago*. Several passages in the novel, including Siberian scenes, were written during that same visit. He must have hoarded them for years, and it is reasonable to suspect that they were first intended for an article he never had the heart to write about Sverdlovsk as an example of socialist construction. Is it not possible that in the third part of 'The Waves', he is considering the duty imposed on writers of expressing just that?

Pasternak and his family ate at the same canteen as the 'experts' employed on the project; it was well stocked, since it was a political police (Cheka) canteen. Outside it there were starving, ragged people begging for food. Boris was unable to bear this contrast; he lost his appetite, sickened and was unable to sleep at night. He saved some bread to give it to a peasant woman, and she thrust a ten-rouble note into his hand; he had to run after her to force her to take it back. The contrast that so horrified him is the most vivid memory of a friend of mine from Moscow in wartime, where he dined or rather banqueted among the general staff with Stalin, while people were dying of starvation in the streets. Boris Pasternak is recorded as having exploded in January 1930 at a banquet given by Alexei Bach, vice-president of the Academy of Sciences, when the Ukraine was starving and people on the Volga were attacking trains, clamouring for bread. As a young man, this same Bach had been a member of the People's Will organisation and the author of a pamphlet on starvation under the Tsars. Pasternak reported to the board of the Writers' Union on his journey, but when *Pravda* asked for his impressions he answered, 'How would you want me to write about that desolation?'

He was on a collision course. Aseev long afterwards, in 1956 when Stalin was dead and the Hungarian revolution seemed for a moment to prophesy a reversal of policies, attacked the cataleptic state of literature that had been Pasternak's experience of life. Critics dared not speak of quality, and editors bowed to a 'single taste'. Aseev was an old futurist, a poet ingenious in the manner of Khlebnikov and Mayakovsky, excessive in alliteration, forwards, backwards and upside-down, and extremely red, who was silent in the last years of Stalin. Kisanov (1909–72) was another old colleague of Mayakovsky and a member of LEF; he wrote a poem in which every one of thirty-six lines began with the letter M; in 1951 he won the Stalin prize, but in 1956, when the old demon was safely dead and buried, he wrote *Seven Days of the Week*, in which the Honest Heart is invented but shoved aside, and the Useful Heart is substituted. Boris Pasternak had an honest but not a useful heart.

The phrase 'socialist realism' came to be an accepted cliché, and to carry such weight as only clichés can. It seems to have surfaced in 'Down to Work', an article in the *Literary Gazette* of 29 May 1932. 'Truthfulness in depicting the Revolution: – this is the demand we have the right to put to all Soviet writers without exception. . . .

The masses demand from the artist sincerity, truth, and revolutionary socialist realism in portraying the proletarian revolution.' It will be seen that this would have put Boris Pasternak in an embarrassing situation, except that he had already dealt with the revolution in terms of 1905. Accounts would be settled only in *Dr Zhivago*, though even there the revolution itself scarcely enters into the action. V. Kirpotin revealed in May 1967 that he wrote the *Literary Gazette* article: the same Kirpotin, as secretary, with the awful Fadeev and with Iudin, a 'philosopher', drew up the statutes of the Union of Writers, including the obligation on members to be guided by 'socialist realism', whatever that may mean. We have met Iudin as the writer of an anonymous editorial in *Pravda*; he went on to scale the heights of power, as editor of the *Cominform* journal in Belgrade, as ambassador to China (1953) and as the author of a statement for the prosecution of Sinyavsky and Daniel. He maintained that Daniel was 'a consummate and convinced anti-Semite'. I stray so far from what threatened Boris Pasternak in order to make it clear how very dangerous his enemies were, and to show that the dead-looking phrase 'socialist realism' was a live bomb.

The Congress of Soviet Writers was not unique: it was Stalin's model, and imitative congresses in other departments of cultural life followed swiftly. The writers who refused the oath of loyalty that the congress demanded consisted almost entirely of hard cases: Bulgakov, Mandelstam, Akhmatova. The cinema, which had been calling for ideological dictatorship since 1928, was an easy victim: it was frankly more interested in masses than in individuals I suppose. One might hazard the view that the improvement of photography, largely due to Hollywood and its star system, has now reversed what swayed the Soviet cinema towards Stalin, by making the individual, as poets create him, the most interesting subject. But there is also the question of money: what directors need is someone to pay for their expensive pursuits, and it is possible they did not have enough wits to understand such crazy phrases as 'ideological dictatorship'. It is also conceivable that they just wanted to get ideology out of the way, by having it agreed or if necessary dictated. The film-maker Dovzhenko said in 1935, 'The artists of the Soviet Union have created an art founded on a *yes*: on the concept, I uplift, I inspire, I educate.' It is some kind of parody of religious education, by which no modern religious artist would accept to be fettered.

But one does not encounter abstract principles head on, however clearly they may be enunciated. One is entangled in concrete events. In November 1932 Stalin finally drove his wife Alleluyeva to suicide, after a furious argument to which there were witnesses. In the *Literary Gazette* of 17 November the whole literary establishment, represented by thirty-three writers, including Pilniak and Shklovsky as well as Fadeev, signed a letter of formal sympathy and sorrow. Boris Pasternak had refused to sign, not because he felt no sorrow, but because his feelings were individual and not properly to be expressed by a formal public letter. Instead of signing, he addressed to Stalin personally a note of his own which was anything but formal, and expressed his personal sorrow very sharply. It was printed as a postscript. No one of course knew then that what had happened was a suicide tantamount to murder; all that was announced was her very sudden death.

'I share the feelings of my comrades. On the evening before, I found myself thinking deeply and continually about Stalin for the first time, from the point of view of an artist. In the morning I read the news, and I was shaken just as if I had been present, and as though I had lived through it, as though I had seen it all.' It is possible that Stalin believed that Pasternak had some kind of second sight, as a Georgian might believe that a poet would have. It is possible simply that he was touched. At any rate it appears that for the next twenty years Pasternak's police file had a mark on it, and that even when he was due to be arrested he never was, because of that mark, that he was in fact protected; it is hard to see by whom if not by Stalin personally. This is conjecture of course; he may have escaped by the shifts of fortune and his own good luck, by his fame or by his innocence. It seems unlikely. If any one reason exists why he was immune, even consulted by Stalin, then this is the most likely.

And why did he insist on writing his own message, rather than signing an ordinary official letter? There is no obvious motive except his nature, his intense feeling of personality in life and in poetry, his curious innocence. But he was conscious of being somebody. Mirsky had written about his *1905* in 1928, Ehrenburg about *The Childhood of Lyuvers* in 1930, 'Pasternak laid the true foundation of Soviet art.' The critic Zelinsky wrote of *Second Birth* that it had 'a special quality of inner wholeness'. Boris had gone flat contrary to every public diktat and convention, and yet somehow by doing so had gone on rising higher in esteem and come closer personally to Stalin. It was an alarming eminence.

# 7

## Insomnia

Many writers of Boris Pasternak's generation lived the natural
length of their lives; they were to some degree privileged because
they were writers, and in the west one would have to be famous
and successful, or have private means, to live as well as they did.
But the strain was great. Stalin was tolerant of them as some
formidable headmaster, interested only in more important
matters, might be tolerant of the sixth-form intellectuals; but when
he struck he did so brutally, and he was in full control of the vast
hierarchy of terror which descended from him. The case of Osip
Mandelstam is an example of this. His poetry had a wonderful
precision of surface, but an ambiguity in its depths. He was such a
crisply accurate maker of phrases that he seemed to write his own
epitaph many times.

> Waiting for death like a wolf in a fairy-tale
> easy living drove us insane . . . (1913)

> Toy wolves from the bushes gaze
> through their burning tinsel eyes . . . (1908)

> What we could not, would not breathe
> an air of ether or of ice;
> now the shaggy reed-pipes sound
> once again their reedy voice . . .

He was not a poet who was going to be at home in Stalin's state.
The peak of his career, when he published *Collected Poems* and the
prose pieces collected with *The Egyptian Stamp* in 1928, coincided
with the moment of Stalin's attaining power. His last publication
was his *Journey to Armenia*, printed in *Zvezda* in 1933. He was

criticised, but no worse than Akhmatova or even Pasternak. Then on 13 May 1934 he was arrested in his flat in Furmanov Street, Leningrad. The offence was circulating and reading aloud a short verse epigram on Stalin. Part of it is as follows:

> His fingers are as fat as worms,
> and his words are hard as sin,
> his huge cockroach moustaches laugh,
> the mountaineer of the Kremlin.

He had met Boris Pasternak in the street and told him the wicked lines; Pasternak said, 'I didn't hear that, and you didn't tell me it.' When Stalin heard about the verses (and at least twenty people could have reported them) he seems to have been amazed at the impudence and curious rather than angry about it. He summoned Mandelstam for confrontation, but apparently remained puzzled. For the previous two years the official organisations had ceased to extend protection to anyone, but Pasternak was brave and generous, indeed he was becoming quixotic. He begged Demyan Bednyi to help, but Bednyi refused. He went to Bukharin and begged him to intercede with Stalin. The result, which was quite unexpected, was a phone call from Stalin to Pasternak in the early hours of the morning. Pasternak agonised over those few minutes for years, and often told the story; there are many versions of it in print, but they do not all agree.

Stalin asked what he thought of Mandelstam as a poet: was he an important poet? Stalin seems to have been surprised at the idea, but not wholly to have discounted it. No doubt he was investigating the world of poets as a schoolboy might investigate a nest of ants, by stirring it with his foot. Pasternak hesitated, not knowing how to answer; he hummed and hawed. Akhmatova, who was a sharp and catlike observer of her colleagues and had a razor claw for men, maintained that Boris always eulogised other poets, never meant a word of it, and never read a word of anyone's poems but his own. He did indeed offer compliments like pieces of candy, and the extremes of affection that he expressed reflected a certain spiritual insobriety, but he would have tried to answer honestly, and he would not have been glib. Stalin cut him off, and he never forgave himself. He begged for a long conversation with Stalin on grave issues: he seems to have believed he could have influenced Stalin and altered Russian history. That is no doubt the kind of temperament you need in order to be a genuinely important poet, who detains the attention of mankind. He could not of course detain Stalin's.

In 1931 he had written a poem clearly intended to influence Stalin towards goodness and mercy, in which he referred to Pushkin's influence over the Tsar. But Stalin was a tougher customer than any nineteenth-century Tsar. Mandelstam was sentenced to three years of exile at Cherdyn on the upper Kama. Apart from the difficulty of earning a living there, I do not believe that Pasternak would have feared such a sentence for himself. Mandelstam protested, and Stalin himself intervened to let him choose his own place of exile. He chose Voronezh, where he wrote his greatest poetry, less neat and dandified, but more magnificent than before. Still, his hatred of the state became very deep and bitter. When his exile was over he came back to Moscow and called on Pasternak, who by then was at Peredelkino. Zinaida thought the Mandelstams were too dangerous to let into her house, so Boris saw them at the railway station. They were particularly enthralled by his conversation on that day, which was about poetry; they let train after train go by without them. Pasternak also gave them money. In May 1938, Osip Mandelstam was arrested again, and sentenced to five years in the labour camps; he died that December, at Vladivostok, ragged, wizened, starving and more than half mad. Boris Pasternak never ceased to feel guilty, just possibly because he never really liked Mandelstam's poetry enough.

The slow time-scale and the gathering momentum of this story are an essential part of it, and characteristic of the thirties. Meanwhile Pasternak's official life preserved the enigmatic look he had adopted in public for as long as he could, but the resulting conflict was sometimes farcical. The first public pressure on him had been a party resolution in 1925; it is plain from his published reply that he had thought through its issues at a deeper level than Trotsky. The resolution claimed, 'we have entered a period of cultural revolution', and we must bear in mind 'the basic fact that the working class has seized power', and 'there is a proletarian dictatorship'. Alone among Russian writers, Boris remarked in reply that all three clauses were poppycock, and nothing should lead people to suppose that a style to suit the epoch was about to be created. Perhaps a new style had been created, but it was poisonous rubbish. Mandelstam himself could not have gone further, yet it was all done rather subtly, wrapped up in admiring language and an apparent desire to be helpful. He did after all believe, and express his belief, in a true historical grandeur to which writers ought to attain. It was this belief, in conflict with most of the concrete results of 1917, that remained his guiding light. His sense of the responsibility of writers, and at first of the greatness, then of the indescribable horror of his times, led him towards breakdown and to the brink of silence.

By 1934 a moment of exaltation about German revolution had given place to serious fears about Hitler. Pasternak assumed he would soon have to take his entire family under his wing in Moscow, and seems to have had that in mind when he moved to large and relatively splendid quarters in the new Union of Writers block in Lavrushinsky Street, overlooking the Tretyakov Gallery. In the road outside the rustle of leaves is the only noise. The Demidoff family mansion, with its pleasing decay, its massive cast-iron pilasters, is now a pedagogical institute. Boris Pasternak was a member of his Union and the Union looked after its own. Its headquarters were in the aristocratic old columned house of yellow stucco that Tolstoy had used as a model for the Rostov town house in *War and Peace*. Its dining-room is the room where Pierre became a Freemason. Boris was right to worry about his ageing parents, but their situation was saved by his sister Lydia's marriage to an English psychiatrist, who installed her in a large house in north Oxford. They were both psychiatrists, and they had children, but the marriage did not last. Her parents followed her to England, and so in 1938 did her married elder sister Josephine. Old Mrs Pasternak died just before the war, but Leonid lived on until 1945.

At the first Congress of Soviet Writers, Boris drew some laughter by leaping from his seat to help a girl with a huge machine over her shoulder, which she carried as the delegate of some industrial union. Babel drew even more laughter and applause, planting his arrows in well-chosen parts of the party's theories. He claimed, since he was not writing much, to be a master of the new literary genre of silence. 'In any bourgeois country I would have died of hunger long ago.' He attacked the vulgarity and triviality of

the Russian press, and artificial, bureaucratic language. 'Vulgarity
is synonymous with counter-revolution. Vulgarity: there is our
enemy, in my view. Stalin hammers out his words.' Babel not only
got away with this speech but was quite fully reported in *Pravda* (25
August 1934). His last story appeared in 1937, he was arrested in
1939, and died nastily on 17 March 1941. The first sign of trouble
for him was an over-expansive interview on the French riviera in
1930, which was published in Poland and noticed in Moscow. He
had openly admitted in it that in Russia he was unable to work
freely. Pasternak's congress speech was nuanced, but as clearly
intelligible as Babel's. 'Poetry is prose . . . prose itself, the voice of
prose, prose in action, not in narration. Poetry is the language of
the organic fact . . . it may be good or bad. . . . Do not lose contact
with the masses – the party says. I have done nothing to earn the
right to use its expressions. Don't sacrifice your personality for the
sake of your status – is what I say . . . there is too great a danger of
becoming a literary dignitary. Keep away from such favour.' In the
course of that congress he was several times attacked for not
making the 1917 revolution the centre of his work, but he got high
praises in a speech by Bukharin: his own contribution was laconic
and modest, and came near the end of the proceedings.

It was soon afterwards that he became ill, with chronic insomnia
and something close to breakdown. He appears to have been trying
to bend his own mind to an enthusiasm for Stalin, and failing to do
so. In his 1935 book he translated flattering poems about Stalin by
his Georgian friends, as of course he was bound to do; but at
exactly the same time he published two of his own in *Izvestia*. Later
in a speech at Minsk he singled out his Stalin poems for contempt,
as the merest cobbler's work, but he coupled with them something
more interesting called *The Artist*, which consisted of four lyrics
inspired by one of his Georgian friends G. N. Leonidze. The series
may represent conversation; it seems to echo the vehemently
romantic views of Blok. It is about the inner struggle for peace and
freedom, the readiness to put everything on to the fire to make
poetry, 'friendship, reason, conscience, daily life', and by this
process to turn all things into blessing. This short series was used in
his collected lyrics, *On Early Trains*, (1936–44) as the first work in
the book, like 'The Waves' in *Second Birth*. There is little to be said
about the two Stalin lyrics.

In landslides they move
inward eternally:
great things resounding in
my immaturity,
in country love and laughter
on the inn's outdoor benches,
in Lenin, in Stalin,
and in verses like these.

The second poem is even more peculiar than the first: tales and relics float over Moscow like the Kremlin, and the ages accept Stalin like bell-chimes. Can this preposterous image allude to the fact that the Tsarist carillon of the Kremlin clock-tower was rebuilt to play the 'Internationale'?

Boris Pasternak wrote at least two letters to Stalin in 1935. The first was a plea for an art historian called Nikolai Punin, freshly arrested, who lived with Akhmatova at the time. Punin was swiftly released, so maybe the poet was right in believing, as he was constantly telling his cousin Olga, that there is always someone to see, something to be done. Later Punin abandoned Akhmatova, which Pasternak thought most ungrateful of him. At this distance it is hard to separate middle-class confidence, and an artist's high-minded directness, from some kind of belief in the system; one must remember that many, many Russians wrote letters to Stalin, and believed that he read them. Akhmatova told people Pasternak was attempting at the time to insinuate himself into Punin's place, which seems bizarrely unlikely.

The second letter to Stalin was about Mayakovsky. Lili Brik, his early mistress and long-term lover, had written to the great man to try to get Mayakovsky's position ratified and made permanent as *the* exemplary and greatest poet of the Russian revolution. She already had the bequest of all his posthumous rights; her letter to Stalin was intended to promote the value of those rights. Stalin answered that 'Mayakovsky was and remains the most talented poet of our Soviet epoch; indifference to his memory and works is a crime.' Pasternak was delighted, because he thought this answer set him free from his own dangerous position. He wrote to Stalin to tell him so, and to express his agreement. 'It rescued me from the inflation of my significance, to which I was first exposed about the time of the Writers' Conference.'

He was suddenly pulled out of a clinic, brushed down, and sent to France. It was the age of international congresses of writers in defence of this and that. Russia was infested with swarms of well-meaning foreign leftists who returned to the west full of the future of mankind. Langston Hughes was the most lyrical, the Webbs were among the silliest, G. B. Shaw praised the vegetarian food, H. G. Wells made friends and influenced people, John Lehmann performed in a particularly dark episode as a communist spy. The Paris congress was 'in defence of culture'. The Russians sent a delegation, but Malraux and Camus noted with disappointment that neither Babel nor Pasternak was a member. They protested to such effect that the two writers were sent at the last moment, and greeted with storms of applause.

Pasternak was ill, and reluctant to go at all. Malraux had negotiated for him by saying, 'Of course I know he's nobody, but things are difficult here in Paris and so it would help greatly if we could have him.' Stalin's secretary suddenly appeared in Boris's room, all arrangements were already made, and he was provided with a top-hat and frock-coat, it being felt in Moscow to be unthinkable that one could represent Russian literature abroad dressed in anything less formal. Ten years later, he told Isaiah Berlin that what he said in Paris was more or less as follows. 'You are organising against Fascism, but it's a mistake. *Don't* organise. Organisation of any kind can be manipulated, and it is always fatal therefore to organise. The only duty of artists is not to organise, not to be organised, to resist organisation.' Malraux in later life could no longer remember whether this was what he said or not, and no record I have found confirms it, but it has a certain ring of truth. He was admittedly by 1945 almost fanatical against Stalinism. On being greeted with 'Well, you survived', he became very worried and angry, shaking his finger and saying, 'You think I did something? Worked for those people?' It is also true that by 1945 he was conscious of his own historical role 'to an almost egomaniacal degree'. Still, I like to believe that the essence of his message to the congress was as I have just recorded it. Some poems were specially translated, and they were well received.

What we have of his official speech is just some exquisite paradoxes that Valéry might have enjoyed. Poetry was the famous heights, higher than the Alps and lower than the grass; one had only to stoop to pick it up. It was too simple to be discussed at conferences, it was an organic part of the happiness of rational speech, so the more happiness there was on earth the easier it would be to be an artist. Behind these high-flown metaphors, the poet seems to be saying something sinister about unhappiness and about those deprived of speech. During the congress he kept Russian hours, rising at noon, eating breakfast at lunchtime, and so on. 'One day I shall tell you in detail what I have been through during those four months. . . . I did not turn away from my best friends.' Here he is writing to Tabidze and names Heinrich Neuhaus and Paolo Yashvili. 'In Paris I met Marina Tsvetayeva. But during this journey, as in the unnumbered, nameless absences in various clinics where I convalesced, I always had for talismans constant thoughts of Zinaida, a letter from R. M. Rilke, and one of yours written in spring. . . . I often put it under my pillow at night in the vain hope it would make me sleep.'

Boris was very low at this time: it would be hard to exaggerate how low. He avoided seeing his parents – which shocked Tsvetayeva – in order to conceal from them the condition he was in. On the journey to Paris they were ill, but Josephine met him at Munich, where she thought his condition terrifying. He spent two days resting with the Lomonosov family in London before returning to Russia by boat. He knew Tsvetayeva was now in such despair that she thought of returning to Russia. He feared for her, but he failed to give her an absolute danger sign, and she failed to read the signals he did give. The only result of their encounter was to add still more to his overwhelming sense of guilt. Akhmatova, whose imagination about men was both jealous and scurrilous, put it about that Boris and Marina slept together in Paris, which is certainly untrue.

While he was in France, he did not sleep once. All day long he had acute pain in the heart and in the arms. 'It was the worst time of my trials, a kind of sickness of the soul, a sensation of the end without any visible approach of death, a quite unimaginable state of depression. . . . I do not want to have any more medical treatment, or go anywhere to rest or convalesce. I want to try to do some work.' He seems slowly to have cured himself. Maybe Peredelkino helped, because in 1936 he got his small country house there, the kind of house a successful Edwardian lawyer or the head of an Oxford college might have taken for the summer in England. The house was in the country and among woods; it was about half an hour from Moscow, which today has crept closer, but in those days it meant he could walk under tall trees and swim in secluded pools like the Samarinsky Prud.

'It is as if one of the midnight colloquies of the eighteen nineties had gone on and on until it became our present life. Then the very madness was enchanting, wreathed as it was in clouds of tobacco smoke, but how completely crazy the ravaging of those revolutionary aristocrats seems now, when the smoke has settled and their conversation has become an organic part of the geographic map – and what a solid part! Yet the world has never seen anything more aristocratic than this, our bare, brutish reality, still calumniated and still deserving all the groans it has been the cause of.' That is how he wrote to Olga's mother, his aunt Asya in Leningrad, who was proposing to invite the family back to Russia, but warning them to bring their own kerosene. To Olga he wrote in 1935 that the longer he lived the more firmly he believed in what was being done, despite everything. 'Much of it strikes one as being savage, and then again one is astonished. There is no denying that taking into account the resources of Russia, which are basically untapped, the people have never before looked so far ahead, and with such a sense of self-esteem, and with such fine motives, and for such vital, clear-headed reasons.'

Probably his most important speech was the one he made at the plenary board meeting of the Union of Writers at Minsk in 1936. He praised Aseev, complimented local writers, and noted the similarity between Tolstoy's views and Lenin's in the nineties. He remarked that 'socialist realism' had not dropped from heaven or been invented by Mayakovsky, but had arisen from Gorky and Tolstoy. He praised Surkov for 'less of that elevated, trumpeting vulgarity' that people thought obligatory. 'We keep putting some kind of extra fetters on ourselves which no one needs.' In about 1922 he had been ashamed of the facile success of poetry in performance. 'I saw that my role lay in the rebirth of the book of poetry whose pages speak with the force of their own deafening muteness; I began to emulate higher models.' He now complained of his own inflated fame. He insisted the 'bad poems' other speakers referred to were only models of bad taste; he accepted only a distinction of good and bad poets, 'whole systems of thinking which either produce something or run idle'. He promised in future to write badly, as he was altering his style to fill 'a space rarefied by journalistic abstractions'. His Stalin poems had been written 'in the heat of the moment, just anyhow'. Hard work was no solution. 'Art is unthinkable without risk and spiritual self-sacrifice; freedom and boldness must be gained in practice, and that is where the unexpected belongs: do not expect a directive about it.' He found himself personally obliged, for example, to reject Demyan Bednyi, a writer of ballads of an awful facility, whom he then praised to the skies as 'the Hans Sachs of our popular movement'. If anyone wanted really to learn from Pasternak, they might have learnt a good deal at Minsk in 1936.

The season of show trials began. They were all rigged, of course, and known to the intelligentsia to be rigged. The first great assault on the Leningrad party leaders was a scheme that Stalin personally cherished. Indeed, this hatred of Leningrad, a fear approaching paranoia, ran its course throughout the war against Hitler; three years of continuous shelling of that unhappy city by the Germans did not for an instant abate the purges and the terror imposed by Stalin just as continually and for a longer period. For the trial of Kamenev and Zinoviev, every stop on the organ was to be pulled out, even down to the *vox inhumana* of a letter from the Writers' Union demanding the death sentence. Boris Pasternak's name appeared with the others, but it remains most doubtful whether he actually signed it. Later, at the trial of Marshal Tukachevsky, he certainly refused to sign any such letter. Luckily for him the authorities were so appalled at the possible repercussions of this that the news of his refusal was suppressed; his signature was printed against his will. It must have been about this time that he refused to translate some juvenile poems by Stalin into Russian, even though Stalin had asked for him as a translator.

'Everything snapped inside me in 1936 when all those terrible trials began, instead of the cruelty season ending as I had expected it would in 1935. My identification with our period of history turned to an opposition I did not conceal. I took refuge in translation: my creative work stopped.' He refused to condemn Gide for *On Returning from the USSR*, and defended his refusal in *Pravda*, on the grounds that he had not read the book. Nor, of course, had the others. He wrote to Olga about his Georgian translations, apologising for 'the rubbish I was forced to include', and to

Tabidze, telling him to keep his faith and ignore the Union of Writers. His cousin had her scholarly book attacked and with-drawn, and he wrote to warn her how such things were organised. First Shostakovich, then Meyerhold and Bulgakov were under attack. Boris tried to defend the others and was met with amazement at his indignation, since he personally had not been attacked. Friends were sent to enquire about his health. He wrote to Bukharin about Olga, but Bukharin was on the brink of his own arrest. Meanwhile, 'I write incredibly little, and such unbelievable shit.' He did publish four short bits of prose fiction, all set in the 1900s and the period just before February 1917. The Moscow secretary of the Writers' Union denounced Pasternak's poems from *The Second Birth* as 'a slander on the Soviet people', but at the height of the Terror, in January 1937, he defended himself vigorously in an open letter to the *Literary Gazette*.

In summer of that year, Titian Tabidze was arrested in Georgia: for years Boris tried to trace him in the vast wilderness of prisons and camps, but he had been shot almost at once. Paolo Yashvili heard of his arrest at the Writer's Union, where he was local secretary; he killed himself at once with a shotgun. Pasternak began without delay to send money regularly to their families.

> My soul grieves
> for all encircling me,
> it is the cemetery
> of these tormented lives.
>
> I dedicate this verse
> to embalm their bodies,
> these strings of bitterness
> and of lament too harsh.
>
> In an age of icc
> like a conscience it stands,
> a wall where ashes end
> and the dead rest in peace.
>
> It bows to the ground
> under their agony,
> smells of dust and decay,
> the morgue and the grave mound.

My soul full of pain
heard all and saw all
and remembered well
and ground all into grain.

Pound, compound and smash
all I witnessed in tears
for nearly forty years,
to compost and to ash.

Boris Pasternak wrote that poem in 1956, when Stalin was dead, to commemorate those closest to him. It has the simplicity of his last poetry. Of his Georgian friends he wrote fully and deliberately in *People and Situations*, increasing a little what he had already written in the final section, 'Three Shadows', of his *Essay in Autobiography*, intended when it was written in 1956 for an introduction to collected poems. The two texts differ very little except in this final section. He calls Paolo Yashvili a post-symbolist. 'His poetry is related to the modern European prose of Beliy, Hamsun and Proust. His poetry is extremely rich in content, and not crowded with special effects, but full of space and air. It moves and breathes. . . . Yashvili was outgoing and centrifugal, Tabidze was centripetal, in every line he wrote and in every step he took into the depths of his soul.' The analysis is finely balanced and effective to this day, but too long to quote in full here.

Boris Pasternak had his calm days, even in the late thirties. Afinogenov the dramatist found him in September 1937 absorbed by his art, taking solitary walks, reading Macaulay's *History of England*, and 'writing his novel'. He wrote to Olga too about 'just standing here' at Peredelkino, until he could work out certain intricate details of plot which held up the novel. He must by now have abandoned the idea of a three volume novel with a revolutionary hero or the revolution itself as hero, which he had once thought possible in the manner of Aleksei Tolstoy. Gorky had spent nearly his whole life trying to write just such a book, *Klim Samgin*, but died before it was finished; the final, triumphant part of that would probably have ended with the arrival of Lenin. Boris had greatly admired the first volume about the young revolutionary, and it throws an interesting light on the way in which he altered the nature of his own hero Zhivago after considering

Gorky's. In Gorky's novel socialism is a gospel, and religion fused into communism: the point is not so much discipleship as that a kind of Christ-like man, who confers immortality, exists or is thrown up by revolution. The confusion of Christ and resurrecton and revolution inspired Gorky as it inspired Boris. The chief difference between them is that *Klim Samgin* is almost unreadable, certainly unfinished, and not thought through. Gorky had died in the summer of 1936. He seems to have been poisoned.

Akhmatova gives a more dramatic account of the Pasternak household of those days than Afinogenov, who is one of the most charming and I think reliable witnesses to the few occasions when their paths crossed. It is our good luck that at least one other, whose accounts are much fuller, takes over at just this time. This was the actor and writer Alexander Gladkov (1912–76; not to be confused with the Gladkov who wrote *Cement*), who, at the age of twenty-four, met Boris and Zinaida Pasternak in 1936 in Meyerhold's house, at a lunch for Malraux. He remembered the wonderful coffee and the brandy for thirty years. A year after that they met in the street, where the poet suddenly gave vent to a powerful diatribe against the atrocities. We shall have reason to return to young Gladkov. Akhmatova's account has a slight touch of comic opera. Zinaida tried to stop them meeting, and by May 1940 Akhmatova on no evidence had decided that Boris was in decline. He was not doing original work, his wife was playing cards non-stop and neglecting the baby (Leonid, born on the last day of 1937). At last he was beginning to be indiscreet about his marriage, she said. He would surely have left her except for the baby, but he was 'one of those conscientious husbands who can't stand a second divorce'. Of course she had always realised what a coarse, vulgar creature Zinaida was, of course everyone but Boris had always known. One must add that Akhmatova was homosexual.

In that year she suddenly managed to publish a volume of poems 'From Six Books' with a few new ones. He wrote her a detailed fan letter. 'When it came out I was in hospital with inflammation of the spinal nerve . . . even there I heard about queues of people two streets long waiting to get it. . . . Platonov . . . has already sold out, and the price for a second-hand copy is 150 roubles.' Publication was soon stopped all the same, according to Akhmatova just as soon as the book reached Stalin's hands, though one may doubt that.

When the end of this period came it was a relief. Boris had been following the war with deep anxiety and grief for his parents, but when Hitler invaded Russia he was relieved. He thought things would go right at last, and that when victory was won Stalin would smile at the Russian people and the Terror would be over. He tried innumerable times to get to the front, and he did at last get there in 1943, but what he wrote was so brilliant and specific it is small wonder that it was no use to Stalin. It was not printed at all until 1965. What Stalin wanted is typified by the crudity and drivel published by Ehrenburg; in England that was called *Russia at War* (Hamish Hamilton (1943), with an introduction by J. B. Priestly); reading it is like eating a peasoup fog flavoured with gunsmoke. But there is 'a steely delicacy and precision' about Pasternak's reporting, as his translator remarks. There are also scenes and sentences in it that recur in *Zhivago*. I believe it was the war that, by removing him from the blocked approaches to his novel, enabled him at last to write it. It revived in him a deep faith in the Russian people, and, with its immediate aftermath, set him loose from the last shackles of subservience to Stalin.

What most deeply blocked him throughout these years was the growing recognition that he must write *Zhivago*. He despised his own verse collection *On Early Trains* (1943), because its publication was an act of conformity; and yet there are poems in it he need not have been ashamed of. Later he added his war poems and called the whole volume *The Breadth of the Earth* (1945), but he was impatient with that too. He had become obsessed with *Zhivago* and its style and its new poems, before he had written it. Where did he learn a style that is so direct and true? Largely in the course of translation, and particularly from Shakespeare, whom it was necessary in Russian and for the stage to simplify. Yet his versions have a power that seems to burn the paper they are written on or the air in which they are spoken. It was in these versions of Shakespeare that he gave the strongest expression to his sense of life in Russia and to his indignation and loathing. One can test this by retranslating into English. People understood it too: there was a day soon after the war when a crowded audience started to hiss at him, 'Sixty-six, sixty-six.' They wanted his translation of Shakespeare's sixty-sixth sonnet, printed in 1940: 'Tir'd with all these, for restful death I cry . . .' Translating the similar lines of Hamlet in act III, scene 1, 'For who would bear the whips and scorns of time . . .', he writes Russian lines resonant with bitter experience, so that scarcely a shell of Shakespeare remains: yet he is the most accurate and best translator Shakespeare has ever had in any language. My only small reservation is that, although the translations were made for the theatre, they were printed and revised for children, so the process of simplifying, and of cleaning up the obscenities, has gone too far at times. But the general effect is of sharpening and tightening the text, exactly as Shakespeare himself did in his own revision of *King Lear*. It is a staggering achievement.

If I offer a retranslation of his Russian for the reader to compare with Shakespeare, it is understood that I am as faithful as possible, but that my version is much weaker than Pasternak, let alone Shakespeare. In *Macbeth*, for example, Rosse describes tyranny, 'Where sighs and groans and shrieks that rent the air / Are made, not mark'd; where violent sorrow seems / A modern ecstasy: the dead man's knell / Is there scarce ask'd for who.' Pasternak has:

> People are used to tears, they go unnoted,
> glimpses of horror and tempest are common,
> all day the bell clangs for someone, yet no man
> stops to consider who goes to his grave.

At exactly this time Boris had just got hold of *For Whom the Bell Tolls*, with its fuller quotation from Donne as the epigraph, and stayed awake all night reading it. The end of *Lear* was revised, very slightly, towards hope for the young. The original is:

> The weight of this sad time we must obey;
> speak what we feel, not what we ought to say.
> The oldest hath borne most; we that are young
> shall never see so much, nor live so long.

Pasternak's 1949 version is:

> Whatever grief ingrows into the soul
> the times enforce us into steadfastness:
> let's follow the example of this shade
> in his survival and longsuffering.

Later on, in new editions of the same play, this becomes:

> Whatever grief ingrows into the soul
> the times enforce we should be stoical:
> the old man has borne all strong and unbent.
> We that are young will never live through that.

As a more characteristic example of the astonishing skill with which he all but matches Shakespeare, it is fair to take a famous and longer passage. It oddly recalls *1905*.

> Her boat burned on the waters like the globe,
> the stern of it was golden, and the sail
> was purple, some sweet fragrance burnt on it,
> and the wind died away in ecstasy.
> So to the sound of flutes the silver oars
> rose in harmony, and shouting waves
> ran after them, pursuing their music,
> Her person cannot be described with words.
> She lay in a gold tent finer than Venus
> who is not real, but only myth and dream.
> By her side like cupids with dimpled cheeks
> stood smiling children holding fans, whose airs
> enflamed the colour glowing in her cheeks . . .

His weaknesses as a translator are really as attractive as his strength. In *Hamlet* he diminishes the sense of physical contamination: 'mutes or audience to this act' becomes 'dumb witnesses of this our finale'; Hamlet is noble, Ophelia pure and beautiful, and there are hints of redemption. Stalin forbade a production of Pasternak's *Hamlet* when it was in rehearsal, because he believed assassination an improper subject and Hamlet a bad hero. In *Othello*, Boris hated the idea of corrupting sexuality. He had trouble making out Iago, whom he called a prehistoric animal. He called Stalin prehistoric too.

He spoke of his translations as hack-work. Afinogenov wrote, 'It's hard work for his wife, they have to get money to live somehow or other, but he knows nothing about how, only sometimes when the money problem gets really severe he starts some translations. "But I'd make just as much as a travelling salesman." ' All the same, the habit of work, quite ceaseless work, does seem to have saved his sanity, and Shakespeare was both a new world for him to explore, rather as Tolstoy and Balzac are to us, and a flexible mask for political self-expression. He was also, of course, the greatest of great poets, and one from whom there is an infinite possibility of learning, most of all in a foreign language no doubt.

The work went with him everywhere, even to the canteen at Chistopol in the Urals, where the Moscow writers found themselves evacuated. The others sat gossiping and complaining in their coats and hats, but Boris Pasternak sat hatless and coatless at work with his English dictionary and *Romeo and Juliet*. The witness is Gladkov, who took the opportunity that winter in Chistopol to deepen his friendship with the poet. Gladkov went to prison in 1948 and stayed there until Stalin's death, but his writing is full of life and light. He calls Chistopol a small, run-of-the-mill, provincial town, with muddy roads and the Moscow papers available only in the party reading-room. Boris Pasternak had stopped reading newspapers years earlier, so that at least would not have worried him.

When Gladkov arrived, Marina Tsvetayeva, a woman surely doomed to tragedy even without two world wars and a revolution, had already passed through. She had trouble with her residence permit, and the police moved her upriver to Yelabuga. She had come back to Russia at the last moment, in 1939, when her husband Efron, a former Russian spy and probably assassin, had already been arrestd. Boris saw her, gave her money and got her work, but she was now alone with one child, whom she called Moor. He was fifteen, wanted to join the army, and quarrelled loudly and furiously with his mother. They shouted at one another most of the night. Next day the whole village was rewarded with bread for helping to make a landing-strip; he went with them, but Marina stayed at home and hanged herself from a farmyard nail. She left Boris a fresh and heavy load of guilt and grief. He wrote a sad, numb poem about her ashes, and the great barges chewing at the unbroken ice. Moor became a pupil of Lev Ozerov, who saw him a few times and tried to help him. Lev even got some cards from Moor, from the army, but he was killed quite soon.

In Chistopol life was strange. Writers wandered around in stylish overcoats and soft felt hats. Some were very rich: one man bought himself a bull to circumvent the meat ration, another bought honey by the barrel. Leonov retained a night watchman to guard his suitcases in the dark. They hired complete houses. Boris had one room. One poor fellow was reduced to selling his wife's underwear in the market. Valentin Parnakh, a poet who used to be a musician and a dancer in Paris, and had his book illustrated by Picasso, 'looked like a parrot in his battered foreign hat', and got two plates of soup a day at the canteen for watching the door and seeing that people shut it properly. Firewood was a problem: it was in a big, frozen stack on the river-bank. A few people hired men to fetch it, but Pasternak cheerfully hauled his own in thirty degrees of frost. Zinaida was teaching in an orphan school where she got two meals a day, one of which she brought home to share with him. His room was freezing and his fingers would go numb, so he used to open the door to the kitchen, where primus stoves would be going full blast, but so would gramophones. He was uncomplaining and pleased to have hours of uninterrupted work.

Once he did beg them to be quiet in the kitchen. They did stop the music, but they muttered about 'all this fuss'. He was so upset at his own bad manners that he was unable to work that day. In the evening he was supposed to read at a public meeting, but, unable to do that either, he made a public apology instead. The writers giggled and the audience were baffled. He fled, and wandered about in the snow with Gladkov. Gladkov was not a formal member of the Writers' Union, which required an election, but he was allowed to run around with the others because he had written a verse play. Pasternak was really encouraging and enthusiastic about Gladkov's work, which was largely patriotic, historical drama. He himself had loved Meyerhold, and to some degree he was stagestruck. He was a very good listener even to ham performances by other writers, beaming with delight and leaping to bring them water or whatever. 'He smiled all the time, and occasionally murmured to himself.' But all his reactions were innocent: he would chew happily on a crust of black bread, he would come in from the cold cheerful and rosy-cheeked. The news that the Germans had done damage to Yasnaya Polyana, Tolstoy's house, shocked and horrified him.

Pasternak valued his freest translations highest, and his *Romeo and Juliet* which I much admire, less highly. He thought the *Hamlet* was best, and compared it favourably with his original poems. There is therefore no doubt that he was conscious of the value of the lessons he learnt from Shakespeare and lavished in translating him. He held the strange view that Shakespeare used to block out scenes in verse and then translate them into his perfect prose. Pasternak's scholarly views are not all masterly, but they are rarely less than interesting. His favourite book about Shakespeare was Victor Hugo's, which is a powerful, engaging and unjustly neglected work. It begins with Hugo and his son staring out to sea in the first days of their exile. 'And how are you going to spend these years?' 'I think I am going to spend them translating Shakespeare.' All the same, the resulting translation was not as good as Pasternak's. Pasternak's interpretations were original too; I am particularly fond of his view that *Lear* should be whispered, and that no productions are any good because the actors always shout. And I greatly sympathise with the attitude he expressed in 1942: that Shakespeare will always be the favourite poet of generations that 'have lived through much and are historically mature'. He spoke of Shakespeare as the highest point of 'the voice of facts, real knowledge of things, and the art of realism, which is serious' – an interesting comment on social realism.

'In every respect he is the child of nature. . . . The explosions of his imagery are unparalleled. His analogies represent the furthest point ever reached by the subjective principle in poetry. He has set a deeper personal imprint on his work than anyone before or after him.' For a moment one thinks this is Victor Hugo resurrected, then that Shakespeare is going to be embraced as an honorary futurist, then that Pasternak is still defending himself against Trotsky and his like. Maybe all of these are partly true, because in his studying Shakespeare things have come together from all over his life. Late in life, he described poetry or the poet as eternity's hostage in the hands of time, and early in life, in *The Black Goblet*, he wrote that 'Eternity is the most dangerous of rebels, its deeds are violent, insistent, lightning-quick.' He wrote in a letter that 'The one thing in our power is not to distort the voice of life which sounds within us.' I find all this Shakespearean at the roots.

He wrote in 1946 some remarks that were printed as a preface to a two-volume Shakespeare in 1949, including a splendid defence of his own vitality and boldness in translation. 'Like the original, the

translation must produce an impression of life, not of literature. . . .
The tempestuous vitality of Rembrandt's, Michelangelo's, Titian's
brush is not the result of a deliberate choice. Assailed by a stormy,
insatiable thirst to draw the entire universe, they had no time for other
kinds of drawing. Impressionism has been characteristic of art since
time immemorial. It is the expression of the riches of man's spirit,
spilling out over the edge of his doomed condition.' The poet uses
metaphors because of the brevity of life and the vastness of his task.
He sees with eagle eyes and 'explains himself in momentary, instantly
intelligible flashes of illumination. That is what poetry is. Metaphor is
the shorthand of the soul.' That sounds more like Boris Pasternak
than like Shakespeare perhaps, but it covers them both. One comes to
see that they really do have unique technical and spiritual qualities in
common. These 'Notes on Translation' are better than almost any
recent writings about Shakespeare.

Before the end of the war he was looking worn out, wrinkled
and older than his age, which was about fifty-four. He warned
young Gladkov that when it was over Stalin would behave like a
drill-sergeant, in which case he was due to vanish among the camps
of the north, 'among so many of my old friends'. In March 1944 he
wrote explaining the change in himself to Nina, the widow of
Tabidze. 'I have often been overworked. This ages me outwardly
and makes me absent-minded. . . . During the last years, and
particularly during the war years in winter, I thought I had got
reconciled to the idea that I lived in a big, big building called the
world, where Titian Tabidze was no longer to be found. That
completely changed reality for me. . . . I became more indifferent,
more courageous, more intelligible. That has not only its bad side:
the bitterness has disciplined me. If it were in the Caucasus, I would
have said a wrinkle of vindictiveness had lined my face and just
dried it up a little. But I'm not like that, and by the nature of my
profession I am influenced by that softening power that teaches
all-forgivness, so the opposite is true.' This letter comes closer than
anything else to explaining Boris Pasternak's *moral* transformation
into the formidable writer that he now was.

> Gloomy the saddened day drags on,
> and past the porch and past the door,
> in through windows standing open
> the torrents of thaw-water run.

. . . Those days are gone, goodbye to them:
Marina it is light labour
to carry home your scattered ash
from Yelabuga in requiem.

And your reburial was kept
solemn, I thought of it last year
along the river in the snow
where fast in ice the barges slept. (December 1942)

A month earlier he wrote a poem on the twenty-fifth anniversary of the October revolution. The poem is a light piece, though serious enough, but it is interesting because of Boris Pasternak's extreme sense of isolation among the Writers' Union writers in Chistopol, and because October 1917 was still what he measured himself by.

. . . I don't regret callow writing
and on this morning of autumn
I greet your coming once again,
still ready for fresh suffering.

To me you mean integrity:
no need to apologise to me,
while the overshadowing war
darkens your anniversary. (November 1942)

His article on a visit to the front near Orel in 1943 has some appalling stories of German atrocities and peasant sufferings: it is written against a background of fire and darkness, like his 'Nightglow', which comes close to being a modern epic; the glow of the title was generated by an artillery barrage that had become perpetual. But his journalistic report is always conscious of history, and of the associations of the region with great writers; near the end, after a lucid and interesting account of tactics ('I see it as a chain of events, link following link in the unfaltering sequence of its moral logic'), he gives us a history lesson. Germany has become a distorting mirror of Russia, and 'no more than a reactionary footnote to Russian history'. In the nineteenth century Russia 'made rapid and successful progress', in a spirit of humanity and broad vision. 'The element of genius which underlay our preparation of the revolution as a moral phenomenon on a national scale . . . could be felt everywhere.' Tolstoy is his example, but before Tolstoy, he suddenly remarks, the same genius was embodied in 'Shakespeare at the very beginning of England's emergence as a distinctive culture'. The war was fought by national genius against hidebound German efficiency, and genius had won.

If I have paid too little attention to Boris's personal life and troubles in this period, it is because what hugely influenced him were greater sorrows and bigger events, and the vast school of Shakespeare. His private life is reflected in his letters to his cousin Olga. The Germans invaded in summer of 1941; young Zhenya was sent to Smolensk to dig trenches, then evacuated with his mother to Tashkent. Zinaida was sent to Chistopol in July with little Leonid and her own son Stasik Neuhaus. Boris chose to remain in Moscow but he was evacuated forcibly in October. The Germans approached within long artillery range of Moscow at that time. Part one of 'Nightglow' appeared in *Pravda* in October 1943, but further parts were rejected. It robustly attacked Stalinist art, and Fadeev persuaded Pasternak not to finish it. He wrote a play about the war called *Life on Earth*, but I have never seen it. When he read it to friends they found it so provocative that he burnt it, except for two scenes, one about Dudorov, who shelters a German on the run, and ponders the differences between Nazi and Soviet tyranny, the other the story of Tanya's childhood, which is reused in *Zhivago*.

Adrian, the other Neuhaus boy, had tuberculosis of the bone. In Leningrad, people died of starvation and the streets were strewn with corpses. There were no lights or telephones, and the sewers were not working. The radio was silent. Olga was very ill and her mother died. A letter from Boris in Chistopol of 18 July 1942 reached Leningrad on 3 August 1943. Olga's letters are courageous and humorous, Boris's passionately affectionate; she writes him excellent literary criticism, discusses Rimsky-Korsakov, and tries to keep working at her *Theory of Folklore*. (She was amazed later to discover that 'a man called Bovra' in Oxford had stolen her ideas in advance.) Boris lost nearly all his Moscow belongings, including his father's drawings; his house at Peredelkino became an army billet, so he stored his father's paintings in Ivanov's house, which burnt to the ground. Zinaida's son Adrian's leg was amputated, and in April 1945 he died.

Boris's own parents died too, and among his close friends so did Serov's daughter Olga and Asmus's wife Irina. In the spring of 1945 Boris was in severe pain, with his right arm in a sling, constant eye trouble and a bad liver; he was writing his version of *Henry IV* with his left hand. In 1946 his cousin Olga suffered from heart disease and nervous exhaustion, but she survived. Heart disease may have been in the family: Boris's son Leonid, who grew up to be a physicist, and was twenty-two when his father died, collapsed from heart disease at the wheel of a car when he was thirty-eight. Boris and Zinaida were observed to be living in imperfect harmony. This is a difficult subject, because there is no doubt that he admired her heroic struggles for the family and to protect the house, and felt love for her. But she was a tough and bossy lady, forty-seven in 1945, who ended up with very few friends among his friends. She was not 'literary'. That does not necessarily mean they were ill matched, though later he was so indiscreet as to say that they were, and that he only married her for Neuhaus's sake – which makes little sense. The war put a fearful strain on marriages of every kind, and it aged people too.

Still, the war was not wholly an evil memory to him. *Hamlet* may not have been produced, but his public readings of it in Moscow were crowded, enthusiastic, and followed by exciting discussions. This direct contact was something new for him, and he found it wonderful. As a book *Hamlet* sold. 'Whether they give me a prize or not, whether they want to know about it or not,' he wrote in 1942, '*Hamlet* spent an incredible, overwhelming winter at the front and in field hospitals, and on the beds of the dying and in forced evacuations.' He had a right to be proud of that, as he was of the circulation of so many of his poems, known by heart and learnt by word of mouth or read in smuggled manuscripts, in the camps of the Gulag. At Chistopol he imagined himself in Pushkin's country house and estate at Mikhailovskoe; in Peredelkino he joined the civil defence and discovered to his delight he was a good shot. He also enjoyed firewatching in Moscow. On at least one occasion he got blown up and knocked unconscious, but it does not seem to have hurt him.

He himself put his years of what he called 'deep spiritual crisis and change' in 1945–6: no doubt what happened was a long-drawn-out process. 'A war', he told a visitor, 'is no mere game of chess; it doesn't just end with white winning over black. Other things have to come out of it. So many sacrifices can't just result in nothing . . . a new view of life, a sense among humanity of its own value.' Zhdanov renewed the persecution of poets who had once been 'fellow travellers' in August 1946, with an attack on Akhmatova; Pasternak accepted the challenge, but that was not his spiritual crisis. Olga Ivinskaya, a young woman he met in an office in October 1946, undoubtedly altered his life and was the love of his last years, but by then his great transformation was over.

The crisis cannot be identified as the decision to write *Dr Zhivago*, because that had been building up for a long time. Zhenya Pasternak, Boris's son, could see it coming before the war. On the other hand, it was during the first two years after the war that it became obvious that the hopes nourished by Pasternak and others, the hopes that had kept them going, were by no means to be fulfilled. Years earlier, in 1932, after a poetry reading by Mandelstam, Pasternak had said to him 'I envy you your freedom, but I need my non-freedom.' If we understand him rightly, that had now altered. The change was spiritually profound, not merely political. It was at this time that he took to annotating a foreign prayer book he had got from somewhere.

When Akhmatova's book had been published he had tried to get her a prize, but, when she gave a reading in 1944 and was received with tumultuous applause, Stalin was told, and his response, which Boris remarked with justice was so entirely typical of him it could not have been invented, was to ask who organised the applause. On 14 August 1946 came the party decree, 'On the magazines *Zvezda* and *Leningrad*'. They were denounced for opening their pages to M. Zoshchenko, a writer of fiction, and Anna Akhmatova. A virulent speech by Zhdanov followed a week later, but the famous insult 'half nun, half whore' was only a quotation from an old encyclopedia. Zoshchenko was attacked for saying that life in the monkey-house at the zoo was more civilised than it was in the Soviet Union. They were not shot, not arrested, only deprived of their ration books and disgraced. Boris was deliberately seen with Akhmatova in public, and privately tucked a thousand roubles under her pillow. It is sometimes hard to tell his quixotic warmth from his considered actions: when he talked to Gladkov in a crowded tram about how thrilled he was that

Gladkov's imprisoned brother had a copy of his poems, he acted in innocence, but on this other occasion he calculated the consequences.

The board of the Writers' Union was summoned to condemn Akhmatova, so he refused to attend and was sacked from the board. When he was threatened with the same treatment as hers because his verse was 'cut off from the people, cut off from the modern world', he answered that he had 'heard all that stuff years ago from your man Trotsky'. Simonov at *Novy Mir* had asked for some poems and he sent them, but the assistant editor Krivitsky sent them back, so Boris rang up Simonov to ask who had dared to hamper the work of the great Simonov. He must print a denunciation of these wreckers and saboteurs. Akhmatova crowed with pleasure; it was a joke in her style. It happens that we have an independent account of this bizarre episode in the memoirs of Chukovskaya, the granddaughter of Boris's friend the writer Kornei Chukovsky. She worked in the *Novy Mir* office and recalls in detail Krivitsky's idiotic criticisms of the poems and his mad rage against the poet; Simonov faltered at first, but when he was forced to the telephone he spoke 'very softly and soulfully' and was much pained by Pasternak's ungrateful reaction. Simonov was a weak, preening, luxurious man, much like a literary functionary in the west: he was not peculiarly Russian or extremely anything.

In March 1947 the novelist Fadeev opened fire on Boris at a literary conference: Pasternak was an alien, not one of us; it was no accident he was so popular abroad. Later in the month the untalented Surkov joined in with an article; both were important literary officials. Boris was called a hermit alien to the age, who referred to the revolution with malice and ill-will. These attacks lacked the ultimate authority of anonymity, and by the strange standards of Stalinist Russia they ranked as mild reprimands. But Pasternak's *Selected Lyrics*, due out in 1948, were withdrawn and pulped; very few copies indeed have survived. Exactly how popular was he abroad? The answer is not surprising really. The leftists and the students took to him in Paris in 1934, and the English slowly and steadily in the late thirties and forties. He was installed in the *Oxford Book of Russian Verse* only in its second editon in 1948, and in America *New Directions* took him up in 1949, but George Reavy, his fan and friend, came across him as a Cambridge undergraduate in the late twenties and wrote about him and translated him in 1930. Cyril Connolly's *Horizon* took up his poetry and his Shakespeare translations in 1944 and 1945, and Maurice Bowra, who followed J. M. Cohen in *Horizon* and did some excellent translations of his own, both in *Horizon* and later in *Orion* and *New Directions*, lectured on Boris Pasternak as Oxford Professor of Poetry soon afterwards. When the lecture was published, he was amazed to get a letter from Pasternak saying it had been his life's ambition to be lectured on by Bowra, but the lecture went beyond his highest expectations. Students of my generation still treasure J. M. Cohen's *Selected Pasternak* of 1946 and we saw the Russian film of *Hamlet*; during the war he once broadcast about Shakespeare for the BBC, but any record seems to have perished.

A more important direct link exists, through Isaiah Berlin's time at the Embassy in 1945–6. 'And so our man is receiving British spies,' said Stalin when he heard of Berlin's visit to Akhmatova. Berlin had left Russia in 1919 at the age of ten; since he spoke perfect Russian and understood American policy, having worked in Washington, he was thought useful in Moscow, but in the event he was scarcely employed there, so he was free to explore. His considered view is that the best accounts of Russian life under the terror and the purges is Mrs Mandelstam's, in spite of its occasional bitchiness; she neither praises nor blames, only recounts. It was not until the war that several writers published in Russia in tiny editions or much earlier discovered their audience; both Pasternak and Akhmatova got a huge fan-mail from the front. If at any public reading they stumbled over a word or a line, there were twenty people who knew the poem by heart. Isaiah Berlin has sparkling recollections of Akhmatova and Pasternak, and also of old Chukovsky. Chukovsky said he loved the poems but had his ups and downs with Boris, who was irritated by his passion for Nekrasov and such writers. Chukovsky maintained that Boris hated populist and committed poetry of all kinds, but in stray references he could be generous about anyone, and he genuinely admired Tikhonov after all. Isaiah Berlin is a good source for Boris's tarter remarks. Of the poet Selvinsky, for example, he said, 'Selvinsky had his hour, but it is, thank God, long past.'

He attacked his own early prose, though not his early verse, saying Beliy was a genius, but a fatal influence. That may well be, and this is the place to note that from certain influences one never wholly escapes; Boris Pasternak never completely escaped from symbolism. Its influence is to be found even in *Zhivago*. How curious it is, then, that Maurice Bowra's *The Creative Experiment* (1949), in which his Pasternak lecture appears, follows on a slightly earlier book called *The Heritage of Symbolism*. There are ghosts whose influence on a writer may seem to him purely negative, yet he is still wrestling in late age with those. Now, Boris told Isaiah Berlin, he was writing something quite different, something new and elegant and harmonious, something well proportioned and classical, 'and this will be my last word, my most important word, to the world'. At times he became strident about all his old selves and all his earlier poems in comparison with the new book. He told Chukovskaya, 'The poems, they're nonsense. I don't understand why people make such a fuss about my poems. The only monumental thing I've done in my life is the novel. And it's not true people value it just for its politics. People read it and they love it.'

He was very keen at this time on a vague philosophy espoused by Herbert Read called personalism, which Pasternak thought derived from the moral philosophy of Kant. Mysterious as his interest may be to us, and vague as Read is about it, this fits Pasternak's views and their history. He got hold of an English anthology, and he used to show it to people and ask what they liked best in it. The trap was to say T. S. Eliot; he was thrilled when Zoe Afanaseyevna said Herbert Read. He knew Eliot was a far greater poet, but he was too gloomy, whereas Read expressed humanity and hope. His English was not good enough to detect the element of cardboard in Herbert Read's verse. His English letters were always stilted. When he heard Shelley's 'Prometheus' read on the radio in English he half understood the words, and thought 'Why, it is by me.'

Isaiah Berlin is inclined to think Blok was the greatest Russian poet of this century, but I have heard him call Pasternak 'a divine poet'. His summary of the impression Pasternak made in the forties is particularly helpful. 'He spoke in magnificent, slow-moving periods, with occasional intense rushes of words; his talk often overflowed the backs of grammatical structure – lucid passages were succeeded by wild but always marvellously vivid and concrete images – and these might be followed by dark words when it was difficult to follow him – and then he would suddenly come into the clear again; his speech was at all times that of a poet, as were his writings. . . . Pasternak was a poet of genius in all that he did and was; his ordinary conversation displayed it as his writings do. I cannot begin to describe its quality. . . . I use the word "genius" advisedly.'

When Isaiah Berlin went home to England, he took with him the first two chapters of *Dr Zhivago*, then called *Boys and Girls, The Story of a Russian Faust: from the unpublished papers of the Zhivago family*. It was intended to depict 'Russia for the past forty-five years', and it was to be 'my only work', as he told his cousin Olga. 'The mood of the piece is set by my Christianity', which was wider than Quakerism or Tolstoyism and founded on the personal meditation of gospel texts. The book was to settle accounts with Judaism, and with every kind of nationalism. He had been writing it since July 1946, and by 5 October he was writing the third chapter in utter absorption at Peredelkino, in the big bow-window on the first floor that looks across country, an empty room full of light. The events of late 1946 that followed the party's decree and Zhdanov's campaign all but passed him by, because he was busy writing.

'One is late in discovering what one needs; only now have I mastered what I have needed all my life. Well, my having done it at last is at least something to be thankful for. And to tell you the truth I am really happy, not in an exalted way, and not by rationalising, but because I am free in spirit, and so far, God be praised, in good health.'

# 8

## *Dr Zhivago*

Thirty years after the death of its author and the hushing of the storm it gave rise to, *Dr Zhivago* retains its freshness and its mystery. Critics have found it many-faceted and enigmatic, but as time passes that does not matter in the least. It is a vast, sprawling, beautiful book, symbolist at times, enormous in scope and range, able to focus finely and to turn on a sixpence. It is certainly a work of genius, but not a Tolstoyan novel, because its lucidity comes and goes, and so does its sense of history; it is not really a novel at all, in any received sense. Some of its most important events happen between sections or chapters, its coincidences are extraordinary, and its time-scale negligent. Somewhere in the course of writing, Pasternak has put in an extra year, but this does not matter at all to the ordinary reader. It is as vast in ambition as any novel ever written, yet at times it has the feel of an allegory or a morality. It strays towards autobiography and it does throw some light on the poet's life, but the light is equivocal because its roots in reality are not single but complex, and Zhivago is not exactly Pasternak. It is the most memorable of Russian novels since Tolstoy's *Resurrection* (1899), which is saying a very great deal, and, more than any other work of fiction, it is the monument of its epoch, though it does not succeed in describing that epoch, 'Russia over the past forty-five years', as he told his cousin Olga.

Gladkov makes a sensible point about it when he complains that it seems to discuss the eternal Russian soul, Bolshevism, Stalinism and the victory over Hitler, and, although it was 'received abroad as something that offered a key to these mysteries, it does not in fact throw real light on any of them.' *Dr Zhivago* is about the world, though, and about real life, though more about life's interaction with the individual and with his soul, and of course with his poetry. As a portrait of a poet or artist it is unique in the history of literature: it is brilliantly convincing, and Zhivago's

210

poems both add to the mystery and intensify the reality. They are the explosive part of the bullet. 'The hero will be something intermediate between me, Blok, Yesenin and Mayakovsky.' He is not just a poet but a great poet, and that in itself makes the book unique. One has only to imagine Auden or Yeats or Eliot writing such a book. Pasternak's sense of predestination, which is both philosophic and religious in colour, makes his book possible where theirs are not, because he believes absolutely in the significance of his story, and he communicates just that.

Feminists object to the women characters, who are pale or play stiff, old-fashioned roles in Zhivago's central light. Perhaps the heroine alters from Zinaida to Olga in the course of the book. The negative critics have come in time to look ridiculous. Akhmatova was often funny about *Dr Zhivago*, which she said contained 'quite unprofessional pages; I think they were written by Olga Ivinskaya.' The idiot Costello, a New Zealander who used to infuriate Pasternak in the forties by trying to persuade him to join the Communist Party, wrote after Pasternak's death, 'Do people still read *Zhivago*? No one can have read it twice.' Sinyovsky called it 'a weak novel of genius'; if he means weak as a technical construction it is a true but misplaced remark, because the weakness is a necessary part of its mysterious and memorable strength: one would not like to read it tidied up by a subeditor. Professor Kermode cleverly calls it 'a heroic if flawed effort to impose upon the matter of realistic fiction the form of a post-imagist poem', but the truth is that such an attempt on such a scale makes no sense at all, and like most separations of matter and form this criticism is itself flawed. What is true all the same is that individual sections are written like lyric poems, with the same symbolist techniques, though the end of one of these poem-like pieces does not necessarily or usually correspond exactly with the end of a section of the novel. The prose wanders off under merely rational control until one suddenly notices another lyric has been crumbled into it. This technique is quite close to Kermode's conception, and helps to account for the extraordinary lyric impetus of *Dr Zhivago*, and its tranquil freedom of spirit. It may well be that, for Boris Pasternak as a lyric poet, *Dr Zhivago* was the breaking of a dam.

This lyrical technique recurs, but I found it particularly noticeable in the first two chapters, so although I intend to enter hardly at all into formal literary criticism perhaps I should give some examples once and for all. Chapter 1 is called 'The Five o'Clock Express', and the train is spectacular, but consider the blowing of the wind in the first sentence and then at the end of the section, then five times in the second section. The wind carries on the chanting at the funeral, bears down on the boy and lashes him with rain, carries the plaintive hooting of engines, makes the acacias dance and the light flicker; its climax 'almost as if the snowstorm had caught sight of Uri and conscious of its power to terrify, roared, howled. . . . The blizzard was alone on earth and knew no rival.' That is the end of the wind, which has served its lyric purpose. Later there are recurring birds, horses, and so on, and the narrative is sprinkled with bits of autobiography unrelated to the story except as symbols: the Kologrivov place in section 4 is just like Obolenskoye, and in Moscow there are addresses the reader of this book will recognise. The novel is in a way about the freedom of spirit necessary to write the novel, about the poet's poetry and love and soul, but not about his biography. Its realism is a huge advance on the early prose and on *Spektorsky*, but it is not the fictional history of modern Russia people were waiting for. As for the formal influences that may help to explain the mysterious construction of what he did write, the only one I can think of that critics have neglected is Charles Dickens's *A Tale of Two Cities*, which his cousin Olga notes was almost always on or near his desk while he was writing *Dr Zhivago*. 'It was the best of times, the worst of times . . .' That treatment of the French revolution throws light on Pasternak's developed view of 1917.

He wrote in his awkward but oddly attractive English to John Harris in February 1959 about how the book is meant to work: 'There are aphorisms, definitions, statements in my novel. But the chief participation of thought in it does not lie in these open sentences (opinions uttered in dialogues, author's notes, etc. etc.) but in the hidden tendency which penetrates the very manner of my display of reality, of my description. Here, in my change of times, style of movement, character of colours, arrangement of groups is my latent unsaid philosophy. I could say more: my philosophy itself, as a whole, is in general rather an *inclination* than a conviction. . . . What matters in this case are not the different, separate notions and sayings, but the constant peculiar light in which everything is seen, lived, reflected and said.'

The light is surely that of Christianity and of poetry: details of the text constantly reflect particular bits of poems as of early prose. The death of the boy commissar Gintz, for example, becomes an allegory or a fable, however brutally it finishes, and the train that carries Zhivago homewards has shadows that leap across it and out of the opposite windows as the lights did earlier. The forest clearing where the soldiers encamp in the same chapter, with its wild strawberries and timber and abandoned huts, is not only idyllic: it is like a poem, though the poem is aborted: it is reduced to an elegiac note or two about the Tolstoyan rebels like English Levellers. The timber of the Cossack horse-vans, reduced by time to a close affinity with natural timber, is part of this lost poem. But Pasternak's letters make clear an overriding mystical and religious intention. I have felt this in many rereadings of the novel itself, even in its small-scale complexities and enigmas. In 1959, when he wrote to Harris, he was getting further away from the writing of the text, and he was a dying man; his interpretations of his book doubtless grew more intensely mystical than they might have been earlier. Still, one must accept both the sincerity and the reality of his vision of what gives meaning to *Zhivago*, and perhaps to life itself.

The epilogue confirms this: it is written in a despair curiously streaked with hope. Pasternak's political view of the first thirty years of his life had probably remained the same or intensified. When Zhivago went home to Moscow from the war, 'Here too were his loyalty to the revolution and his admiration for it, the revolution in the sense in which it was accepted by the middle classes and in which it has been understood by the students, followers of Blok, in 1905.' Later his experience became wide, and he saw human consequences work themselves out: hence the vast range of the book. But still 'civic institutions should be founded on democracy, they should grow up from below, like seedlings that are planted and take root in the soil. You can't hammer them in from above like stakes for a fence.' His old metaphor had been that Mayakovskian poetry would become compulsory, 'like potatoes under Catherine the Great'. His hope for Russia, and the meaning that he saw in history, could be more easily stated in religious or mystical terms than in any others. He wrote in August 1959 to Stephen Spender that he had seen nature and the world as a kind of painted canvas roof, pulling and blowing and flapping in the air, 'an unknown, unknowable wind'. In the same letter he says, 'there is an effort in the novel to represent the whole sequence of facts and beings and happenings like some moving entireness, like a developing, passing by, rolling and rushing inspiration, as if reality itself had freedom and choice and was composing itself out of numberless variants and versions.' This is not a Hegelian or a Marxist or any other classic philosopher's view of history; it is his own.

But the story, like every long story since the *Iliad*, consists of its details. The multiplicity of its characters is so dazing that at one point the Collins translation leaves them out; this occurs early in the book with a long list of guests at a pre-war party, which in Russian, as the English critic Ronald Hingley points out, is as resonant as 'Old Uncle Tom Cobbleigh and all', but has no other obvious place in the strategy of the novel.

After five or six full rereadings I still find it as hard to remember who is who in *Dr Zhivago* as in the *Iliad*. *Dr Zhivago*, like the *Iliad*, is based on earlier attempts, and in that way it can be studied as a development of themes. The history of the text was fully rehearsed in *Novy Mir* for 1988, no. 6, and in the Moscow edition of *Dr Zhivago* (1989). The prose fragments written between 1937 and 1939, to which one may add the mastery of style in his wartime reporting, show a particular affinity with the novel, discussed in detail in Henry Gifford's *Pasternak* (pp. 176ff.) But only in *Zhivago* does he call Lenin 'vengeance incarnate' and Stalin a 'pockmarked Caligula', and deride Marxism as unobjective, uncontrolled, unscientific, and having something in common with medriocrities and 'victims of the herd instinct'. In the concrete, in terms of characters, he is less harsh and more penetrating. He is excellent at the old, embittered railwaymen, like grim and silent gods at whose feet the revolution laid its smoking sacrifices. No writer has been more conscious of the paths of young extremists or of the irony of events. Vignettes of characters tied loosely to the edges of history and of this book are like separate short stories, but their oblique, sometimes unspoken, commentary on the central narrative is essential.

What makes *Zhivago* different from other books and, as Boris Pasternak knew, quite different from his earlier lyric poetry is the fullness of its integrity and the range of its wisdom. There are awkward sentences in it, which Akhmatova swatted like midges, but no unreadable pages, no boring paragraphs. One reads and re-

reads it, continually enthralled, and entering into a world one cannot really know. Why? Because it is written in what Eliot called a 'condition of complete simplicity, costing not less than every-thing'. And what is this work about? Not religion, not even poetry, though its poetry is essential to it as the fine point of Zhivago's expression, and the assurance of his immortality. It is about suffering, about war, civil war, revolution and the hell of life, and among these the tracks of love, which are so painful and so moving and without which we could not live. It is a love story as his own life was: the women characters are multiple, but Tanya has a bit more of Zinaida in her youth, and Lara more of Olga Ivinskaya in hers.

Before going through the book or the affair of Boris and Olga in any more detail, it would be best to look closely at the Zhivago poems. Some of them can be attached to precise places in the prose text, but some cannot, and it does not seem to matter, since they form a series, and they are all written by a mature poet who has turned his back on the state and intends to tell the truth about it. His simplicity has become stony and prose-like, but that only means that one can feel the force of prose behind the force of poetry, as one often can in the mature poetry of Yeats. That analogy is worth pursuing, because they both had to extricate themselves from dream-worlds, from symbolism and from a prose habit which was relatively arty. It was Yeats who began the *Oxford Book of Modern Verse* with Walter Pater's prose statement about the Virgin of the Rocks: a rare example in English of the German *Kunst-Prose* Boris Pasternak admired. The Zhivago poems are on the whole hard and clear, more so than those of Acmeist poets, who are more like French Parnassians such as Heredia; but at this time the lonely survivor of that school, Anna Akhmatova, had changed her style too.

The order of the poems is probably important, since it draws attention to a correspondence between the first poem and the last. We know independently that Boris Pasternak took a high view of Hamlet, whom he thought a noble character, no mere ditherer, and we know that his poem 'Hamlet' was in a way prophetic of the storm that would break on his head when *Dr Zhivago* was published. The book was written knowingly, but Boris had early experience of the role of reluctant Hamlet from the twenties and thirties; it may even have been basic to his psychology. In these poems Hamlet is like Christ, and the series ends with Christ in the garden of Gethsemane, a Christ who is like Hamlet, longing for the cup to be taken away. But this restatement of the Hamlet theme, which obsesses several poems at the end of the series, adds a prophecy.

> The book of life has turned the page
> to what is holy and most precious to men,
> what is written shall be fulfilled:
> so be it. Amen.

> Look. Centuries of years like parables
> passed, each on fire as it went:
> in the name of its terrible majesty I shall go
> freely down to the grave through torment.

> And on the third day I shall rise again,
> like rafts going downriver, like a long line of barges
> they shall float down to me from their darkness
> to be judged, and I shall judge the centuries.

To take these last poems first, the whole Christian section is in the position of climax at the end. It begins with 'Christian Star', a long Dutch Nativity scene with the rhythm of a gentle snowfall, which we know from early in the novel to be a tribute to Blok. 'It occurred to him that Blok was a manifestation of Christmas in the life and art of modern Russia – Christmas in the life of this northern city, Christmas under the starry skies of its modern streets and round the lighted trees of its twentieth century drawing-room. There was no need to write an article on Blok, he thought, all you needed to do was to paint a Russian version of a Dutch Adoration of the Magi, with snow in it, and wolves, and a dark fir-forest.' The poem is original and surprising; it is a landscape poem and one that casually makes itself a position where there seemed no room, a poem that makes itself at home among all existing poems, yet with no concession to cliché. 'Angrier and wickeder the wind blew from the steppe', though there are no wolves. At the end, 'Gazing at the Virgin like a guest, the Christmas Star was standing in the doorway'.

Next comes 'Daybreak', a poem that expresses charity, a

Christian outlook. It is a restatement of the title poem from *On Early Trains*, about travelling into Moscow on the community train. One might have taken 'Daybreak' to express socialist warmth and camaraderie. 'All night I read your testament . . . I want to be among people . . . and bring them to their knees. . . . In me are people without names. Children, stay-at-homes, trees. I am conquered by them all, this is my only victory.' It goes deeper than the poem it restates, though that does not necessarily make it a better poem; the context makes it more powerful, that is all. 'The Miracle' follows: it is the miracle of the barren fig tree that Christ cursed, here applied not to Israel but, I assume, to Russia. The next poem, 'The Earth', is about spring in Moscow. Zhivago (or Pasternak) feels his calling extends to a responsibility 'that the distances should not lose heart, the earth should not feel lonely'. So he gathers with his friends, 'and our evenings are farewells and our parties are testaments', like the Last Supper, we must assume, 'So that the secret stream of suffering should warm the cold of life.' This looks like another poem of applied Christianity, sandwiched like 'Daybreak' between two mythological Christian poems. The series ends with 'Evil Days', which is about Christ when the crowd turns on him, then the two 'Mary Magdalene' poems, of Bach-like grief and redemption, and 'Gethsemane'. The last stanza of 'Evil Days' is about Christ's memory: the fluttering candle goes back a long way in Pasternak's poetry and life.

> And the poor in their hovel, gathering,
> and going down to the vault, candle lighted,
> and the candle in terror snuffing out
> when Lazarus stood up out of the dead.

Those of these poems that are not about fear like Hamlet's transformed to Christ's (a theme that first appears, I think, in *Lieutenant Schmidt*) are all touched with the Resurrection. They were all the more of a wonder in Russia, because this kind of poetry, which in England might almost have been written by a rural dean in the eighteenth century, simply does not exist in Russian. Its formal source for Boris Pasternak was probably in Lutheran hymns. Congregational hymns of that kind do not exist in Russian either. The Russians have splendid and far more exciting kinds of religious poetry. Pasternak has made native in his

language a new kind of poetry, and done so with complete
assurance. When the question of printing *Dr Zhivago* arose again in
the eighties, it appears to have been these innocent religious verses
that struck longest in the craw of the authorities, but they were
printed in the end in 1988, first of all in *Nouy Mir*.

The poem 'Hamlet' which opens the entire series and echoes
right through it, is famous. Robert Lowell translated it as the
second part of what he calls 'Hamlet in Russia: A Soliloquy'. For
the first he adapts a poem we have already looked at, about a boat
throbbing on the water and the trailing willow, with the sudden
cry 'My sister life . . .' But the 'Hamlet' part is fairly accurate, and
like all Lowell's *Imitations* (1962) it has a force of its own.

> The clapping stops. I walk into the lights
> as Hamlet, lounge like a student against the door-frame,
> and try to catch the far-off dissonance of life –
> all that has happened, and must!
>
> From the dark the audience leans its one hammering brow
>     against me –
> the thousand opera glasses, each set on the tripod!
> Abba, Father, all things are possible with thee –
> take away this cup!
>
> I love the mulishness of Providence,
> I am content to play the one part I was born for . . .
> quite another play is running now . . .
> take me off the hooks tonight!
>
> The sequence of scenes was well thought out;
> the last bow is in the cards, or the stars –
> but I am alone, and there is none . . .
> All's drowned in the sperm and spittle of the Pharisee –
>
> To live a life is not to cross a field . . .

The last sentence is a pre-existing proverb. There follows a
poem called 'March' seething with rustic life, then 'In Holy Week',
relating the natural countryside to the Orthodox liturgy and lightly

tinged at the end with the coming Resurrection. It is not as forceful as the later Christian poems. 'White Night' remembers Petersburg; it is a memory of a girl student from Kursk, 'daughter of a small landowner of the steppes'. I am unable to fit this poem exactly into the novel, but nor can I find poems to fit all the moments in the novel when Zhivago writes them. This poem is light and generous, and its nightingales are thunderously loud in the woods. 'Spring Floods' has nightingales even more prominent, and linked with the nightingale of a famous and ominous folksong from southern Russia called 'Ilya of Murom and Nightingale the Robber'. 'Sparks and fire poured from his mouth and nostrils, he piped like a nightingale, roared like an auroch, and hissed like a dragon,' says the epic, and his whistle caused an earthquake that destroyed the city of Kiev. Pasternak was fond of him, and in this poem it seemed he would come out of his forest lair to meet the partisans. This poem and the next, 'Explanation', which is about a difficult love affair, can be more or less anchored in the novel; so perhaps can 'Summer in Town', which is about a woman, and 'Wind', if only because *Dr Zhivago* is full of wind-blasts and storms. Akhmatova said once how thrilled Annensky would have been to see his storm-winds lashing the pages of Pasternak's poems: this is just, but by now Boris Pasternak more than any other modern poet had made bad weather his own.

The poems deliberately move on through seasons. After the slight love-epigram 'Intoxication', which is love in the open air, we come to 'Indian Summer', 'The Wedding-Party' and 'Autumn'. They are magnificently direct poems about happy days: they fit precisely into the novel. But after 'A Fairy Tale' we are back to 'August'. I had thought this poem was sad, even tragic, and that its unhappiness probably placed it here. But the third part of it transforms all into an allegory of love overcoming dangers and lasting as it seems for ever. No doubt Zhivago is writing later, thinking back to the lost summer. After this comes one of the most mesmerising and beautiful of all his lyrics, 'Winter Night'.

> Snow sweeping across earth
> sweeping from end to end,
> on the table a candle burned,
> only a candle burned.

> Like swarms of summer gnats
> that the flame draws
> flocks of snowflakes
> pressed to the windows.
>
> Driven snow drew shapes
> on the glass without end,
> on the table a candle burned
> only a candle burned . . .

I despair of conveying the spirit of this simple and perfect poem. It is powerful in the same way as a Victorian poem, yet it is perfectly modern, indeed it is almost prose. It reads as if Zhivago has taken over from his creator and developed a life of his own, as so often happens to novelists, so that Pasternak was seeing with his hero's eyes. 'Parting' and 'Meeting' convey the same sensation, and then we come to 'Christmas Star'. If I have dwelt a long time on the Zhivago poems it is not just because I think them so remarkable: they are not more remarkable than the prose text. But they give that text a powerful charge of emotional force, and of what I can only call inner life. By more directly expressing what Zhivago himself most deeply means they show you what the book means. They are arranged in a series in which his happiness in love reaches a climax in the summer and his deeper Christianity, which comes at the end, is more slowly achieved. Hamlet becomes Christ so slowly that one hardly notices. It may be worth adding that those who see *Dr Zhivago* as an epic novel (a phrase I personally find inappropriate) should consider the strange sub-epic narratives of Russian tradition, the folksongs of the Kiev cycle, which have had a more formative influence on Boris Pasternak than Homer and Virgil and Milton. 'Nightingale the Robber' is the only direct allusion, yet one often feels that folksongs are in the back of his mind. They may well have helped him attain the clarity of his narrative in *Dr Zhivago*, which is like spring water.

Dr Zhivago is written as a novel in two parts, with seven chapters in each, then a conclusion and an epilogue at the end of the second. The big division comes after the revolution, at the arrival near Varykino, far to the east, at the far side of the Urals. The first part is Zhivago's pre-war life, his marriage, the war and its consequences, including the revolution. But it is only in the second half that the poet finds himself; the lover follows a path far beyond normal matrimony, and it is fair to say that he both suffers and grows accordingly. The revolution also begins to sort itself out. The fact that old characters recur seems to me to mean only that this is what might become of such a type, such a person, a man in such a job, or such a man's son. Certain characters do remain enigmatic, though they are probably meant to be intelligible enough, such as Pasha Antipov and perhaps Yevgraf. Numerous events which were once taught in schools are now beginning to fade from memory, but Pasternak wrote for those who knew them; he wrote about what happened thirty years earlier, expecting much to be familiar. The names of characters are often apparent hints to their meaning, but are not systematic or very helpful. Yevgraf means 'good recorder' or 'evangelist'; he is possibly a sort of good angel. On the other hand Mikulin is named after a river. Zhivago means 'Life', or 'Doctor Lively', but I understand Boris Pasternak found the name, however pleased he was by finding it, on the iron cover of a manhole somewhere in Moscow. The book may be pregnant with hidden symbolism, but not to me, so having recorded this aspect of the book I will now ignore it.

'The Five o'Clock Express' is a lyrical introduction to what were meant to be some principal themes of the entire book. New characters occur on every page, and we see a variety of provincial places and railway trains. The first section is the funeral of Zhivago's mother. He climbs on top of her grave and all but howls like a wolf. The wind and the rain lash on him, then his uncle Kolya, a distinctly unmotherly unfrocked priest, leads him off to a monastery where they spend the night. Kolya works for a progressive newspaper in a provincial town on the Volga. The evening is cold and spooky, and the snowstorm howls, roars and terrifies the poor child. He is ten years old, deserted by his father long ago in favour of 'wenching and carousing'. Two years later the boy is taken to see another progressive writer in the country, which he hears is ripe for revolution. Kolya becomes for a brief moment interesting, because he is a man going somewhere unknown: the books that will make him famous are still unwritten, he has been a priest, a Tolstoyan and 'a revolutionary idealist', his mind moves freely and 'welcomes the unfamiliar'. But the progressive writer, who lives on the estate of a progressive millionaire, is as dry as dust; his conversation has a period flavour,

as Pasternak intended. Kolya explains how Christ has altered the
meaning of death, and refers in passing to the deadness of Rome
and the horrors of its pockmarked Caligula: surely Stalin.

Young Zhivago is twelve, but he weeps himself into fits for his
mother, on his own in the woods. Meanwhile an express train has
halted in the marshes, because of a suicide, which is actually that of
his father, though no one knows that except the reader. The father
was travelling with a 'thick-set, haughty lawyer' who will turn out
to be Zhivago's evil genius, and the same train is full of characters
we shall meet again. Misha Gordon is a Jewish boy, and with him
the problem of Jewish consciousness is squarely faced, though it
never gets developed. There is also an old woman whose husband
was burned to death in an accident, and whose sons are engine
drivers. We enter quite deeply into Misha and his problems, and
into Nicky, a boy in the house, two years older than Zhivago and
the son of a terrorist and a princess. Nicky tries to kiss a girl on a
lake, but they both fall in. So far, almost none of these expansively
sketched characters have met or talked to one another. It is as if
Pasternak were merely experimenting, but that is the end of the
chapter. Nicky's adolescence will have to do for Zhivago's, and
Kolya and his writer friend will have to stand for a generation.

Writers do not have many themes or devices, they constantly
re-use the same ones, so it is easy to pick up allusions to Boris
Pasternak's own life, but at a deeper level: there is no tendency to
autobiography here, rather the opposite. Why do both Zhivago's
parents die? I think simply to get them out of the way. The riches
that were lost are just romance: the smell in the woods reminded
him of his mother at Antibes and Bordighera, and there was once
an estate like an enchanted kingdom. You could tell your sleigh
driver to take you there: can it have been Samarin's Peredelkino?
'The park closed round you as quiet as a countryside; cows
scattered the hoar-frost as they settled on the heavy branches of the
firs; their cawing echoed like cracking wood; pedigree dogs came
running across the road out of the clearing where building was
going on and where lights shone in the gathering dusk. Suddenly it
all vanished. They became poor.' How beautiful it is, and how
strange, this extremely Russian paradise lost.

'A Girl from a Different World' begins in 1904 or 1905. It might
as well be called 'Youth'. The wicked lawyer Komarovsky features
here, and it all happens in Moscow: a mean hotel in Oruzheinyi

Street, a repellent old dressmaker and her daughter Lara. In this chapter Zhivago becomes friendly with Misha and hears about his father's death. There seems to be a lot of Dickens in all this. The characters are so numerous they even include a canary in a cage called Kyril Modestovich. When Lara goes to sleep her thoughts are Boris Pasternak's, of the stuffed bears in the windows of the coachmakers' and the dragoons parading at the barracks. There are magnificent station scenes, and we meet Antipov's father, the track overseer, and an entire interlocking world of railway workers and their families. It was obviously Pasternak's intention to use these people, whom he knew from childhood, to show how the revolution had happened, and to people it with human faces. At times he overdoes the typical: 'As usual the old foreman, Pyotr Khudoleyev, was walloping Yusupka the apprentice.' But it is here and among railway workers that the plot begins to be gripping. We have had no high-life characters except the ghastly lawyer. The demonstration at the Arts School is formalised like a tale too often told, but the charge of the dragoons is brilliant, unexpected and sickening. Meanwhile Kolya has come to Moscow to write and sees the dragoons from his window. Zhivago now has lodging with a professor whose daughter is Tanya; Misha is close to them both. The young people read Tolstoy's *Kreutzer Sonata* and believe in chastity: this may or may not throw some light on Boris Pasternak's adolescent hang-ups. Kolya warbles on about the inward music of man, 'the irresistible power of unarmed truth', and Komarovsky corrupts Lara.

In the middle of all of this, the Presnya rising takes place. Nicky and Pasha go to the barricades. People poured over them bucket after bucket of water, which froze immediately and must have made them formidable obstacles to horses. Nothing else could explain why determined cavalry was not able to clear the streets in an hour. 'The two boys were playing the most terrible and adult of games. . . . Good decent boys, thought Lara, it is because they are good they are shooting.' Zhivago really is just a boy, and he and Misha go with the doctor for fun for what turns out to be a gruesome visit to Lara's mother's attempted suicide. They are both embarrassed, but Zhivago's feelings are distinctly ambivalent; sex raises its head for him, and he has seen Lara. Throughout this chapter, as history and the novel gather pace, the most gripping element is the tiny details of railways and cold weather. Pasternak has not only created world beyond world of people but, more difficult still, a city. 'The air smelt of early winter in town – of trampled maple leaves, melted snow, and warm engine soot and rye bread just out of the oven (it was baked in the basement of the station buffet). Trains came and went and were shunted, coupled and uncoupled to the waving, furling and unfurling of signal flags. The deep engine hooters roared, and the horns and whistles of the guards and shunters tooted and trilled. Smoke rose in endless ladders to the sky, and hissing engines scalded the cold winter clouds with clouds of boiling steam.'

'Christmas Party at the Sventitskys'' sees Tanya ready to graduate in law, Misha in philosophy and Yura Zhivago in medicine. His youth has therefore passed with only those incidents recorded which might have personal or do have historical significance. These experiences have been unpleasant, but it is hard to see that they make any difference to him in the future, since he emerges as sage, middle class, a doctor and a poet. Yet the book is cumulative, so one senses the suffering in its early chapters as if it were always present in him, and as if it somehow explained his quality of love, and the hidden impulse of his poetry. The superficial roots of poems occur in this third chapter, which begins and ends with death, resurrection in all its forms still being the conscious subject-matter of the whole work. Even in the dissecting room, Zhivago is thrilled by the mystery of other lives, and in section 3 he makes his first attempt at talking about the conquest of death. He is completely serious about this religious or philosophic comfort, of which Russia was deprived not by fashionable atheism but by the state. What he says therefore emerges with great force. No doubt that is also the point of the Christmas party. The roots of the poems appear superficial, yet the poems themselves are deeply felt. They are 'Winter Night' and 'Christmas Star'.

The melodramatic event of this chapter is Lara's shooting of Kamarovsky; it stands out even more vividly than the background rumble of history and the oddly beautiful process of the growing up of Lara and young Antipov, but the themes of life and burial are more deeply dramatic than any melodrama, and here they surround the shooting like heavy black edging on old letter paper. The wound is not at all bad. 'Well, you've been lucky. It's not even worth bandaging. A drop of iodine wouldn't do any harm though.' It is little more than symbolic, like a slap on the face, but the pistol no doubt derives from old stories about girls of the People's Will association in the last century, and the pistol-owning girl in *Spektorsky*. Yet as fiction it is perfectly judged, it seems the exact truth. One cannot imagine a Lara who would slap the lawyer's face, or a Lara who would be a good shot. The shooting gets a further revolutionary colouring from the presence of Kornakov, a prosecution lawyer against the railwaymen who in real life made a fanatical speech against them.

'The Advent of the Inevitable' takes us to 1917, to the excitements of the first revolution. Lara ends it remembering 1905, 'but how much more frightening it was now! You couldn't say, It's the children shooting, this time. The children had all grown up, the boys were all here, in the army.' It is interesting to what degree Lara rather than Zhivago is the consciousness and conscience on which the revolution registers. There is something persistently pure about the way in which she sees things: Zhivago by comparison is just a benevolent liberal, passive because he is a poet, no doubt. We begin with Komarovsky in the ruins of Christmas; Lara is ill and recovers, Pasha marries her and hears her past, so that he never recovers. The Antipovs move away to Yuryatin, where Lara's parents had lived, Zhivago is shown brilliantly at work in a hospital, his wife Tanya has a son. He goes on to the war, where he behaves with a patience and devotion we are beginning to recognise. The minor characters conduct their lives with passionate unsuccess. Antipov dislikes Yuryatin; he feels that what Lara loves is only her own heroism, and sets off on that ruthless intellectual journey which will transform him into the terrible civil war figure of Strelnikov.

But Boris Pasternak adores Yuryatin, so to dislike it is to fail as his reader. Lara loves it. It stands on the railway and on a big river; in fact it sounds much like Chistopol. 'A sign of approaching winter in Yuryatin was that people took their boats out of the river. . . . The sight of the boats with their light, upturned bottoms in the shadows of the yards meant in Yuryatin what the migration of the storks or the first snow meant in other places. . . . Lara liked Yuryatin's provincial ways, the long vowels of its northern accent and its naïvely trusting intellectuals in felt boots and grey flannel sleeveless coats.' The war zone is treated as a vast, smouldering chaos, like that of the Orel front in 1943. It is magnificently awful, and its violence is unpredictable. Pasternak shows with intelligent economy how it becomes a way of life. Its astonishing coincidences are always connected with death, but it has unaccountable islands of safety. Pasternak has considered the styles of war journalism quite carefully, and in section 12 we get a sharp analysis of what is wrong with them, which turns to analysis of nationalism, Judaism and the gospels. 'Why don't the intellectual leaders of the Jewish people ever get beyond fashionable *Weltschmertz* and irony?' Why in fact are they not Tolstoyans? These two or three pages of powerful polemic are difficult to answer, and have therefore caused great offence; he is never so rude about Russians.

'Farewell to the Past' follows with stunning swiftness. The technique of leaving things to happen between chapters means that Pasternak seems to be bursting with things to say. The revolution was passed over with some criticism of the Tsar and a paragraph or two of shooting in Petersburg. 'Farewell to the Past' begins with Lara as a nurse and Zhivago as a doctor setting up the future affair which is going to consume them both. A lot of space is given to the strange but probably typical episode of the independent republic of Zabushino, which Pasternak links to the seventeenth century. It was a millennial kingdom set up by the local miller, who was a Christian of some strange sect and had corresponded with Tolstoy. It was an independent republic of one village and some armed deserters, ruled by a council called the Apostolic Seat. Of course it was crazy and doomed; it lasted just over two weeks in the June of 1917.

Its meaning for Pasternak is its comparative authenticity, its wildness and unregenerate peasant quality, on which the official revolution closes in. We see the machinery of repression beginning (inevitably of course) to operate. The death of the young commissar Glintz who falls into a water-butt, gets shot and then bayoneted to death, is its symbol. The tall and ghostly figures of the mounted Cossacks with swords drawn among the trees, standing in a circle round the clearing ready to move in, is equally unforgettable. From this episode Zhivago goes home to Moscow by train. He travels with a deaf-mute who gives him a duck, having been on a shooting expedition. Is this the same deaf-mute who took part in the brief republic? Who is he? The incident remains so far as I can see enigmatic, as if Zhivago were like a character in *The*

*Magic Flute*, searching for the right way among events he was unable to decode.

All these seven chapters, even though they constitute half the book, were intended to set up Zhivago's adventures in the Urals, so both Yuryatin and the vivid forest clearing of Zabushino are foretastes. One has the impression that by the end of chapter 5 Pasternak was hurrying to get to the main unfolding of his story in part two. Chapter 6 is 'Moscow Bivouac': at the beginning Zhivago is in his slow train, and at the end he sets out for Yuryatin. 'It had seemed to Yuri that only the train was moving, that time stood still and it was still only midday.' In Moscow the squares were crowded but there was nothing to buy and they were unswept. 'Already he saw, shrinking against the walls, thin, decently dressed old men and women, who stood like a silent reproach to the passers-by, wordlessly offering what no one needed.' At home he finds 'streets dirty, roofs leaking, bellies empty. . . . There will be all sorts of horrors this winter, famine, cold . . .' He loves his child but he finds himself isolated: even Uncle Kolya has come home as a Bolshevik, and Nicky is keen on Mayakovsky, though Zhivago is not. Maybe in real life Zhivago would have been closer to the Acmeists? But the scarcely submerged Christian and socialist disturbance of the Zhivago poems would have torn apart any formal surface: he was himself alone, and isolated. In section 4 we see that the revolution had not yet reached its flood-tide.

'The town is getting to be like a forest. There's a smell of rotten leaves and mushrooms.' The streetlights are so weak you bump into them, muggings are on the increase. Pasternak shows the breakdown of civilisation with exquisite precision. His hero rescues a street victim, who protects him; the author feels that is necessary in the suspicious world of 1917. Fighting breaks out in the street, and Soviet power is proclaimed in the papers. Zhivago reads about it by a streetlight in a snowstorm: an oddly un-forgettable vignette. 'He was shaken and overwhelmed by the greatness of the moment, and thought of its significance for centuries to come.' He brings home this broadsheet, which he feels is a work of genius; 'Only real greatness can be so misplaced and so untimely.' It has Pushkin's directness, he says, and Tolstoy's bold attachment to the facts. These praises are in no way exaggerated; if the early weeks of the revolution gave us nothing else, they gave us

an incomparable boldness of style, just as the American revolution
did. But trouble of many kinds follows, including typhus. His
enigmatic younger half-brother Yevgraf looks after him when he
has fever, and advises the family to clear out of Moscow, so they set
off for Yuryatin. Zhivago plans a poem about Christ in the tomb
and 'Time to awake and get up, time to arise, time for the
resurrection.'

The last chapter of the first part is about the journey east. It opens
with an even more withering depiction of conditions in the new
Soviet state. Even the sweet old family servant can no longer be
trusted. 'At the militia post which he had selected as his political
club, he did not actually say that his former masters sucked his
blood, but he accused them of having kept him in ignorance all
these years, and deliberately concealed from him that the world is
derived from apes.' There really was a Tsarist decree against the
dissemination of Darwinism. The party leave at dawn, in a fall of
snow, to join the gypsy caravan of the long train. 'Tanya had never
travelled in a freight truck before.' They have plenty of time to
meet conscripts, co-operativists and peasants, whose intertwining
stories we learn. It is as if by merely being on this train they are
plunged into the heart of the Russian people. Any reader of
Maurice Baring's account of Russian journeys twelve years earlier
will recognise the truth of this, though in his day the first-class
carriages had a library, a piano, and real bathrooms.

As they approach the end of their journey, the state of civil war
begins to press around them. The signs of hope are natural: a
morning of sawing in the forest, an overwhelming leafless wood
with a mighty waterfall, a few wild cherry trees in blossom. But
Yuryatin is under siege, and Zhivago has an ominous wayside
conversation with Strelnikov, whose name means Shooter,
though they nickname him the Executioner. Zhivago turns out to
have been 'twice wounded and invalided out', which is new to us:
Pasternak does not bother about such details until they seem useful
or necessary. 'These are apocalyptic times,' says Strelnikov, 'this is
the Last Judgement. This is a time for angels with flaming swords
and winged beasts from the abyss, not for sympathisers and loyal
doctors.' Zhivago refuses to have it out with him, but the
conversation, we are warned, is only postponed.

The second part of the book opens with chapter 8, 'Arrival', of
which the climax is a conversation about Pasha Antipov, who was

such a good science teacher, and was killed in the war. (In fact he was taken prisoner, as we already know.) 'Some people say this scourge of ours, Commissar Strelnikov, is Antipov risen from the dead. But it's only a silly rumour of course. It's most improbable. Though who can tell, anything's possible. A little more tea?' The chapter is not otherwise very exciting: they are swallowed up slowly into local interests and local perspectives before arriving. Zhivago makes his cutting and very important attack on Marxism to a local bigwig, and at the country station they are befriended by the ancient station master, who knows Tanya's family of course, though he warns them to be careful about mentioning that connection. They are driven to her confiscated parental estate by a white mare with a black foal, and for a moment life is lyrical. 'Everything pleased and astonished them, above all the unceasing chatter of their cranky old driver, in whose speech archaic idioms, traces of Tartar influence, and local oddities of language mingled with those of his own invention.' Whenever the foal lagged behind, the mare waited for him. They confuse the driver with a figure from a folk-tale, and he sings a folksong, a debased jingle from the pre-war factory, but with a beauty of its own as such ballads have. His language is well observed and beautiful too. The superior peasant family in possession, the Mikulitsins, receive them suspiciously but take them in.

Chapter 9, 'Varykino', opens with the core of the entire novel, Zhivago's diary. At the end of it he has met Lara in Yuryatin, he knows who Strelnikov is, and as he rides home he is captured by the partisans in the forest. I do not know how far the analogy can be pressed, but if there is something in common between the circles of this novel, pressing spiritually inward and physically outward, and the circles of Dante's heaven and hell, then the circle of this chapter is a kind of paradise. When the partisans take him away, one thinks at once not of his fate or his deserted wife and child, but of the forest and of his love of the people. The scene for that feeling has been set by the old man who drove them from the station in chapter 8. His diary deals seriously with poetry. It begins by quoting Tyutchev:

> What summer, what summer,
> this is magical indeed,
> how did such days fall upon us
> unlooked for and unmerited?

The record of Zhivago's happiness and his hard, physical work recalls nothing in Boris Pasternak's life but Peredelkino. There he dug his own potatoes and cultivated what in England would be an allotment, and was often seen doing it. The others employed gardeners, but he really enjoyed the work. When someone toasted him not as a poet but as a working man, the stonemason of Russian literature with his sleeves rolled up, he cried out, 'That's right, that's what I am, a working man.' Lev Ozerov remembers the occasion, which anyway was not unique. I find Zhivago's diary, which is written with the laconic delicacy of which Boris was a master, the best part of the book. Everything that went before it was necessary in order that we should believe in such a man, writing such a diary as he writes, at such a time. For one thing, it brilliantly carries on the narrative, through what might have seemed static. 'We have been lucky. The autumn has been dry and warm. It gave us time to dig up the potatoes.' His potatoes have become more exciting to the reader than world politics. The diary is also extremely beautiful.

They re-read *War and Peace*, *Eugene Onegin*, all Pushkin's poems, Stendhal's *Le Rouge et le Noir*, Dickens's *A Tale of Two Cities* and Kleist's short stories. If ever there were a heavy hint about the formal origins of a book, no doubt this is it. 'We go on endlessly re-reading *Eugene Onegin* and the poems.' He considers art in section 4, and style in section 6. 'We go on discussing Pushkin' and the choice of metre in his juvenilia. He comes on a nightingale in Pushkin which is conventional, but it excites him to quote 'The Nightingale the Robber'.

> At the nightingale's whistle, the wild forest voice,
> The grass was a-trembling, the petals were shed,
> And all the dark forest, it bowed to the ground,
> And all the good people were falling down dead.

He remembers Turgenev on the nightingale, and records its notes as he heard them: *Tyock-tyock-tyock*. At this point Yevgraf appears again as a *deus ex machina* with unexplained powers. I believe one must assume that is how Pasternak believed in his own protection and survival, not as the influence of Lunacharsky or Bukharin, still less of Scriabin's cousin Molotov, but as something magical. Or can it be that Yevgraf is an invented apotheosis of his younger brother Sasha, or that he had to invent Yevgraf, as I think most likely, in order to explain the survival of a poet unlike himself, one without acquaintance with Lunacharsky or Bukharin, a poet of absolute integrity? 'In the distance, where the sun was refusing to go down, a nightingale began to sing. "Wake up, wake up" it called entreatingly; it sounded almost like the summons on the eve of Easter Sunday: Awake O my soul, why sleepest thou?' He is going to meet Lara again, and Tanya's marriage is doomed.

Chapter 10 is called 'The Highway', chapter 11 'The Forest Brotherhood' and chapter 12 'Red Rowanberries'. This forest episode with Zhivago among the partisans is quite a large slice of the book, much more than a tenth. The episode is set among archaic Cossack villages along the old post road into Siberia. Pasternak remembers with awe the old political prisoners: tea, bread and pig-iron travelled one way, and prisoners in chains the other. Village to village, and town to town, the people were linked by friendship and by marriage. In the distant past before the railway came (not so very distant) the mail went by troika, and the condemned 'walked in step, jangling their fetters – lost, desperate souls as terrible as heavenly lightning – and around them rustled the dark, impenetrable forest.' When he wrote that, did Pasternak know about the modern counterpart of these men, even more miserable? Undoubtedly he did. Zhivago arrived in a village on a Holy Thursday, and the narrative hints at the liturgy, but with no hope of the Resurrection. The partisan leader believes that 'only through the Soviets can the alliance between the town poor and the country poor be achieved', but we shall see that hope fail and the depths of Russia betrayed. The portrait of these peasant partisans is as full as *The Burghers* by Franz Hals: they are most carefully observed. The depiction includes an Easter feast, political argument and the dramas of the day. This tenth chapter might almost be by Thomas Hardy. I do not understand how Boris Pasternak knew so much about these people: one must assume he learned it during a couple of wartime winters. Or did he remember Samarin's stories? We know that he read what books there were.

The doctor has been a conscript, almost a prisoner with the partisans. In the transition between chapters, two years pass. He has tried to escape, but all attempts have failed. With typhus in winter, dysentery in summer, and more and more wounded, he is up to his eyes in work. The civil war is more ghastly than the war.

An amulet on the chest of a dead man contains a text mistranscribed
from old Slavonic, a jumble of words from the ninety–first psalm.

> He that dwelleth in the secret place of the most High, shall
> abide under the Shadow of the Almighty. . . .
> Thou shalt not be afraid for the terror by night; nor for the
> arrow that flieth by day.
> Nor for the pestilence that walketh in darkness; nor for the
> destruction that wasteth at noonday.
> A thousand shall fall at thy side, and ten thousand at thy right
> hand; but it shall not come nigh thee.

The words are a mere jumble, though being used as magic. The
partisans and the Whites, the anti-communist army, swing backwards and forwards in a deadly wrestle like Balin and Balan. Civil
war is in the first place a shock. It is at least thinkable that it was
with the Whites as much as the communists that Pasternak now
intended to make his peace. That may be going too far, but he was
deeply a Tolstoyan, and in section 5 of 'Forest Brotherhood'
Zhivago says so. In this encounter with the partisan leader, I have
the impression that Zhivago's quarrel with the state reaches its
deepest: it grounds on an absolute. He demands to be released. But
the season moves slowly, creeping towards winter, and he remains
enmeshed. The weather is still and dry, the woods are brilliant with
ripe berries. An old man called Pamphil loses his wits and goes
beserk with an axe.

'Iced Rowanberries' begins with the arrival of partisans'
families, including a witch who interests Pasternak greatly. She
must be drawn from life, but where and when? All these three
astonishing chapters are written as if he had actually lived the life of
Zhivago. They ring completely true, yet they are as distant from
us, or far more so, than *The Mayor of Casterbridge* or *Under the
Greenwood Tree*. Boris Pasternak has a freshness none of his
contemporaries achieve. In 'Iced Rowanberries' the weather
deteriorates. 'The rain skimmed and smoked over the pinewoods.'
We hear the witch's spell, which ends with a bit of an ancient
chronicle. Zhivago dreams of Lara, though earlier he dreamed of
his wife. 'High winter came with its grinding frosts', and he
escapes. 'Isn't that just like a gentleman's folly! Who's ever heard of
picking berries in winter! Three years we've been beating the

nonsense out of the gentry but they're still the same. All right, go and pick your berries you lunatic. What do I care?'

There are only two chapters left of the body of the novel. The thirteenth is 'The House of the Caryatids'. It begins when he gets into Yuryatin, and ends with a goodbye letter from his wife, who has got to know Lara and finally gone abroad. 'I am thankful to her for being constantly at my side when I was having a difficult time and for helping me through my confinement. I must honestly admit she is a good person, but I don't want to be a hypocrite – she is exactly the opposite of myself. I was born to make life simple and to look for sensible solutions, she – to complicate life and confuse the way.' This letter gives him a heart attack, and the few sentences I quote indicate the situation of Zinaida versus Olga Ivinskaya more than any other in the book. Indeed, Zinaida was to such an extent a protectress that she made various Stalinist remarks recorded by her enemies, though no one can know whether she made them for repetition, for the record, or for the microphone (as I suspect).

When Zhivago returns to civil life in chapter 13 he finds himself without papers and grossly disadvantaged. Nothing really happens except this tragedy working itself out; the good news is that he finds Lara. 'He had complained that Heaven had cast him off, but now the whole breadth of heaven leaned low over his bed holding out two strong, white woman's arms to him. His head swam with joy, he drifted into happiness as though he were losing his senses.' We are told that their conversation was like the dialogues of Plato, and that what united them was their hatred of 'shrill, textbook admirations, forced enthusiasm, deadly dullness', which sounds a little like Olga once again. In section 17 we get another sermon about Christianity, once again from a minor character such as Plato uses. Its principal interest is to illuminate the poems about Mary Magdalene.

The last chapter is called 'Varykino Again'. Komarovsky turns up, they flee to rustic solitude, and Zhivago writes poems. There he persuades Lara and her daughter to leave as Komarovsky suggested; in a sense, Komarovsky wins. There also Zhivago settles his account with Strelnikov, who is now perfectly friendly and a hunted man. The chapter ends with his death: Lara had been left alive only as a lure to him. If the diary was the core of this novel, then the poems Zhivago only now writes are its climax. The narrative is engrossing and swift, and Komarovsky as the devil's advocate gives it a smell of burning wheels. In section 8 Zhivago writes out his old, finished poems, 'which had taken the most complete shape in his mind', such as 'Christmas Star' and 'Winter Night'. He goes on to others, unfinished or only begun. 'After two or three stanzas and several images by which he himself was astonished, his work took possession and he experienced the approach of what is called inspiration.' Language itself took him over and 'turned wholly into music'. We are not told what he wrote in that state, which is fully described, but only of Zhivago's prayer to God, 'and all this is for me? Why hast thou given me so much. . . ?' He sees the white flame of light playing on the shadowless snow, and in the distance the wolves. One should notice that the creative moment for him is when language conforms miraculously to music.

In the next few days he goes on writing 'Fairy Tale'; he must find a connecting theme; he cuts the rhythm to lose its pomp 'as you cut out useless words in prose. . . . He heard the horse's hooves ringing on the surface of the poem as you hear the trotting of a horse in one of Chopin's Ballades.' But the wolves disappeared and the moment was over and Lara went away. I take it that this sad desertion was planned from the first page of chapter 1. He loses Lara just as he lost his mother, and well he might howl like a wolf. 'Do you hear? A dog howling. Even two of them I think. Oh how terrible. It's a very bad omen. Well, bear it till morning, and then we'll go, we'll go.' Too late of course.

'Conclusion' is a dead-pan record, like the conclusions of Dickens. 'All that is left is to tell the brief story of the last eight or ten years of Zhivago's life, years in which he went more and more to seed, gradually losing his knowledge and skill both as a doctor and as a writer.' Had Pasternak known such people? One fears he had. Zhivago came back to Moscow in the spring of 1922; at first he wrote booklets which a peasant friend printed, then he drifted. Once again, Boris Pasternak has an extremely sharp eye for the downward social history of Moscow. Zhivago settles in with his servant's daughter and has two children by her; he meets Misha and Nicky again. 'People who have sufficient words at their disposal talk naturally and coherently.' He gets interested in a persecuted priest, and he hears from Tanya in Paris. He writes articles without end and incessant poems, and suddenly he dies.

'Perhaps the mysteries of transformation and the enigmas of life that so torment us are concentrated in the greenness of the earth, among graveyard trees and the flowering shoots that spring up from graves. Mary Magdalene not immediately recognising Jesus risen from the dead mistook him for the gardener.'

Lara finds him dead, and starts to sort out his poems. 'One day she went out and did not come back. She must have been arrested in the street, as so often happened in those days, and she died or vanished somewhere, forgotten as a nameless number on a list which later was mislaid, in one of the innumerable mixed or women's concentration camps in the north.'

How after that can there be an epilogue? Yet there is one, in 1943, on the Orel front. Misha is a lieutenant, Nicky is a major; they are talking over their extremely grim lives, and agreeing together that, whether one was in a university or a concentration camp, the war came as a relief. They consider cold-bloodedly how collectivisation was a mistake and how private judgement had to be stamped out. They discuss a horrifying tale of heroism. They still have hope, like an inextinguishable natural force. Yevgraf is a major-general, and his role now is to look after Zhivago's lost child by Lara, whom he discovers. No real summary is possible. 'A thing which is conceived in a lofty, ideal manner becomes coarse and material. Thus Rome came out of Greece and the Russian revolution came out of the Russian enlightenment.' But that is not an adequate verdict, and Pasternak knows it is not. In Stalin's last few years, Misha and Nicky meet again. 'To the two ageing friends sitting by the window it seemed that this freedom of the spirit was there, that on that very evening the future had become almost tangible in the streets below. . . . ' The final paragraph is moving, because somehow one believes it, God know why.

Although I have travestied the plot of this book, I hope I have given its spiritual skeleton. There is nothing more to say about *Dr Zhivago* except that it is a great masterpiece in its queer way, beyond the reach of any other writer in this century, and an extraordinary monument to humanity and to poetry and to grief. One seems to experience in it without mediation things that are otherwise more obliquely conveyed. In spite of its faults, which are ludicrous and childish, it seems to me better and more tragic every time I read it.

# 9

## The Nobel Prize

Life does not stand still for a writer while he writes a book, particularly such a long one as *Dr Zhivago*. It was then that his affair with Olga Ivinskaya began to dominate him, and I have no doubt that her magnetic attraction had a more and more powerful influence on the plot as he went on; she took over his interest from Pasha Antipov, until that enigmatic and alarming figure became shadowy, and from Mrs Zhivago, whose dismissal from the plot was summary in the end. Be that as it may, Olga certainly disturbed or excited Boris so that he felt himself renewed. He could not bear to desert his wife, a second divorce was more than he could contemplate, but effectively he now had two households. Olga has written a full account of this, though she is not always a good witness: her observations convey a strong subjectivity which is not matched by balance; she is confused and confusing. All the same she is an important source of information, and played a role in his life that came near to being central for a time.

The trouble with Zinaida, Boris is supposed to have told Olga, was that she came from the family of a colonel of gendarmes. We know that she made oddly Stalinist remarks, but one does not know whether she was talking to a microphone in the wall. We know also that she tried to protect Boris from his quixotic generosity to the imprisoned and their families, and it is hardly surprising if she was worried by *Dr Zhivago*, and hostile to Olga. It is Olga who maintains that Boris never truly loved Zinaida, that he knew nearly at once this marriage to her had been a mistake, that he loved her only for the sake of her husband, and her husband only for the sake of his piano-playing. There is a good deal of evidence against that point of view, even if, under whatever emotional hammering, he expressed it. In the case of a normal human being one might rule it out at once; only in the case of Boris Pasternak I admit there is just a flicker of the plausible about it.

236

Olga was the daughter of a provincial schoolteacher who moved to Moscow when she was three, in 1915, so that when she graduated at twenty-one in 1933 Pasternak was forty-three and the greatest and most famous poet in Russia. She was mad on poetry, above all on his. She may well have driven her first husband to suicide; as soon as he was dead she married his rival and arch-enemy, who died in his turn not long afterwards. In 1943 at thirty-one she went to work for *Novy Mir*, where she met Boris Pasternak three years later. She left the magazine to work with his help at verse translations. She was appealing as well as sexually attractive, she had a romantic tale to tell, and a daughter eight years old called Irina, whom the poet loved. Her good qualities were her warmth, her intense loyalty and her understanding of him. The affair began in the autumn; they were city lovers who sat in public gardens and met at the statues of great writers or on the boulevards. But her life was tragic: in October 1949 she went to prison until Stalin's death in 1953. There is no doubt at all that she was imprisoned as a hostage for Pasternak's good behaviour and as a threat to him, as Akhmatova's son was three times imprisoned, and Beliy's wife was imprisoned.

They tried to make Akhamatova's son admit his mother incited him to try to murder Zhdanov. Why should the government be too delicate to imprison the writers themselves? The psychology of such people is a mystery. We know that in prison Olga bore Boris Pasternak a son who was stillborn, and that the police played cat and mouse with him over that too.

After Pasternak's death in 1960, while the storm created by *Dr Zhivago* was still vaguely raging, she was arrested again, and so was her daughter, who was now twenty-two. Irina was released after two years, probably by the diplomatic intervention of Sir Maurice Bowra through the poet Yevtushenko. In 1964 Olga was released too, though her sentence had been eight years; she had been charged with a currency offence in connection with the publication of *Dr Zhivago* in the west. The offence appears to us rather technical than substantial, her daughter had nothing to do with the matter, the trial was secret, and it appears extremely likely that Olga was innocent anyway. She was alive when I visited Moscow in 1989, but she was old and ill and nervous and there was no point in bothering her with precise questions to which she might not remember the answer. The important thing about her is that Pasternak adored her. Her loyalty to him in prison, her refusal over a long period of questioning to implicate him or to drag him down, as she might easily have done, must have forged an unbreakable link, but the sense of renewal of life that runs right through *Dr Zhivago* and all its terribly real love poetry, belong to her.

Her picture of Pasternak and of the times is grimmer than others we have seen, but he was older and the times of course were worse. It is she who records him saying that after a conventional writer's visit to a collective farm in 1935 'for a whole year I could not sleep'. She says that from 1948 on he began to regret time spent on translations, and that he found himself unable, not unwilling, to get new work into print. (She is not too good at dates.) 'If they publish you, you can't write as you please, and if you write as you please, they won't publish you.' He was not allowed to write the substantial introductory essays he intended for Shakespeare and for Goethe, because 'we have specialists for that kind of work'. His *Faust* ran into trouble with critics who demanded to know what had become of Goethe's progressive ideas. 'What progressive ideas?' he wondered. He thought much of the second part of *Faust* was drivel. When the thaw began after Stalin's death and Fadeev as a guilty official shot himself, Pasternak said, 'This I can understand.'

Meanwhile his own writing altered him: that is the secret purpose of poetry, that it changes the poet, as he wrote in a letter to Georgia. 'One must write in a way never known before, and make discoveries, so that unheard-of things happen to you – that is life, and the rest matters nothing.' I cannot imagine a more romantic view of the poet, or a truer one of Boris Pasternak. He knew that he needed his huge audience, because once it is written 'poetry exists only in the others, in the readers', and now he had reached them. And behind all that there was by now a granite integrity, the result rather than the cause of *Dr Zhivago*, which he defined in a letter: 'The one thing that is in our power is not to distort the voice of life which sounds within us.' That is the distillation of sixty years of his life. 'The fabulously small part of me that represents me in my true essence I have distilled into my essays and my novel.' The difference between Stalin and Khrushchev was to Boris Pasternak the difference between a madman and murderer and a fool and pig, someone like Piggy in *Animal Farm*, who ought to have worn his collar as a ring through his nose. Had he always talked like that? No one has told us so.

In 1953, when Olga was amnestied with many others at Stalin's death, Pasternak was still writing *Dr Zhivago*. He did not finish it before 1956, but as he was finishing it he wrote a note that gives a view of his own history over the last twenty years. He and Olga were more deeply entwined than ever, and his gravely written note expressed his life from the strongly anti-Stalinist perspective for which he has become well known in the west. It is not unbalanced, but the accents might have been less powerful and the tone less absolute if he had written earlier. This note survived in Olga's possession, added in pencil to a typed copy of the cycle of poems that opened with the two slight *Izvestia* poems of 1936, which we know that he vehemently rejected by 1946.

'A sincere and one of the most intense of my endeavours – and the last of the period – to think the thoughts of the era, and to live in tune with it. Today [17 February 1956] . . . coming across this, I am vividly reminded that I wasn't always what I am now, as I finish the second book of *Zhivago*. It was actually in 1936, the year that all those terrible trials began (instead of the years of cruelty coming to an end, as I had believed in 1935), that everything snapped inside me, and my attempt to be at one with the age turned into opposition – which I do not conceal. I took refuge in translation. My own creative work came to an end. It awoke just before the war, perhaps as a premonition of it, in 1940 [*On Early Trains*]. The tragic and harrowing wartime period was a *living* one, and in this sense a free and blissful restoration of a sense of community with everyone else. But when, after the magnanimity of Providence had expressed itself in victory – though bought at such a cost – and history had proved so generous, there was a return to the brutality and chicanery of the darkest and most imbecile years before the war, I had for the second time (since 1936) a sense of shock and revulsion from the established order, stronger and more categorical than before. I would like to convey something of this in the autobiography which is meant to introduce the one-volume edition.' I do not think that he quite succeeded in doing so, but the note does it, and his stance in the face of persecution over his finished masterpiece does it very well.

Around 1955 he wrote in a letter of how nineteen years before he had sat in the big upstairs room full of light at Peredelkino, unable to proceed, yet now he sat by the grace of God in the same room, writing the end of *Dr Zhivago*. In the meantime he had been thrown off the board of the Union of Writers for refusing to attack Akhmatova, and perhaps for protesting over Zhdanov's attack on Shostakovich, who alas made nonsense of the protest by grovelling to his accusers. Boris Pasternak suffered his first heart attack in 1950, and his second in the autumn of 1952. He was seriously ill then, with three months in hospital and two in a convalescent home. In hospital he seems in his weak condition to have experienced something almost mystical, and his new inner strength dates from that time. Gerd Ruge, one of the handful of new friends who later wrote about him, and one of his many correspondents in the last decade of life, records that he said of the first decision to write *Zhivago*, 'I thought to myself, you must stand to attention before your own name. I felt that I still had to earn this name by writing not verse, but prose – something which would demand more work and time and effort and might even cost me a good deal more besides.' Olga says, 'He always felt hopelessly in debt, not only to his readers, but simply to people in general – to all those together with whom he lived and suffered on earth.' In the end he was Tolstoy's best disciple.

He worked unbelievably hard, and liked others to do the same. He thought his first wife's painting was an idle way of filling the time, but he admired Zinaida as an excellent housewife and gardener, and although a lot of contradictory gossip has been repeated about the matter, some printed and some not, it seems to me that the evidence is clear that at the end of his life he went home to Zinaida to die, and refused to let Olga visit him on his deathbed because he did not want to upset Zinaida. But that was still in the future. Before her arrest in 1949, Olga was passionate and threw tantrums, and her mother was no help. While she was in prison and at the labour camp, her daughter could not have survived without him. When she came out they soon decided to live virtually together and in 1954 she was pregnant again. Unhappily at the end of August, after a long, bumpy ride in the country west of Moscow, that child also was stillborn. Boris was bitterly grieved.

In the summer of 1955 Olga took rooms in Peredelkino, in a sort of glasshouse overlooking the great dish of Izmalkovo lake, which had a long wooden bridge. In the winter she moved to somewhere warmer in the village, to a house surrounded by big poplars, and in

1959 to a bigger place with a garden of its own, looking across a valley at Fadeev's tavern, so named because Fadeev used to frequent it. Of Fadeev after his suicide, Boris Pasternak declared in a resonant voice as he stood before the open coffin, 'Alexander Alexandrovich has rehabilitated himself.' For Olga, the few years from 1956 to 1960 were the happiest of her life.

For Boris that can scarcely have been so. The novel was read by friends or usually read aloud to them as he finished each section. This must have been known to the police. When Olga was first arrested in 1949 they pressed her about anti-Soviet conversations and about a supposed plan to flee abroad, but they were also curious about his novel. The first two chapters had already reached England with Isaiah Berlin, and Katkov, that most Russian of the Oxford Russians, used to steal little bits to read over the BBC radio. As the novel approached its conclusion, Boris read it out more and more. He sent it as it was written to the poet Sergei Spassky in Leningrad and almost complete to the art historian Alpatov, both of whom wrote him considered and extremely encouraging letters. In spring 1954 a few of the Zhivago poems had appeared in the magazine *Znamia*, with a note that the book treated a period from 1923 to 1929 and would be finished within the year, with the poems in full as the final chapter. Bound copies of the two parts or volumes were taken to the publisher in summer 1955, and to *Znamia*, and an unbound copy to *Novy Mir*. Like other writers, Boris had wept over the death of his hero, but he was as thrilled as other writers are by the sight of his bound and corrected typescript.

At the end of August 1955 Krivitsky at *Novy Mir* said the novel was too long for him, but Simonov was away and had some chapters with him, so there was still a possibility of printing extracts. In autumn Boris was quite clear in his mind that they were never going to publish it, and determined 'to pass it around to all and sundry' and give it to anyone who asked for it. Early in 1956 the publishers said they were ready to produce a big single-volume edition of the poems, in which Pasternak decided to include all the Zhivago poems, which constitute the whole final chapter of his novel. He believed now that all the poems scattered over his lifetime were only steps towards that one full statement. In May 1956 the Italian-language service of Moscow radio announced that the big book was about to be published. At the end of May, while *Novy Mir* still murmured about extracts, Boris handed over *Dr*

*Zhivago* to two strange emissaries from the Italian publisher Feltrinelli.

One of them, Sergio d'Angelo, a communist working for the Moscow Italian radio, was acting for Feltrinelli, the other, a certain Vladimirov, came from the Soviet embassy in Rome. Boris had told another Italian that he was ready to face any kind of trouble so long as his novel appeared; 'I've had enough of such trouble,' said his wife. It is perhaps important to realise that Italian communism was at the time a good deal less monolithic than Russian: Gramsci was still an influence and Togliatti was alive. Also the area of foreign relations and office politics suggested by the presence of Vladimirov was a labyrinth. Maybe someone wanted the novel published, maybe someone wanted to tempt Pasternak to a fatal step, maybe someone was playing both sides against the middle. The essential clue is probably in the nature of Feltrinelli himself: he was a dashing leftist, an agonised communist and a very sharp publisher indeed. Just recently, when the Russians finally did print *Dr Zhivago*, Feltrinelli as a firm sued them in their own courts, using Russian lawyers, and established their own right to the Russian as well as the foreign-language texts of the book worldwide. Sergio d'Angelo wrote an account in 1968 of what happened. The last thing Pasternak said to him at the garden gate was 'You have invited me to take part in my own execution.'

The single-volume Pasternak poems were held up because of severe doubts about the introductory essay. Its editor, Bannikov, became terribly agitated when the anxious Olga told him about the Italian arrangement. 'But what has he done! Doesn't he know that this is a period when the novel might eventually be published?' Khrushchev and Gromyko took much the same line. None of these people could begin to understand why there should be such a fuss about a book, or why it should matter so much to its author. They did not understand the reception of *Dr Zhivago* in the west until too late. In those first days Olga was as busy as a disturbed ant. She tried to get the novel from d'Angelo and failed. She gave a copy to a woman who used to be a concentration camp commandant and now worked as a publisher; it was to be passed on to Molotov, Scriabin's successful kinsman. Olga went to see the editor of *Znamia*, who said, 'How like you to get mixed up with the last romantic in Russia.' He put her in touch with Polikarpov, the new head of the cultural department of the Central Committee. The novel 'must be returned at all costs. . . . The question of what happens to it must be settled here.' But Feltrinelli was intransigent. Polikarpov then tried to rush the book through its Soviet publisher with changes and cuts as necessary, and of course a binding contract. Pasternak wrote that he did not care to have his novel appear in something other than its original form. So far, all this was a game of chess, and he was winning it.

The Russian publishers now wanted to do both the novel and the book of verse, but the Union of Writers under Surkov and Markov approved of neither. Surkov had called Pasternak 'an unsuitable guide for the young' in 1934, and denounced him in 1947, and it was he who was amazed at a great burst of applause in the forties when he was reading an indifferent poem, only to discover the applause was for Pasternak, who had entered the platform behind his back. That reading was part of a peace campaign of Stalin's, but Pasternak told the applauding crowds that he had nothing to say on that subject, so he would read some Shakespeare. They yelled for sonnet 66 until he read it. Surkov must have really hated him.

The Hungarian revolution of 1956, about the repression of which Pasternak was the first to protest, had poisoned the atmosphere of Moscow even further. In September 1956 five members of the editorial board of *Novy Mir* wrote a long letter to the poet refusing *Zhivago* on ideological grounds: at least they were to produce such a letter in 1958, probably backdating it. In 1957 Pasternak was in hospital again, this time with arthritis, but there he received the proof copy of his poems, which is as far as the book got, though in the summer *Znamia* and an almanac called *Literary Moscow* were still begging for his newest poems, and for the *Essay in Autobiography*. Pasternak continued patiently playing chess with everyone about what should appear where, but by now he was like one of those masters of chess who defeat five different opponents at once.

For instance, he was made to send a telegram to Feltrinelli demanding the non-publication of *Zhivago*. He was stubborn over this at first and irritated the authorities, but in the end he calmly signed the document in the secure knowledge that it would not prevent publication, and that photocopies of the book were already in the hands of the publishers all over the world. He also sent a letter telling Feltrinelli to disregard the telegram. When the book appeared he wrote a long and interesting letter of gratitude to

William Collins, among others. He had always known it was obvious that the wording of the telegram was not his. Surkov went to Italy in October with a gang of official poets to make a protest about publication 'against the author's will', which was now imminent. 'The cold war thus invades literature. If this is artistic freedom as understood in the west, then I must say we take a different view of it.'

When Boris was told Surkov had called *Dr Zhivago* an anti-Soviet novel, he remarked, 'He is right.' He was summoned to a secret meeting of the secretariat of the Union of Writers, but he refused to attend it, so they passed a gigantesque resolution against him. 'There's nothing to be done about it now,' he told young Gladkov; 'the order from above has already been given. . . . I'm in for trouble this time, my turn has come.' *Dr Zhivago* appeared in November 1957 in Italian and very soon in other languages, and the world was stunned by it. It was read in huge editions in twenty-four languages within a year or two. This progress around the world really was by now beyond his control. At this point, to alter the metaphor of the game of chess, the score was game, set and match to Pasternak.

He knew just where he stood. In spring 1958 he was in hospital again. He wrote to his Moscow publisher that he knew the feeble stirrings over Russian publication of his poems would lead nowhere, that the rumours of his affluence were unfounded, and that he would like his *Shakespeare* reissued. The journal *October* had offered to send him to Baku to see the oil rigs; to them he wrote asking instead to be transferred to a private room where he could work and spread out his books. 'Although this seems even to me an excessive request and something quite unheard of, I have done enough to merit an exception of this kind being made for me.' To a Georgian publisher he wrote that he hated reminiscences about the past, particularly his own. 'My future looms immeasurably larger, I cannot but live by it, and I have no reason to look backwards.' That was in May 1958, when he was sixty-eight years old.

His own book now moved him as a reader of it, and so did the world's reaction. He wrote: 'It seems the hunger in the whole world for freedom and simplicity is so great, that everybody is glad of *Dr Z.* as a happy excuse for a kind of self-emancipation', and again, 'Soon you will read my book, and weep uniquely justified and grateful tears, such as I could not restrain myself when I read the French translation.' That was to Renate Schweitzer, who had once sent him an opera adapted from Hoffmann to music by her father; she published his letters at Munich in 1963. Was it only because of the language that he spoke of relighting the candle of 'Malte Laurids' (that is of Rilke), and spoke with passion of the streets and the art of before 1914? He thought Rilke had no subject-matter, but now there was so much. Elsewhere he remarked that there was something wrong with Proust, whose works somebody had sent him, however beautiful his writings were. He could measure himself against European literature.

He was terrified that he might get the Nobel prize; he had been a candidate a few years before, but this year he hoped it might go to Moravia. As for his being a candidate, Maurice Bowra suggested him annually, but it was only with *Zhivago* and in 1958 that the sackfuls of his fan-mail and his consciousness of his great fame began. So far as he could, he still replied personally to all letters. Innumerable short correspondences resulted. His letters to the American monk Thomas Merton are fascinating. On 23 October 1958 he was awarded the Nobel prize. For a moment he wondered if he could now repudiate his novel, but he decided he was still proud of it. 'The fat is in the fire now: Fedia came round and told me I must give it up. He looked as if I'd committed a crime. He didn't congratulate me, only the Ivanovs did: what enchanting people.' The furious Soviet reaction began on Saturday, 25 October. There were official demonstrations, letters in the papers, betrayals by pseudo-friends, and a particularly wounding visit from two young men he had helped with money, asking his permission to attack him for the sake of their careers, which of course he gave. They disappeared down the road to Peredelkino station, skipping with glee. He was like some great wounded animal, terribly alone in those days. His 'Hamlet' poem had come true.

Since this is the biography of a poet, and of a very complicated man who by this time had lived through a long period of remarkable historical change, it has little room for the deafening crash of international reaction to the prize. The applause was impressive and all but universal. Moravia, the other candidate, Camus, the 1957 prizewinner, François Mauriac, T. S. Eliot, Edmond Wilson, and many more great men, expressed enthusiasm and delight. Foreign communist parties including that of tiny

Kerala, an Indian state then communist-controlled, protested against the Russian attitude. Inside Russia the storm raged all the more furiously. Surkov, who truthfully remarked that he had 'come to literature from communism rather than the other way round', was for throwing Pasternak out of Russia. Markov, who is still as I write technically in office in the Union of Writers, grimly and malevolently annotated the secret documents in the case, of which I have a photocopy.

Surkov expressed the usual party line when he claimed that the awarding of the Nobel prize to Pasternak was an act of deliberate, provocative, political hostility to Russia. That is not true, or not the whole truth, because the Swedish committee genuinely admired *Dr Zhivago*, but one may note without impropriety that no one who received the Lenin prize for literature had ever gone on to get the Nobel prize, at least so far as I know. If there is an exception it appears to be the Icelandic poet Halldór Laxness. Bunin got the Nobel as a Russian in exile, but Gorky never got it. The only crumb of comfort for the Russian government was that, when they persecuted Pasternak, Sartre, who had tied himself into a complicated knot at that period of his life, refused to protest. The best account of all this is in a powerful polemical book which stands up to the most acid and hostile kind of close reading: Robert Conquest's *Courage of Genius* (1961).

In the year after *Zhivago* Pasternak got no work to do except from Poland, that unruliest of Russian subjects. 'I am very happy, but you must understand', he told the *New York Times*, 'that I am confident that I shall move immediately into this new, lonely role, as if it had always been so. . . . I have not been singled out for special treatment. Under the circumstances, nothing else could have been done.' The storm was certainly intensified by the Nobel prize, but not caused by it. He told both the *Guardian* and the *New York Times* that he was very pleased by the award, but that his pleasure was lonely. He thought at first with relief of a journey to Stockholm. The first powerful denunciation of him was an anonymous article on 25 October in the *Literary Gazette*, printed with the backdated letter rejecting the novel. It had little to do with literature. Pasternak had already sent a telegram of acceptance, and now he sent another: 'Immensely thankful, touched, proud, astonished, abashed. Pasternak.' Next day *Pravda* joined the chorus, with a coarsley written onslaught by a journalist called Zaslavsky, whom Lenin had called a hack who should never be allowed to cross the threshold of a Bolshevik newspaper. The next day again, Pasternak was expelled from the Union of Writers. Other attacks followed. The Kalmuks, deported *en masse* in 1943 and rehabilitated only in 1957, attacked him for writing absolutely nothing about the happy life of the Kalmuk people. On the 29th it was suggested at a public meeting of the Young Communist League, in the presence of Khrushchev, that Pasternak ought to be expelled from Russia.

He sent a telegram the same day: 'Considering the meaning this award has been given in the society to which I belong, I must reject this undeserved prize presented to me. Please do not receive my voluntary rejection with displeasure.' He assured a correspondent that he made this decision quite alone, consulted no one, and had not told his friends. Only a few days before, according to Olga, he had written a letter to his Union saying that nothing would make him give up the prize, though he was ready to give the money to a peace committee. When she heard of the telegram she was astounded. By this time Tsvetayeva's daughter Ariadna Ephron, a forthright lady who had a moving exchange of letters with Boris Pasternak from prison, was living with Olga. When she was asked why Boris felt so guilty about her mother she said 'Because he knows he has not gone through what I went through'. She became a painter. Now she was the first to congratulate him, not because she agreed with his telegram, but because it could not be altered, and what he needed now was support.

But he had sent another telegram to the Central Committee saying he had given up the prize, and asking for Olga to be allowed to work again. If that was a chess move it was finely calculated, because it did not suit Polikarpov, whose aim was to achieve humiliation and self-criticism. That was the last thing in Pasternak's mind. He went to Olga to suggest suicide, alone or together, with some Nembutal he had. She put it off and went to tell Fedin, a man who as Pasternak remarked used to put on his smile as if it were his hat. Both he and Polikarpov told her if the suicide happened she would be 'aiding and abetting a second stab in the back for Russia'. It was in fact the sort of suicide of which Horace writes, taking for his example some lines by Euripides where the god himself is disguised as the god's servant, in the hands of a tyrannical king. '"I will take away everything from you, put you in prison." "The god himself will free me when I will." By this he intended death, the end of all accounts.' Suicide had become his most powerful weapon. For a moment he thought of accepting exile, wrote a letter and tore it up. He wrote to Khrushchev refusing to go. 'I am tied to Russia by birth, by my life and work. I cannot conceive of my destiny separately from Russia, or outside it.'

That letter was published the next day, and having taken his line he wrote another, published four days later on 5 November. Solzhenitsyn as a young physics teacher at Ryazan was shocked by these letters, and still more shocked later when he considered them in retrospect as a hardened convict. He felt it intolerable that one should put personal ties before 'duty'. Had he known the letters were drafted by the pragmatic Ariadna, by Olga and her daughter, he would doubtless have been still more shocked by them. Rostropovich certainly thought they meant defeat. To me they look like one of Pasternak's most brilliant manoeuvres. He was not going to use the final weapon of suicide, but everyone was going to live. His book was out, it was famous, nothing could stop it. His position was strong and clear, and people knew what he stood for. He could afford to write a letter to *Pravda* which made it extremely difficult to go on attacking him.

He insisted that all that happened was the natural consequence of his actions, and all his own actions were free and voluntary. He was delighted by the prize, which he assumed was literary. 'But I was mistaken. I had reason for my mistake, because I was a candidate for the prize five years ago when my novel did not exist.' He had then observed 'the political campaign around my novel' and freely and voluntarily rejected the prize. That we know to be true, and as for the anti-Soviet campaign in the west it was indeed amazing, as I remember well after more than thirty years: I was shocked by it, and very surprised when I read the novel that it was so mild and so beautiful. He goes on to express his identification with the Russian people though never with the party. He notes there are obstacles to this closeness to the Russian people, 'engendered by the novel through my own fault'. That is almost over-delicately phrased, but he does not repudiate his novel.

He had meant no harm, but *Novy Mir* had warned him how the book might seem to strike at the October revolution and the foundations of the state. 'I did not appreciate this and I regret it now.' Since the one thing the book did not do was attack the revolution he appears justified in this piece of extreme politeness. If the publication had been suspended he 'might have succeeded at least partially in correcting' the idea that revolutions are always historically illegitimate, but, as he says, 'the book has been printed and it is too late to talk of this.' He emphasises that his life and liberty have remained secure and his actions voluntary. 'It goes without saying that no one put any pressure on me and that I am making this statement of my free will, with a bright faith in the future of society and in my own, with pride in the time I live in and the people who surround me.'

That was always his most valuable possession as a writer. The reader may wish that he never wrote this letter, but only consider its elaborate irony, the things it refuses to say, and its cool and gleaming good nature. It is a letter for the connoisseur of Pasternak as stylist. He gives away nothing but an apology for suggesting a position he had genuinely never held. And with that letter began a few years of late sunshine, before he died in 1960 at the age of seventy. It was a master-stroke, because now there was little more they could do to him. 'There is no security in property. . . . We are the guests of existence, travellers between two stations. We must discover security within ourselves.' That is what I think he had discovered, and that is how he was able to play with his persecutors with such apparent ease, like a fish in deep water, with the run of the tide on its side.

The interventions of foreign writers on his side were in many cases most moving. 'Will you really allow people to be gathered from the face of the earth like mushrooms?' asked the Yugoslavs. Halldór Laxness appealed to Khrushchev to 'mitigate the malicious onslaught of sectarian intolerence upon an old, meritorious Russian poet, Boris Pasternak'. The Russians were 'arousing the wrath of the world's writers, intellectuals and poets against the Soviet Union. Kindly spare the friends of the Soviet Union an incomprehensible and most unworthy spectacle.' Under these circumstances, the case of *Dr Zhivago* was bound to become entangled in the cold war on both sides, and little more sense was to be made of it except in the context of that furious coldness. The book itself remains: whatever readers it has lost in the west, it has recently gained many Russian readers, and Boris Pasternak's star as a poet and as a man is in the ascendent there.

Things were still not easy for him, though there was a kind of false dawn at the end of his life. 'It continues in all strictness. My situation is worse, more unbearable and endangered than I can say or you can think of,' he wrote in August 1959 to Stephen Spender. He felt that the police and the party were closing in, and that he would come to a bad end. There is no doubt that he feared for Olga, and no doubt that her arrest, which so swiftly followed his death, had been prepared before it. Possibly the authorities were worried about papers he might have left, but that was not all: the old game of using one person to trap another or just as a hostage for another was still being played. There was no genuine liberalisation. In July 1960 Khrushchev, in a speech to writers, recorded with glee the effect of his own thunders and lightnings in 1957. 'It is better to warn a man in sharp terms and at the right time. . . . The development of literature and art in a socialist society proceeds . . . planwise as directed by the party.' Most of this speech is simply too repulsively stupid to repeat; there is a long metaphor about levers and transmission belts and spiritual weapons all working as a single mechanism. Even the Popes have seldom attained a prose style to rival his, though some of them would I suppose have burnt Pasternak alive.

Yet, as things were, Boris Pasternak had his enemies at a disadvantage. It is possible that Olga's verbal reporting may be unreliable, but I do not think she is wrong about atmospheres. After Pasternak's letter to Khrushchev he went with Olga by appointment to see Polikarpov, who was trying in an elephantine way to make friends. First Polikarpov rose solemnly to his feet and announced that in view of Pasternak's letter he would be allowed to remain in Russia, but he would still have to make his peace with the Soviet people. 'People!' said Pasternak. 'People! As though you had them in your trousers pocket! You really shouldn't use such a word.' Polikarpov gasped loudly, walked up and down a bit, and then attempted a friendly gesture, patting the poet on the shoulder. 'Goodness me, old fellow, what a mess you've landed us in.' Pasternak was furious and brushed the hand away. Olga says he hated being called old in front of her, since he thought of himself as young and healthy and the hero of the hour. 'Will you kindly not speak in that tone; you can't talk to me like that,' Polikarpov insisted, as oily as old cheese. 'Come now, there you go, sticking a knife in the country's back, and we have to patch it all up.' The banal jargon about the stab in the back enraged Boris. He leapt to his feet and made for the door. 'Take that back. I refuse to talk to you.' Polikarpov was in despair. 'Stop him! Stop him! Get him to come back.' It will be seen by what an easy mechanism Boris Pasternak took control of this encounter. Olga was now an intermediary useful to both sides, but Pasternak's treatment of Polikarpov face to face expressed the reality of the situation not only as he saw it but as Polikarpov saw it too.

Of course, in spite of his loneliness, Boris had friends. Olga exaggerates his loneliness because her own lodgings and her tiny family group were already cut off, lonely and under close surveillance. In the village lanes life was tense: he came to her once with tears in his eyes to say the village policeman had said good morning to him. But Boris had a home after all, and did not lose his allies. Yevtushenko was a young poet whose work he knew and admired from a Georgian edition, who in turn admired him passionately and remained loyal. In his own generation Ehrenburg replied to all invitations to condemn Pasternak in his own unmistakable voice on the telephone. 'Ehrenburg has gone away and won't be back.' Even Sholokhov condemned Pasternak only to the minimum necessary degree, making his interviewer suffer considerably in the process. There is not the slightest question about Kaverin, Asmus and the Ivanovs, his friends since the twenties, or so far as I know Aseev or Tikhonov. It is almost more important that the tempest that broke so suddenly over his head was concentrated indeed, but it did not last long. His private replies to public abuse were withering, but their tone was always cool and level.

He surely had consolations we still know nothing about. He planted and lifted his own potatoes, he swam in the lakes, he was at ease with the working people of the village. Katkov told me that one day Boris Pasternak had a workman in to repair his roof. When the job was done, knowing that money must not change hands, he asked the workman what he could do for him in return, how he could serve him. The workman asked for the honour of drinking vodka with him. So they sat at the long empty veranda table with two glasses, a bottle and a loaf of black bread. 'This isn't much,' said Boris. 'Isn't there anything else I can do?' The workman banged the table with his fist. 'Lead us!' he said. 'Lead you! How lead you?' 'Lead us! Lead the country!' 'But I can't lead you,' said Pasternak; 'I am not a man of that kind. There are some men like – like banners, they bend in the wind, they move, they go forward. But I am like a tree. It has roots in the earth. The wind may blow and it bends, but it has roots and it can never move.'

Gerd Ruge, a friend and journalist, estimates that Pasternak got twenty or thirty thousand letters after the Nobel prize.

> Along the paths of cat and fox
> with piles of letters I go home,
> walk to the house where I will sit
> and read my letters with delight –
>
> Countries, frontiers, mountain, lake,
> peninsula and continent,
> view and review and reflection,
> children, old men and young men . . .

As he wrote in 1959 to the émigré Zaitsev, who had been in Paris since 1924, 'It has fallen to me as a great and undeserved bit of luck, that towards the end of my life I have entered into a direct personal relation with many estimable people in the vast and distant world, and I have begun an intimate and informal and important conversation with them. Unfortunately this has come late in the day.' The reader may be delighted with the old man's pleasure, with his taste of the full blast of fame for which he had hungered, but the letters kept him so busy now that one is relieved so much of his life had passed in undistracted literary pursuits, and in poetry. But there were still the long summer evenings on the veranda with his friends, the endless lunches at the weekend, and many external signs (however misleading) of a very happy life.

Maybe his most revealing letters were those to his cousin Olga Freidenberg in Leningrad. When he was starting *Dr Zhivago* at New Year 1946 he had written to her, 'Now that the scandal and the misunderstanding about me have taken such deep root, I wish to become a human being in the full sense of the word . . . I want to write something deep and true.' In childhood he could not bear to be criticised; now it had become one of his most important stimulations, and his last few years were extremely fruitful. In

October that year he had already written two or three of the ten chapters of what he still called *Boys and Girls*, 'to encompass the four decades from 1902 to 1946 in ten chapters'. He was as interested in his cousin's ideas as in his own. In mid-novel, we find him writing to her about the emergence and essential nature of lyric poetry in Europe. He thought it arose, presumably in Greece, simultaneously with a new philosophy, that it meant a shift in world outlook to that of people living in a social world. 'The myths of the gods become the biographies of poets.' He touches on something in common with Uncle Kolya's ideas in *Zhivago*, something one would like to hear about at much greater length, because at the core of that novel, and of Pasternak's attitude to what followed it, lies certainly the mysterious self-definition of a lyric poet. He does not, to put it mildly, behave like an ordinary novelist.

Sometimes he could write only 'in the twenty-fifth hour of the day'. His industry is almost inconceivable to us. In five weeks he translated 2500 lines of Petöfi, including a narrative poem of 1500 lines. He did *King Lear* in a month and a half. Meanwhile he was working at his novel. While he was finishing what he had begun to call part one of *Zhivago*, he was re-editing seven translations of Shakespeare for different editors in different offices, with different views of their own. He raced through Goethe. 'There are people who love me very much (only a few) and I feel that I owe them something. It is for them I am writing this novel, as if it were a long letter to them, in two volumes.' His letters to his cousin Olga are well worth reading in full, because her situation complements his, and although she achieves a certain inner peace, her smaller-scale scholarly or intellectual triumphs are the more moving for being less exciting than his; her despair and the shock of the siege of Leningrad affect her deeply, and the comfort he is desperate to offer scarcely touches her. They write to one another as if between two dimly lighted planets where two astronomers sit, each conscious of the blackness of the universe.

Pasternak's letter to his cousin about the 1954 Nobel prize which he so nearly got, shows just how shrewdly he foresaw what the consequences would have been. 'You cannot imagine how strained my relations with officialdom are and how terrifying it is to have attention drawn to me. On the least provocation they assume the right to ask questions about my basic views, and there is no force on earth that can compel me to answer such questions in the way everyone else does. . . . It is expedient that I live secretly and withdrawn.' It is clear from the context that he alludes here to Olga Ivinskaya, who makes him happy but at the same time complicates his life and confirms his instinct for the shadows. He would like to go abroad but he could not go like a mechanical doll as others do. 'I have to think of the lives of my loved ones, of my unfinished novel, and of how to keep my position from becoming even more precarious. Ah me! The Babylonian captivity. But the Lord seems to have shown mercy; the danger seems to have passed.' His cousin died soon afterwards.

In the summer of 1955, when he was working hard on the end of *Zhivago*, and a lot of people had already read part one, he wrote that he 'could count on the fingers of one hand the number of those who like it'. He already felt that it was 'a work of love, which will never, or only in the distant future, see the light.' He was in disgrace at this time for taking little interest in the family events and diseases, because he was working so hard and seeing nobody. In February 1956 he was expected to respond to the news that a big cast-iron model of his Uncle Misha's linotype machine had been placed on show in the Moscow Polytechnic Museum. There was a problem, as there still is, about his father's paintings.

There is no doubt that Boris Pasternak despised his critics. The letters to his cousin give evidence that he was quite conscious and rather gleeful about the irony with which he handled them. This sense of being above the dusty world of such people is an important ingredient in the novel itself, and explains why he was willing that if necessary it should be corrected, though not by an enemy, for Russian publication. He wrote a note on the envelope of a letter from the scholar K. Bogatyrev, a specialist in German who was then in a punitive labour camp, who wrote to him in April 1954. 'The politically unacceptable barbs not only place the manuscript in jeopardy, but also squaring accounts with the directives of the age is trivial. The novel is opposed to this in tone and scope. So it was in the preceding parts, and so it must be from now on. There is no need to yield to an open, negative treatment of contemporary dogmas in the dialogues of characters: dogma should be ignored, disregarded.' It was of course just this disregard and small esteem that so maddened and confused his Soviet critics.

It still requires a difficult act of historical imagination to grasp just how original and how appalling his treatment of the revolution of October 1917 seemed to be. People had not thought of it like that; they had not been told about it. It had become a myth or a holy icon in which the entire nation believed. (There is an example of this in Solzhenitsyn's novel *August 1914*, in which so many western readers were disappointed.) It turns out that its extreme originality as a Russian novel went unnoticed in the west, and lay in its relatively fair and decent treatment of tsarist officers and even members of the royal family, who in the myth and icon of the 1914–18 war had become the scum of the earth. In Russia as we have known it in our lifetimes, and of course as it was in Tolstoy's lifetime, realism has always been shocking, it has always been a powerful weapon. In the hands of a great writer it is devastating.

But already in 1954 Boris Pasternak foresaw other writings: he wrote of the need to finish *Zhivago* 'and one or two other things' before he died, of the need to write prose 'because it brings me nearer to the absolute' (a most interesting and unusual reason) and at the same time to go back to writing lyric poetry, which he found easier and knew more about. He did write one more brilliant collection of lyrics before he died, but he also wrote a play, constructed like a tragedy in three acts, of which two were more or less written before he died but only one has been translated complete. The play, *The Blind Beauty*, preoccupied him at the end of his life: it was to have the scope and range of *Zhivago*. In 1959 he had completed an early rough draft; he intended to treat the emancipation of the serfs, around 1860, with 'realistic verisimilitude', including serf actors, artists in bondage, duels and other melodramatic complications, but the point of it, as of *Zhivago*, was to be 'a conception of life in general, of life as such, of historical being or existence'. He wrote all this to his Swedish publisher. He wrote to Jacqueline de Proyart that *Zhivago* was a foretaste of it; it was going to 'continue and deepen' that book.

Was this an old man's folly? It is obviously unfair to judge very severely the text we have, because it was unfinished and unrevised, and bears little obvious relation to the high hopes he had of it. It reads as an excellent, melodramatic piece, with a realism as solid as Balzac's with some moments of coincidence, but with real development of interesting characters and of their interaction. I would guess it was the unfleshed ghost of the skeletal draft of a great play, a sketch scribbled by a great man dying rather than a piece of apprentice work for the theatre like Henry James's *Guy Domville*. We have it at the *Boys and Girls* stage of *Zhivago*: it needed a few more years of his work on it, and of the play of life on his work. It is at any rate not like any other play: it is yet another work of startling originality, in which I detect a faint overtone of Dumas, as of Dickens in *Zhivago*.

As for the serf actors, they existed, of course, and there was a famous case of a squire falling in love with one. Their theatres are on the ordinary tourist circuit from Moscow: Sheremetov's theatre at Ostankino, where there is now a museum, is a good example.

The whole of the historical background that Pasternak sketches is exact, strange as it may feel to us. It is even true that Dumas, who according to Pasternak is snowed up in a local inn, visited Russia in 1858. The account of his journey, *From Paris to Astrakhan*, was published the next year. Boris Pasternak intended a play within a play, with Dumas among the spectators, and an argument about art between Dumas and a serf actor. The play within a play was to be called 'The Suicide', and written in the style of a popular melodrama of the mid-century. In the third act the serf actor was to be free and successful, enjoying the early eighties, and the old butler Prokhor, who was sent to Siberia and came home to be an innkeeper earlier in the play, was to be a successful bourgeois from that middle class 'who did so much for Russia at the end of the nineteenth century. Imagine someone like Shchukin, who collected all those beautiful French paintings in Moscow at the turn of the century.'

The first act, which takes the form of a long Prologue and is most of what he had actually written, is meant to represent Russia at its rawest and meanest, 'like the first part of Gogol's *Dead Souls*', untouched by spirituality. Gogol could never write the second, redemptive part of *Dead Souls*, because it implied a moral regeneration in which perhaps he scarcely believed, taking place in the future. It will be seen that in *Zhivago* Pasternak wrestled with precisely the same problem, which is literary but with far deeper ramifications. I would contend that as far as possible he solved it. Only the possibility of grace makes history bearable: that is what he essentially believed. Sinyavsky puts this better than I do in his introductory essay to Pasternak's *Poems* (Moscow, 1965), and Max Hayward repeats it in his Foreword to *The Blind Beauty* (1969).

When we consider what Boris Pasternak most deeply felt or

believed, we are bound to look closely at his last poems. One of them for a somewhat comic reason survives in two versions, neither of them in the usual collections. In one version he all but names Ivinskaya, but since it touches on a significant event he was terrified Zinaida might come across it among his papers, and wrote a special, less obvious version to keep at home in case she did. It is called 'Nobel Prize', and it was written in January 1959: it is a protest, almost petulant, and yet profoundly optimistic. There was trouble for him when the *Mail* got hold of it, and printed it in his lifetime. No doubt it is partly an attempt to exorcise fear by expressing it and by wrenching it towards a deeper hope. His late style in poetry is really too simple to be translated, but this poem sums up his experience and is worth recording even in a feeble version.

> I am snared like an animal:
> where are men, light, liberty?
> and at my back the hunt,
> there's no escape for me.
>
> Dark forest or lake-shore,
> malicious trunk of a tree.
> Cut off all ways. Let it come,
> it is all one to me.
>
> What is the evil I did,
> murder or robbery?
> I made the whole world weep
> for my beautiful country.
>
> Yet even at my grave's edge
> I believe a time will come:
> over all malice, all wrong,
> the victory will be won.

He turned naturally to hope as a magnet turns to north, and as he turned towards women. With Ariadna Ephron his relationship was a continuation of the one with her mother, only less painful, less intense. 'Don't think I'm starting a romance with you,' he wrote to her early in their correspondence, 'I love you anyway, without that.' He sent her in her camp his father's illustrated *Resurrection* of Tolstoy, and poems from *Zhivago*. She wrote of how she recognised him in her mother's poems, 'same hair, same sins. . . . In her notes and drafts there is a lot about you. How she loved you and how *long*. She only loved Dad and you and never ceased to do so. She didn't exaggerate. Those whose love she did exaggerate were dethroned after sufferings.' She sends him a marvellously sensuous love poem from her mother, but apparently he knows it already, because the same images turn up in *Zhivago*. 'I touch your nakedness with my fingers quieter than the waters and lower than the grasses.' Small wonder he loved Ariadna; he had known her first as a girl of twenty-three in Paris in 1935, and he was a man haunted by the whole of his past, not just by one part of it at the expense of other parts.

Ariadna Ephron was born in 1912; at eighteen she went to work for the French-Russian Society as a publisher, and in 1937 she was estranged from her mother and went back to Russia, where she was arrested in 1939, two months after her mother's arrival. On that occasion she served a sentence of eight years, which at least kept her out of the war, but in 1949 she was arrested again. It was then that Boris wrote to her and she to him. She was exiled for life to the Krasnoyar region, but rehabilitated in 1955 'for lack of a charge'. She worked for twenty years on her mother's archives, and published her own memoirs in Paris in 1979. The story is worth setting down here only because it is typical, almost average. She was never a central figure in Boris Pasternak's life, but he saw her a lot and she was on its margins: indeed, its margins were thick with such people. It was habitual in his circle to refer to them as martyrs. Akhmatova was 'the greatest martyr', and he wrote to Ariadna in prison, 'I love your life, my poor martyr.' As he had written after Tsvetayeva's death, 'It is still hard to imagine you dead, miser millionairess among starving sisters. What can I do to please you? Tell me what I can do. In the silence of your going away there is an unexpressed reproach.' When they came out of prison, he kept Olga and Ariadna in the same lodgings at Pevedelkino.

# 10

# The Hands of Time

The storm that struck Boris Pasternak over *Dr Zhivago* was intrinsically short-lived, and its chief issues were the Nobel prize and the threat of exile: it lasted essentially ten days, and certainly less than a month. He was terrified but he kept his footing and the government suffered far worse than he did because it had somehow tied its own hands. It could not suppress the book without his co-operation, which was not forthcoming, and it could not punish him without being seen to do so by the whole world. By choosing to accept a minimal and ironic apology, it had left him secure at Peredelkino, which became a place of pilgrimage, as Tolstoy's house had been. Police surveillance added only a touch of the ridiculous.

What did he live on? Since Stalin's death his *Hamlet*, his *Faust* and his *Maria Stuart* of Schiller had been performed in the theatre, and his translations made money. Indeed, he was still giving away money, to Lina Prokoviev for example. Nor did his expulsion from the Union of Writers mean that he had to leave the house they allowed him at Peredelkino: that organisation was not as mono-lithic as it pretended, and he had many friends in it. It even contributed a handsome sum, when the time came, for his gravestone, through a nineteenth-century organisation called Litfund, of which Dostoevsky was once secretary. Polikarpov nourished a particular hatred of Zinaida, whom he thought unacceptably blunt, but she went on living at Peredelkino, paying rent as is customary for literary widows, until her own death in 1966, when she was buried beside Boris.

Pasternak's life in his last two years was essentially unaltered. His voice was deeply nasal and his vowels were long-drawn-out; he was by now a great public reader. Yevtushenko says he was 'as crisp and sparkling as fresh lilac'. He got about thirty letters a day and sat up late at night answering them; he got books from abroad,

259

not all of which he appears to have kept, but including most of the modern classics, some of which he was doubtful about, and on his seventieth birthday received such unlikely gifts as an engraving of Jena and an antique silver candle-lighter. His walks were swift, and in spite of his white hair his face was still youthful and apparently blazing with health.

He got up early, did some habitual exercises, breakfasted well, worked, and then washed his face at the yard pump in winter before lunch, or dipped his head in the river when there was no snow. After lunch he lay down for a little, then he worked until maybe nine or ten o'clock in the evening. His walks could take more than two hours; he spoke to everyone he met and kept sweets in his pockets to give to children. He had given up reading the papers in the thirties, and those who have seen Russian papers will understand why; they are meagre, official sheets. He had given up the radio too as a kind of echo-chamber, and almost never watched television. He grew marrows and cucumbers and some fruit, as well as his potatoes, and he helped his wife gather kindling in the forest. One cannot imagine a more ideal life for an elderly writer.

One day he met his friend Gladkov by chance on the bridge at Peredelkino, so they went for a walk. 'I remember everything just as if it were yesterday – the light grey waters of the lake with the purplish-pink glint on them, the bank with its willows and the black-edged white posts going all the way round, the beautiful old limes, cedars and larches in the surviving part of the former estate to which Pasternak took me, and his beloved voice, with the intonation I loved so well. He showed me the old house with the colonnade – once the estate of the Samarins, described in his poem 'The Old Park'. . . . Dmitri Samarin was evidently the real-life original of Yuri Zhivago, at least as far as the biographical externals go.' This is the only confirmation I have ever found of my view that Zhivago in Siberia must owe something to Samarin. 'We strolled around for about two hours. . . . His manner of talking had not altered, his sentences piled up rapidly in dense, urgent clusters, he interrupted himself, wandered off into digressions, seeming to lose his thread until you got used to it and understood the relentless logic behind it.'

But there were dead people he could not forget, and whom he lived to commemorate, not only in verse but now in prose, in his *Essay in Autobiography* and its later version *People and Places*. As he rewrites and rewrites it becomes stronger and stronger until it ends as a kind of roll-call of his dead friends, the young Mayakovsky, Tsvetayeva and his beloved Georgians. Gladkov notices that, so far as it concerns Pasternak himself, it does not concentrate on the lyric poet but the writer who was going to produce *Dr Zhivago*. He still saw Nina Tabidze, and when Macmillan visited Moscow the government hastily flew him down to Georgia for a last visit, for fear Macmillan might ask to see him. The autobiography in its new form opens with Tolstoy, Beliy and Blok, the challenge of Rilke and the only two who met it face to face, Aseev and Tsvetayeva. Two of these names need explaining. Beliy had died in 1934: he had lived with Rudolf Steiner from 1912 to 1916, and welcomed the revolution as some kind of liberating storm like Shelley's 'West Wind', as of course Pasternak did; he wrote an excellent appraisal of Blok in *Novy Mir* in 1933. Aseev was quite a good friend at Peredelkino, where he hastily planted Boris an orchard to prevent his garden there being taken over as untilled ground. He got a Stalin prize in 1941 for a poem about Mayakovsky. When Pasternak was buried, like Fedin he darkened his windows and did not appear, possibly from timidity.

These autobiographies were written with calm self-control; they dwell not on death but on the continuity of art. Pasternak seems pleased to have publicly written that 'The fate of these two men [Yashvili and Tabidze] and the fate of Marina Tsvetayeva were to become my greatest sorrow.' I do not think it is my fantasy that what he intends is a roll-call of the dead. He had wanted to use an epigraph from Proust for his 1955–9 poems, *When the Weather Improves*: 'Un livre est un grand cimetière où sur la plupart des tombes on ne peut plus lire les noms effacés.' Gladkov found 'a studied dryness, a marked severity of judgement' in the whole essay; that was clearly intended. He gives the names of those he underestimated too. It is as Gladkov says 'an agonised reappraisal' of the past, and perhaps a portrait in a distorting mirror. One must remember that Gladkov was by no means best pleased with *Dr Zhivago*, though he loved its writer, who welcomed him back from prison (where he spent 1948–54) with extraordinary warmth. Gladkov is a critic of intuitive power and great integrity, with whom one must come to terms. He is also a witness that in August 1957 Pasternak 'clearly understood what was in store for him'.

Poetry spilled out of him as if by mistake. After the Moscow

Arts Theatre produced his *Maria Stuart*, he wrote 'Bacchanalia', 'contrary to everything I have written either before or since', and to the grave disgust of certain of his friends. It reads like a 'given' poem, but in fact he worked on if for several days, as he always did on any poem. It is a sort of showpiece, with old women in church at night, a blizzard in the street, shattered opinions and rugged simplicity, the theatre and the black-market ticket-sellers. Maria Stuart goes to her execution rather as Hamlet expects his future in the earlier poem.

> Pounding against her ribs life, liberty:
> prison cannot crack her with a stone
> she is as restless as a dragonfly,
> born to enslave hearts, to hurt her own . . .

Then we return to the blizzard and for a moment to the church. The whole poem is episodic and fragmentary, but its source and background seem to be in this lightly sketched ecclesiastical scene of 'foreheads at prayer, vestment and cloak, old women weakly candle-lit.' The church is that of St Boris and St Gleb, and because Pasternak is called Boris this night service must have to do with his patron's feast. The title must refer to the night life of Moscow, including the Schiller play, but this is a long and not simple poem, in which one image is more deeply mirrored in another. After the second reference to the church comes a party, with 'Stairs, doors, laughter, opinion, baskets of lilac, icy cyclamen', and the food, which is sketched in with minimal and brilliant lines. Pasternak had certainly not lost his appetite for life. 'Deadlier than small-shot the mouth-line. . . .' It is unfair to attack this poem, because it is mostly no more than this sort of *tour de force*. Even the condemning end is brilliant and unexpected, 'with snatches in their ears of the thirty times repeated telephone. . . .' It is as if Pasternak had quite suddenly, gleefully and successfully invaded the territory of Pushkin or Byron and modernised it. But it is also beyond doubt that he so enjoyed drawing the social picture that it far outgrew what was originally to have been its frame. Was the birthday party of the poem really a party for him as a translator, or did it coincide with his name-day, or was it a theatrical party at all? It is utterly untranslatable, I fear.

Many of the poems written between 1955 and 1958, of which

Nikolai Tikhonov in old age. He was a popular writer of patriotic ballads. Boris Pasternak admired and liked him.

Nikolai Aseev, a poet of the Soviet literary establishment who remained on friendly terms with Pasternak, at least until *Zhivago*. When Boris died, he blanketed the windows of his house, and did not appear at the grave.

Some of Pasternak's favourite photographs of himself, chosen in old age, and given to Zoe Afanaseyevna for copying at the time of his death.

Boris Pasternak close to the time of his death at the age of seventy. The pictures on the wall are his father's.

Akhmatova, 1889–1966. A poet born close to Odessa of aristocratic parents. She belonged to a less wild group than the young Pasternak, but became close to him as a friend under pressure of Stalin.

Olga Ivinskaya, Boris Pasternak's mistress, photographed in old age in her flat in Moscow.

there were more than thirty, carry the resonance of his moral crisis, but many are remarkable in other ways, as the *Zhivago* poems are. These are immediately dramatic, and yet mysteriously inexhaustible. I am still bemused with admiration and curiosity over some I have known for thirty years. Part of his objective charm is that of his personality, with the added attraction of his privacy: he knows he has attained fame but he does not overvalue it.

> . . . Merge into privateness
> like country into mist,
> blinding the passer-by
> with a mere nothingness.
>
> Other pairs of feet
> will tread in your footsteps,
> not for you to reckon
> victory or defeat.
>
> But you must still defend
> inch by inch where you stand
> to be alive, only alive,
> only alive to the end.

The poem is so simple and so morally clear that one would have to search back a long way to find another poem of the same kind that was as strong. The Russian is as laconic as it is potent; poetry of the kind can no more be perfectly translated than it can be imitated, it is the reward of a lifetime and comes in one language only. The poem 'Soul', with which I have already dealt, comes from the same collection. It is fair to say that only a poet who has written his *Dr Zhivago* could write this. In the moral verses I have just quoted, only one thing is happening, but in other poems, including one from the very end of his life, we have weather, memory, art and a prophetic strain: it is called 'After the Thunder'. It is cosmic and intensely invigorating as if the weather had finally got into his bloodstream.

> The storm wears out, the air is full of it.
> All lives, all breathes, like earthly paradise.
> With all its groping clusters of purple
> the lilac drinks a waterfall of freshness.

Things revive with a change of weather.
Drainpipes are overflowing with rainfall,
behind the storm-clouds a light sky
towers high and hill-blue over all.

The artist's hand is still more vigorous
to wash the impurities of the world with.
Life is new-dipped in colour, transfigured
into brand-new reality and myth.

Half a lifetime's memories go to sleep,
they recede like the storm and they grow dim.
This century has grown out of its childhood.
Clear the way for whatever is to come.

It is not earthquake, it is not upheaval
that lead us to the life of our desire,
but generosity and open truth,
and visions in the soul, visions of fire.

This simplicity has a direct message, where the complexity in a youthful poem of Boris Pasternak reveals no more than a state of mind: its message was a paradox or existed only in order to hold the poem and the state of mind together. The consequence is that in late poems what the poet has to say has become habitually so clear that it may emerge baldly from its music and its imagery. 'Women in Childhood', for example, is a Proustian evocation of women, but its message is just a raising of the hat to them. The exciting part of the poem is simply an old man's memory: 'a side-street tenebrous as a stone quarry', onion-domes and the shadows of poplar-trees, and 'the frothing blossom of the cherry-trees washing at the windows'. But the end of it, which I will give in Michael Harari's translation, is simply this:

You had to grin and bear the twittering lash
Of women's tongues, an education
In passion like a science,
Heroic adoration.

To all those women who flickered here and there
Along my life, and turned another way,
I send my thanks
And own a debt to pay.

We knew already that the roots of his attitude to women went
back to childhood: whose do not? But he is not writing now like a
man in love: he is affectionate, even gallant, but one feels there is
safety in numbers. Is he thinking about Zinaida? She seems to me
likelier than Olga. But he is certainly still capable of love, and in
other poems even the memory of love is incandescent.

My winters are on fire
with winter solstices,
the unrepeated days
repeated without cease,

gathered in memory
until they can fulfil
the circle of time
when time was standing still.

Winter, near midwinter,
the detail and the peace:
wet road and streaming roof
and sun basking on ice,

two lovers in a dream
longing themselves to one,
hot trees, steaming wet,
with starling boxes on,

clock-hands dazed with sleep
sticking to the clock's face,
days like a hundred years
and kisses like the days.

This remarkable poem is prefigured in part three of 'Fairy-Tale'.
Winter was his time, of course, as autumn was Milton's. There is a
fineness about winter scenery and a liberty at the heart of it, when

snow has obliterated nine-tenths of the world. In a way he would have preferred to be Chekhov, photographed as happy as a schoolboy in the snow outside his cottage, in a village within calling distance of Peredelkino. In the early stages of *Zhivago*, he wrote to his father how he thought always of Chekhov. I had always crudely supposed that it was Chekhov's example that made Zhivago a doctor, a profession of which Boris seems to have had only the vaguest of ideas.

These late poems of his are lit up by memory, a light somehow brighter than that of pure fiction, fuzzier perhaps but more pleased with what it sees. The same light shines, of course, here and there on details in his prose, but in the poems it falls more evenly and more vividly. He remembers Christmas in a more thrilling scene here than the Christmas party in *Zhivago*. It is more innocent, and he does not have one hand of his metaphor-making imagination tied behind his back. 'The shivering candle-light turns the faces to stone . . .' Who would have expected that line in such a context? The whole poem, 'Winter Holidays', ends with a faint touch of the end of 'Bacchanalia', but not inappropriately, and it is interesting that the innocence of the poet that criticises the adults is here unabashed and childlike. Something in him really was like that. As I have said, he almost uniquely exemplifies the general truth that genius is the survival of the powers of childhood among adult techniques, and this seems to be truer as he grows older.

The last of these very late poems is called 'God's World'. It is the poem in which he discusses his foreign correspondence, readable letters from men that are 'dry witness to good sense', and letters of surprising and fervent allegiance from women. It is a piece of light verse, nothing more, and it ends with an invitation to stamp collectors, 'If you could stand a moment in my unlucky shoes'. This mild and rueful joke recalls the Horace of the hexameter poems: it defuses a poem instead of letting it explode into fire, and the poem is none the worse for that. But I do not think an English writer would have made that joke about stamp collecting, because to us foreign letters are part of daily life, and the activity of collecting stamps is banal, it has lost the romance it had for King George V. Russia really is a distant and was an isolated country: one could scarcely overemphasise the joy and the excitement Boris Pasternak got from his letters from abroad, even so late in his life.

That is why he begins by making you feel the woods, the tracks of cat and fox, and the pleasure of meeting the postwoman.

In October 1958 he wrote several times to Thomas Merton at his American monastery. The first letter Pasternak sent, thanking him for a book, was dated 'Holy Cross day, 27 September', and several further letters followed in the course of October. Merton wrote a note on *Dr Zhivago* as a work of genius for the *New York Times*, and protested about the events of those days to Surkov and Khrushchev. In November he wrote three articles about Pasternak, for one of which he found himself in ecclesiastical trouble. He had called Boris a 'Christian Anarchist', but that was not the objection, which was simply that monks ought not to meddle with such worldly things as novels. Merton felt that *Dr Zhivago* challenged both Soviet atheism and western Christianity, of which he was in a mood to disapprove at that stage of his life. Later he modified his claim for *Zhivago*. In November he heard from Pasternak through a certain John Harris, a country schoolmaster who had written Pasternak a fan letter and got a reply. 'Write if possible to the poet and prosaist Mr Thomas Merton . . . his precious thoughts and dear bottomless letters enrich me and make me happy. At a better and easier time I shall thank and write him. Now I am not in a position to do so. Say to him his high feelings and prayers have saved my life. I intend to name him in my short immaterial (not concerning things and goods) commemorative testament of these days and few lines.' He wrote again to warn Merton against reading poems written before *Zhivago*, because 'The most part of my mature years I gave off to Goethe, Shakespeare and other great and voluminous translations'.

The 'commemorative testament' was never written so far as I know, and the letters he wrote in such numbers lack the discipline of light verse. He wrote again to Merton in February 1960, 'I shall regain myself from that long and continuing period of letter writing, boring troubles, endless thrusted rhyme translations, time robbing and useless, and of the perpetual self-reproof because of the impossibility to advance the longed for, half begun, many times interrupted, almost inaccessible new manuscript.' His heart murmured and he ignored it; now he was ill again. The manuscript was *The Blind Beauty*. 'But I shall rise, you will see it. I finally will snatch myself and suddenly deserve and recover again your wonderful confidence.' The kind of directness and warmth that appeals to us in Russians appealed to him in foreigners: all the same, the sweetness that Merton drew from him is something special.

Such a correspondence throws a flickering light on his character and his biography, his circumstances, but it loses sight of what I cannot but call his genius, which with the partial but considerable exception of *Zhivago* lies largely in his poetry. The poems are so lively and so engaging it is rather hard to get to grips with them. Dale Plank in his *Pasternak's Lyric* (1966), based on a thesis under Victor Erlich at the University of Washington, made a determined onslaught and got closer than most people, at least to the poems from 1916 to 1932. His central intuition is that 'Pasternak's poems have the peculiar ability to engage the reader in the poetry as process, as activity.' That is true, for example, of a late poem like 'July', about a summer ghost in the house. Dale Plank plunges among Russian critics, to suggest that 'the better half of his poems are about poetry' (yet 'July' is not), and that you cannot but spot the opaque, elemental, chaotic gift 'that gave rise to them, and so not only the coldness of experiment but the cruel failure of a poet' (which have quite disappeared in the poems of the fifties).

What I think gave rise to these early poems, and can be called an opaque, elemental, chaotic gift, is simply the art of poetry itself, which fails all poets, at least all young and modern poets. But Boris Pasternak combed out his language in the end as Alexander Pope combed out his. Long ago Jakobson reproved him for his 'passive lyrical hero', but in his late poems the hero is by no means passive. These are abstruse ruminations, but they do throw light on his nature and circumstances, on his biography. As a poet, Pasternak can dissolve into an old photo, a garden, a falling pear, and it is then that he most lives.

> Poets and lives of poets: I'd leave them
> to live only the life of my poem.

Luckily we have a text that shows him at his clearest and best about just these questions. The series of interviews with writers in the *Paris Review*, reprinted as *Writers at Work* by Penguin (Series 2, 1977), is probably the most telling of all the French, German and English interviews that were recorded with the poet at the end of his life. This one was written by a Russian lady, Olga Carlisle, who brought him presents and messages from her parents, who were old friends (Andreev). Her parents recollected that like many Russian writers of his generation he had held open house on Sunday afternoons. The day was sunny and the snow was glittering; Peredelkino was a village from another era – low, ancient-looking log cottages, a horse-drawn sled, kerchiefed women in a group by the small, wooden church. Today the place looks like something from the 1920s, but thirty years ago it looked like the last century. What remains the same is the small, winding roads among tall, dense, coniferous forest, with a few twittering birds high up in the trees. At the time of Mrs Carlisle's visit, Fedin had succeeded Fadeev as first secretary of the Writers' Union, Chukovsky was alive, and the house where they arrested Babel was well remembered. The fences around every plot in the cemetery were painted bright blue, and the crosses stood at drunken angles. The poet had an old note in English pinned to his door: 'I am working now. I cannot receive anybody, please go away.' He was on his way out, not wearing the flat cap of his summer photographs, but an astrakhan hat.

'Usually, one walked into Pasternak's house through the kitchen, where one was greeted by a tiny, smiling, middle-aged cook who helped to brush the snow off one's clothes.' Then came the dining-room with geraniums in the big bay window, and drawings by Leonid on the walls, including the portraits of Tolstoy, Gorky, Scriabin and Rachmaninov, and of Boris and Sasha as children with their sisters. 'We stepped out into the brilliant sunlight and walked through the evergreen grove behind the house in rather deep snow . . . on particular spots he would take my arm, otherwise he gave all his attention to the conversation.'

His language was that of his poetry, full of alliterations and unusual images, 'with waves of words and images following one another in a crescendo'. When she told him so he sensibly replied, 'In writing as in speaking, the music of the word is never just a matter of sound. . . . It results from the relation between the speech and its meaning. Meaning – content – must always lead.' His face was extraordinary, with the long arching neck as he welcomed people, and the long equine lower jaw thrust out; at certain moments he became self-conscious, half closing his slanted eyes and turning his head away. He was intensely aware of others, reacting to every change of mood, grasping the most elusive thoughts at once. 'It is hard to imagine a more perceptive conversationalist.'

At that time he was translating a Czech surrealist poet called Nezval, whom he found excruciatingly boring. 'He is not really bad, but all this writing of the twenties has terribly aged.' His last-recorded official job, so far as I can discover, was to make the Russian version of Brecht's speech of acceptance of the Stalin prize, but nothing is recorded about any encounter; I think there was none. With Olga Carlisle he discussed mostly *Zhivago*. He was alarmed by Edmund Wilson's tendency to turn it into theology. 'One must live and write restlessly, with the help of the new reserves that life offers. I am weary of this notion of faithfulness to a point of view at all costs.' He thought one should alter one's way of looking at least once in every ten years. The devotion to one point of view meant a lack of humility. He cited Mayakovsky as someone unable to accept what was altering 'within himself, or around him'. Pasternak refused her a formal interview, because he was too busy, but several visits to him merged into one long literary conversation.

Once she arrived in a full-scale snowstorm. The snow intensifies with incredible swiftness, and it darkens. 'It was about four o'clock and the room was dark and warm, shut off from the world with only the sound of snow and wind outside.' He talked about her grandfather's stories that 'bear the stamp of those fabulous Russian nineteen hundreds', discussing Nietzsche, and the Russian longing for the extreme. 'In music and writing, men had to have this enormous scope before they acquired specificity, became themselves.' Gorky was impregnated with him. 'Actually, Nietzsche's principal function was to be the transmitter of the bad taste of his period.' Kierkegaard, unheard of then, was more of an influence now. 'I would like to know the works of Berdyaev better . . .' He was impatient as usual with his own early verse, but now with a difference: they were slight sketches; 'just compare them with the work of our elders. Dostoevsky and Tolstoy were not just novelists, Blok was not just a poet . . . they were three voices that spoke because they had something to say – and it sounded like thunder.'

That seems to me to be the true criterion that he had secretly applied to his writings all his life. It was something more than a romantic ideal of the artist or an apocalyptic idea of art or a childish notion of greatness, but it was very slightly tinged with all three. Yet his criticism is admirably mature. 'Our success' (as opposed to his father's agonising) 'was partly due to chance. My generation found itself in the focal point of history. Our works were dictated by the times. They lacked universality, now they have aged. Moreover, I believe that it is no longer possible for lyric poetry to express the immensity of our experience. Life has become too cumbersome, too complicated. We have acquired values which are best expressed in prose.' All that one can say to that is that thirty years later the supremacy of the Euro-American novel does not look quite as overwhelming as it did: the supremacy of the classical, nineteenth-century novel may be unshaken, but it can no more cope with the modern world than lyric poetry can. And one may add that the nub and the essence of *Dr Zhivago* is its poetry, and that Pasternak went on writing poetry. He speaks of 'The falling apart of form, the poverty of thought, the unevenness' of twenties poetry as alien to him, though he loves Yesenin and puts Tsvetayeva highest, 'a greater poet than Akhmatova, whose simplicity and lyricism I have always admired'.

This interveiw is the classic statement of many of his well-known views. He is fastidious over 'dreams of a new language, a completely original form of expression', though a critic might insist he himself had meddled with such dreams and experiments as a young man. 'The most extraordinary discoveries are made when the artist is overwhelmed by what he has to say. Then he uses the old language in his urgency, and the old language is transformed from within . . . today's poetry is often rather ordinary. It is like the pattern of wallpaper, pleasant enough but without real *raison d'être*. Of course some young people show talent – for example Yevtushenko . . . prose is today's medium, elaborate, rich prose like Faulkner's.' He complained of the demands of 'scholars, editors, readers' and above all translations: 'this is my only serious problem, the terrible lack of time.'

Olga Carlisle's last visit was on another Sunday of brilliant sunlight on snow: Boris was out for a morning walk and she waited in his study, the big, bare, sparsely furnished room on the first floor, windows blazing with light, with the view of a field of virgin snow. There were postcards from abroad like flocks of butterflies pinned to the walls. The poet when he came in looked gay and healthy; he wore a navy-blue blazer. He discussed the new play at some length. He had set his sights on Gogol: 'I hope that my plays will be as real, as involved with everyday life, as *Dead Souls*.' He admired the English for cutting Shakespeare to emphasise what was significant, and he was annoyed with the French for not cutting Racine. As for Shakespeare, it is a pity Boris did not live to read the modern research which shows the poet himself cutting his own works in exactly that spirit; but it is evident from Pasternak's translations of Shakespeare that his view was old and deep-seated. 'Only what is expressive today, what works dramatically should be staged.' This is a step beyond the victory of the novel at the expense of the lyric: it is the victory of the essential and the significant over the theatre and the novel. One is tempted to wonder if he might have ended, had he lived long enough, like Isaac Babel, paring down sixty pages into six. *The Blind Beauty* would surely have passed through many alembics of essential-isation.

Unfortunately *The Blind Beauty* was very much news at the time of this interview, and so Olga Carlisle devotes too much precious space to it. For a time at his death and at Olga Ivinskaya's arrest, which followed so swiftly, the play was thought to be lost altogether. Now that a large part of it is translated, it turns out not to live up to his conversation about it: at least it is not another *Zhivago*: it is less complex and less overwhelming in its pulse of life. In Pasternak's conversation it is simply thrilling. 'The play opens with a snowstorm. . . . Alexandre Dumas is invited to attend the première of a new play, *The Suicide*. I might write it – a play within a play as in *Hamlet*. I would love to write a melodrama in the taste of the middle of the nineteenth century. . . . We see the local executioner and his aides stop at the inn' (where Dumas is snowbound). 'They are travelling from town to their residence deep in the woods – by custom they are not allowed to live near other people. . . . Agafon [the serf actor] dreams of going abroad, of becoming a Shakespearean actor, to play Hamlet.

'At first, I consulted all sorts of documents on the nineteenth century. Now I'm finished with research. After all, what is important is not the historical accuracy of the work, but the successful re-creation of the era. It is not the object described that matters, but the light that falls on it, like that from a lamp in a distant room.' Until the final phrase, this sounds like an almost insouciant modernism, but with those last words we are suddenly back in the world of his father's charcoal drawings, on which he must constantly have meditated, until they became second nature to him. It is true indeed as L. P. Hartley said that the past is another country, and for an artist of seventy there is none stranger or more absorbing. *The Blind Beauty* was a historical work intended to explain his personal memories and the world of his childhood: it did not exist for its own sake. In the same way, Tolstoy's obsession with the Decembrists and the whole of *War and Peace* were an attempt to make sense of the Volkonsky family history, his mother's princely family.

> Our fathers' story's Stuart history,
> beyond Pushkin, which in a dream we see.

The lines are from *1905*, and Olga Carlisle quotes them.

The dinner or lunch party that day was mostly a family feast: his wife Zinaida, his elder son by his first marriage who was an engineer, and his young son by Zinaida who was a student of physics, Zinaida's first husband Professor Neuhaus of the Moscow Conservatory, a famous Chopin teacher, 'quite elderly, with an old-fashioned moustache, very charming and refined', and two ladies 'whose exact relationship with Pasternak I did not learn'. The table was covered in a white linen cloth with red cross-stitches, with simple silver and china, and a vase of mimosa, imported in that month in great quantities so that everyone gave it to their friends and carried branches of it as they strolled in the streets. Someone would have brought that from Moscow. There were bowls of oranges and tangerines, and hors d'oeuvres which people passed to one another: caviare, soused herring, pickled vegetables and a macédoine. Boris poured the vodka, then homemade kvass, which sometimes ferments too actively and pops its cork at night with a bang like a pistol shot. The main food was a game stew.

Conversation was about Hemingway, whom the ladies found monotonous, but Boris defended him. 'The greatness of a writer has nothing to do with subject matter, only with how much the subject touches the author. It is the density of style that counts. Through Hemingway's style you feel matter, iron, wood.' He had not always been so positive about Hemingway, and even now he admitted he preferred Faulkner, particularly *Light in August*. They discussed fine points of Chopin interpretation, and once again the poet returned to an old theme. 'Chopin used the old Mozartian language to say something completly new – the form was reborn from within.' He thought Proust echoed 'some of the ideas that absorbed us in 1910', and his own lecture on 'Symbolism and Immortality'. 'Although the artist will die, the happiness he experienced is immortal. If it is captured in a personal and yet universal form it can actually be relived by others.'

He was sad about Chopin because he was thought old-fashioned in America, and because Stephen Spender had failed to publish his Chopin essay, but he was thrilled to hear how Gide loved to play him. 'I have always liked French literature. Since the war I feel that French writing has acquired a new accent, with less rhetoric. The death of Camus is a great loss to us.' In the past, he had not known much about Camus, who was badly viewed in Russia and not printed there, but what arrests interest in that brief sentence about Camus is the word 'us'. It does not stand for all writers, all readers, or an international republic of letters, but for 'us Russians'. 'French literature is now much closer to us,' he went on. He hated French writers about politics: 'they fancy they must be absolutists, like Robespierre or Saint-Just.' He must surely have been thinking of Sartre.

Lights were turned on, it was long past six, so she left. The evening was blue and snowy. Pasternak's last message was to tell his friends abroad that he was well, that he remembered them even though he had no time to answer their letters. Then he called her back. He stood bare-headed under the door light. 'Please', he called out, 'don't take what I have said about letters personally. Do write to me, in any language you prefer. I will answer you.' It was the end of an ordinary Sunday afternoon, important because it gave a vignette of his friendliness, of his ordinary life, of his conversation unilluminated by storms or lightning-flashes, and of how he behaved to women.

*When Skies Clear* or *When the Weather Brightens Up*, a collection of forty-four lyrics, which was his last, was tranquilly spirited abroad for publication just as *Dr Zhivago* had been. With the exception of three or four poems, it was added to his *Collected Poems* in Moscow in 1965, when the so called thaw had gone further than it had in 1960. It appears to me that this foreign publication confirms Boris Pasternak's victory. The government may have been furious, but there was nothing they could do about him now, and if they would not publish him he could and would reach a vaster audience, in the end even a Russian audience, by publishing elsewhere. The question of which poems they found offensive and why is of minor and merely political interest. Akhmatova's view has more interest because of her eccentricity. She thought that of seven or eight poems he showed her four were marvellous but the others stank. The names of the stinking ones are not recorded, though I recollect that she disapproved of 'Bacchanalia'.

She liked 'In Hospital', where the dying man muses through his sedatives on the presence of God. 'I feel your hands . . . replace their handiwork, like a ring in a jewel-box.' The sharpness of that final simile is so sudden as to imitate death. The poem opens with ambulances and policemen and streets, as if the death were Zhivago's, but ends with this coldness and stillness, this un-warmth. The second half of it, from where the patient begins to speak, 'O Lord how perfect are Thy ways . . .' is perhaps the most deeply religious set of verses that Boris Pasternak ever wrote, and its end is awe-inspiring as well as chilling. The other poems that Akhmatova liked are 'Foul Weather', 'Night' and the title poem of the book. Her taste is more Parnassian than mine, but if Russian is not one's language one is in no position to argue with her. They are certainly fine poems.

> No sleep, no sleep, but work,
> no wavering, and get
> no sleep, wrestle with it
> like pilot or planet.
>
> No sleep, no sleep, artist,
> because sleep is shame,
> eternity's hostage
> in the hands of time.

That is the end of the poem 'Night', but, as I have said before, as they get simpler and more dramatic these poems become far harder to render in acceptable English. This one has an irresistible rhythm: 'Nye spi, nye spi, rabotaï . . .' (No sleep, no sleep, but work . . .). It is close in English to traditional children's verse, but its language is of course wholly adult. The accent falls on the second and fourth words and on the second syllable of the last, so the internal rhyme is slightly syncopated. The whole two stanzas have a hard, metallic ring. I am not arguing that this is great poetry; indeed, although it is exciting, it is committed in some ways to slightness, to minuscule conjuring tricks, but I want to explain how different its texture is from anything we know, and really how sound it is, what a wonderful artefact or little object, yet which breathes deeply. It is just what Akhmatova could not resist.

Personally I like the ends of all the poems, 'the green of birches and dark grey of plough', 'city playing its passions like a game', 'river-sculpture of beech and fallen tree', even better than their bold, surprising opening lines. And like other readers I have been particularly excited by 'The Wind', four fragments in tribute to Blok, the payment of a lifelong debt, since he admired Blok before ever he tried to write poems, and still passionately admired him when poetry was over and nothing remained but his death-bed. What the word 'poem' meant to him when he tried to write them, and what the word 'poet' meant to him all his life, derived partly at least from Blok, whose works these four pieces suggest that he meditated ceaselessly. His opening is harshly ironic.

> The influential yes-men know
> whom the critic must call great,
> whom the critic must criticise
> and whom he must exterminate.
>
> Without those PhDs of theirs
> to fill the universe with light
> and call Pushkin a national gem
> we would now know Pushkin could write.
>
> But Blok is different, thank God,
> from the condescending clerisy
> marching down Sinai's rocky flank
> in search of their own progeny.
>
> No school, no system pickled him
> alive in glory, what he wrote
> keeps him alive, not reheated
> or stuffed down anybody's throat.

So far this is light verse, though it has a stinging note not usually to be found in the verse we call light. It is an extremely articulate, unhurried whiplash, exactly applied, and of course true about Blok in Pasternak's lifetime. An English equivalent is hard to find, because our academic machine sucks up literature and canonises it almost more swiftly than new reputations arise; in Russia of course the canon was more severe and was imposed, and had political backing. As the poem goes on, Pasternak considers Blok more deeply.

> He blasts like storm-wind. Like storm wind
> roaring across countryside in the days
> when Philip the Outrider galloped by
> whipping up his six horses, his six bays.

> The grandfather of Alexandr Blok
> a radical crystalline soul,
> the grandson blasting like storm-wind
> an old man's image and equal.

> For better and for worse Blok's poems
> are resonant with the whistling of the wind,
> storm-wind whistling in through the rib-bones,
> and the wind whistling in into the mind.

> The wind blows where it wills to blow,
> among houses of men and among trees:
> it blasts among the rain and in Book Three
> through the Twelve and through death, among all these.

The poem retains its fastidious apparent lightness of form, and yet it begins to bite. It is a wonderful piece of praise, but the wind or the spirit has got out of control, and goes beyond the poem. The soul, which in the third stanza I called 'mind', goes beyond the poem too. At this stage it is as if the subject of the whole poem, the four fragments, were too great to master or to comprehend. Blok's grandfather is a master-stroke. The third part is calm and beautiful, a pastoral interlude.

Wide, wide, wide,
spread stream and meadow,
the rustle of harvest,
reaping, threshing, shadow.
No time for the reapers
to stare into the shallows.
Harvest draws men in,
Blok is the squire's son
taking a sickle on:
lucky at the first go
he misses a hedgehog
and cuts a snake in two.

He hasn't done his homework,
they grumble Lazybones:
singing from the meadows,
childhood's leaden lessons.

Clouds in the east at sunset,
north and south warring on:
wind hurls itself on sickles,
savage, out of season,
bleeds on the blades of rushes
that crowd the river bend.

Singing from the meadows
childhood's leaden lesson.
Wide, widely, without end,
spread meadow, stream, shadow.

I have taken a few small liberties with this wonderful summer chant, because I could not resist the word 'shadow': the Russian summer is harsher, but I hope I have not softened it. The poem is an enchanted croon, and it says something about Blok that we do not usually hear. It says something at least as interesting about Boris Pasternak and the enduring influence of the summer holidays of his childhood. Would he really have been allowed to join in with a scythe or a sickle? I doubt it, but it must have been what he wanted most in the world, around the summer of his thirteenth year. In the fourth part the thunderstorm bursts. This is more familiar territory but it has startling vividness. It begins as a variation on part three.

> The stark horizons threaten
> twilight unhealed from wars,
> bleeding and bruised like reapers,
> their legs criss-crossed with scars.
>
> The sky livid with gashes
> says storms and destruction,
> the marshes smell of rust
> and water and iron.
>
> On roads, in woods, in bottoms,
> villages big or small,
> still the cloudprinted zigzags
> promise a rainfall.
>
> But ruins of purple rust
> round the great city track
> down pompous state events,
> cyclones poise for attack.
>
> Blok saw the patterned heaven,
> noted its prophecies,
> and waited, while bad weather
> assembled its forces,
>
> exploded, shook the earth, signed
> life and poems in dumb
> and flaming strokes, with a fearful
> thirst for what was to come.

In some ways this last piece might be thought to recall the early Auden, but it is less knowing, less psychologically overweening, and has much less appetite for disaster. The comparison is indeed unfair, because Auden had not lived through the storm, though he sang like a missel-thrush at the sight of a thundercloud, and Auden's signs of doom were not so rustic. For an English analogy one would have to go back to Marvell, but Marvell is playful with omens, the Russian country had scarcely emerged from the seventeenth or sixteenth century, and in Pasternak's hands the strange sky is deadly serious. The poem evokes Blok with an unexpected and oblique strength and makes one want to read him again, which is its purpose. Maybe I have delayed too long over this book simply because it is the last, but I do not think so. He is paying off old debts in it: a piano building a High Mass or a forest out of notes, the symbol of a blessed privacy, and of his beloved Chopin and Tchaikovsky. About the simplest things he is always perfectly fresh. 'Geraniums reach out for the small white stars of falling snow beyond the window.'

Maurice Bowra always feared that Boris Pasternak's poems showed a falling-off from his early abundance and brilliance: some other critics have felt the same. Angela Livingstone has expressed stern doubts about what I have called the light-verse aspect of the final book, which personally I like and welcome as if it were 'Beethoven unbuttoned'. It was Auden I suppose who cured us all of being too earnest about poetry, even great poetry. It may even be, as I was recently told by a pupil, that the ability to write light verse has become a criterion of seriousness in our time. We have no need to enter into that paradox in order to spot the bold incisions, the technical swiftness, and the flashes of brilliance and great, childish beauty in Boris Pasternak's last poems.

Ronald Hingley has justly observed that the poet was always uneven, and continued so to the end, as Akhmatova noticed. 'But how startling, forceful and enchanting he is at his best . . . unique, original, and dazzling.' Chukovskaya calls him the only non-tragic Russian poet: I am not sure about that, but he was a life-affirming, life-enhancing writer. It is true, as she says, that every year he contrived to marvel at all four seasons all over again. At any time he could rise to his full height, and on these occasions his poetry was awe-inspiring. An instance of that (at what was mostly a bad time for him) is the poem 'Pines' (1941), which is too long to quote here, being eleven of his usual four-line stanzas. It was well translated in Richard McKane's *Shalford Book of 20th Century Russian Poetry* (1985), and bravely in the Penguin *Pasternak*. He could have been the poet of one phrase, remembered like Lady Winchelsea only for 'dying of aromatic pain' at the smell of a daffodil, but he coined a thousand or ten thousand phrases as memorable: 'the gelatine of blind midday and yellow spectacles of pools', and of two dead lovers, in a version by that ancient wizard J. M. Cohen (1946):

> That we should deafen someone's ears
> with our married harmony
> and with all we drink and sip
> and shall sip with our mouths of grass.

Renate Schweitzer visited him in April 1960, at his last Easter. His letters to her were somewhat exalted, as his letters to women often were, and he seems to have gone further on paper than in cold blood he intended; in a few letters he speaks of cutting off the Platonic growth. Now he was pale and ill-looking; he ate little, but Zinaida said he often ate little. He knew he was not well, but recalled his Moscow clinic in 1958 with real dread: 'It was terrible, I wouldn't want to relive it.' Renate noted his foreign books with some surprise: among the books she brought him, he was most excited by Albert Schweitzer's *Civilization and Ethics*: he felt a kinship with Schweitzer, with his compassion and 'reverence for life'. He got Renate to distribute 5000 dollars from his accumulating western royalties to those he thought needy. When he died he left all foreign-rights negotiations and money matters to Olga Ivinskaya, who was therefore swiftly arrested on a charge of currency offences. He met Leonard Bernstein, and they wrote to one another. In April he wrote a few more optimistic letters about the visionary future, but by the 20th he had taken to his bed with severe pain in his chest, back and left shoulder. He had to stay there, fretting as usual about his friends and his letters and the fate of his family, and hating the idea of doctors. Early in May he began to have blackouts. Olga was not invited to visit him.

Doctors came in the end, and he was taken to the Kremlin Hospital, but there he was refused entry. The reason was not necessarily political or personal; the bureaucracy of the Soviet health system is wellnigh incredible to this day, and anything can happen to anybody. All the same, who knows. On 17 May he suffered another severe heart attack. Ten days later the heart specialist Nikolai Petrov discovered that he had cancer of the lungs, and that the cancer was at least two years old. This had now spread to his heart, so the diagnosis came too late. The *Harper's Magazine* correspondent got him some penicillin from an embassy. A West

s

German journalist told his friends outside Russia. He lay in an oxygen tent in the music room on the ground floor. His family and closest friends were with him, including Nina Tabidze and his kinsman Nikolai Vilmont. But when they were all out of the room for a few minutes he died quietly and alone, late in the evening of 30 May 1960. Only a nurse was present.

It was full spring, as hot as midsummer. All the apple trees in the ragged orchard were in blossom, and there were wild flowers in the grass. His funeral became a vast, uncontainable public demonstration of grief and of respect, with anonymous handwritten notices pinned up in Moscow railway stations and a crowd of many thousands that the village could hardly hold. For several hours musicians, one of whom was Sviatoslav Richter who played Chopin, played music for him in his coffin. The procession wound past the long row of writers' houses, down across the bridge and up again to the small church, then down again to the pine trees he could see from his windows, at whose feet he had expressed a wish to be buried. Formal notices of his death were printed in the literary press by the Litfund: 'The board expresses its sympathy to the family of the deceased.' Pasternak's pallbearers were his sons, and among others his friends and disciples Sinyavsky and Daniel. Asmus the philosopher, who was a neighbour at Peredelkino, made a brief speech. The rites of the church had been read over him quietly in private the evening before, ending as always with the words, 'May his memory remain with us for ever.'

Asmus said, 'We are here to say goodbye to one of the greatest of Russian writers and poets: a man with every talent, including even music. One may accept or reject his opinions, but as long as Russian poetry has any voice on earth, he will stand among the greatest. His quarrel with our times was not with one regime or one state: he desired a society of a higher order. I have never talked to a man who demanded so much of himself or spared himself so little. Few equalled him in the honesty of his convictions. He was a true democrat, and he knew how to criticise his fellow-writers. He will remain an example for all time, as a man who defended his convictions in the face of his contemporaries: he was deeply convinced that right was on his side. He had the power to express humanity in the noblest of terms. He lived a long life, but it passed so quickly, he was still so young at the end, he had so much more to write. His name will live for ever as one of the noblest of human beings.'

The informal recitation of poem after poem went on until it was dark.

# Appendix

The following poems may be useful to the reader. The first four translations are my own, the later ones are by Richard McKane.

In old days in the kingdom
of fairyland
a horseman went spurring
over the broad land.

The knight went to the battle
clouded in dust,
and there rose up to meet him
darkness and forest.

Anxiety stroked his heart
as light as feathers,
fear water, tighten up
your saddle leathers.

The horseman would not listen
to anxieties,
he galloped his horse on
uphill among the trees;

he followed the dry channel
of a dead stream
past meadows, where the hilltop
awaited him,

strayed down to a ravine,
found animal traces,

and followed them downhill
where the water is.

He was deaf to warning,
by will and force
by forest tracks to water
he rode his horse.

★

Over the shallow ford
where the water runs bright
opens the cave, burning
with sulphurous light:

smoke billows crimson
clouding the sky,
and sounding through the forest
an uncanny cry.

He grips his lance in rest
and still he rides on,
till his horse stands breathless
facing the dragon:

green scales wrap the girl
three times around,
and the fire-breathing nostrils
scorch the ground,

and the great body sways
as the knight comes, step by step,
its neck over her shoulder
like the lash of a whip.

In the country of that forest
it was usual
to give girls to the dragon
youthful and beautiful.

This tribute the poor people
payed to the Worm
to protect their tumble-down
dwellings from harm.

The Worm luxuriated
with the girl it got,
tightening round her arms
and round her throat.

The rider muttered one prayer
to heaven's height,
and took a grip on his lance,
ready to fight.

★

The mountains and the clouds
and the closed eyes,
rivers, the shallows, years
and centuries.

Horseman fallen in battle,
his helmet gone,
his faithful horse had trampled
on the dragon.

Dead horse, dead dragon
lay side by side.
Horseman knocked out, the girl
dazed but untied.

High vault of midday
blue with gentleness,
who is that girl? a queen,
or peasant or princess?

At times excess of joy
made them weep and weep,
and at times they were held
deep in their sleep.

And at times he could feel
health returning,
and at times he lay still
from his long bleeding.

And still their beating hearts
struggled to wake, and deep
still he fell, still she fell
back into sleep.

The mountains and the clouds,
and the closed eyes,
rivers, the shallows, years,
and centuries.

### Magdalene (1)

Night falls, the devil's by my side
like a debt owed to my past,
memories of debauchery slide
into my heart to break their fast,
memories of a self who'd feed
all whims of men, fool, madwoman,
sheltering in the street at last.

Only a few minutes remain
before the silence of the tomb
brings down eternity again,
but at the edge where I have come
I break my life to bits and drain
its scent on you from the smashed pot.

O where then, where would I now be
my teacher and my Saviour,
if this were not eternity
sitting at table here with me,
Death, my fresh client quite ready,
my fish netted and pulled ashore.

Tell me the meaning of my sin
and death and hell and fire to me,
when everybody's eyes have seen
me growing into you in grief
as the graft grows into the tree.

Jesus, your feet are on my knees
and as I cry and never cease
maybe I learn how to embrace
the square shaft of the holy cross,
and fainting, straining at your peace,
prepare your body for the grave.


## Magdalene (2)

Cleaning before the Festival:
out of the crowd I sit
to wash your innocent holy feet
with myrrh from a bucket,

I feel in vain for sandals,
see nothing, weep, despair,
my eyes are covered with a veil
by the strands of my hair.

Jesus, your feet are on my hem,
I have watered them with tears, wound them
with strings of beads from round my neck,
and in my hair I have dressed them.

I see the future in detail
as if frozen by your decree:
at this hour I can prophesy,
like a sybil I can foresee.

The veil of the Temple shall be rent
tomorrow, we'll huddle away,
the earth will sway under our feet
out of pity of me maybe.

They will form the guard in columns,
all the horsemen will have gone,
the cross will strain above my head
like the vortex of a storm.

And in silence I'll bit my lips
at the foot of the cross then,
your arms will spread out on the arms
of the cross to embrace too many men.

But for whom in all this world
must your arms embrace so wide?
And for whom have so much pain
and so much power cried and died?

In the whole of this world
can there be so many souls,
villages, rivers and forests
between the poles?

Three days shall pass by
while in my black dejection
I shall grow through emptiness
into your Resurrection.

## Parting

A man looks over the threshold
of his own house, not knowing it;
remains havoc everywhere,
her departure was like a flight.

Every room is in chaos,
and his tears and headache blind
him from seeing the whole truth,
how utterly he is ruined.

That morning, light rang in his ears
like drink: awake, dreaming or dead?

Why do the waves of the ocean
keep breaking in his head?

When frozen windowpanes have blanked out
the world you touch and see,
despairs are doubly like
the deserts of the sea.

She was so close, so dear to him
as is the wave that makes
in to the shore, in all her ways
as any wave that breaks.

As after storm the water floods
to shore and the sea surges,
in the deep water of his soul
her memory submerges.

In years of trial of a life
lived inconceivably
she had driven in on him
by surf of destiny.

The sea through countless obstacles,
unending dangers, bore
her past all hazards
home to his shore.

Now she was gone so suddenly,
what force dropped them alone?
Parting consumed them with ruin,
grief-eaten to the bone.

He looked around inside the house:
at the moment of leaving
she turned everything upside down,
drawer by drawer, everything.

He roamed around till it darkened,
and drawer by drawer,

he put back scattered bits of stuff
and patterns of paper,

pricked himself on a needle stuck
in sewing, and he sighed,
and suddenly he saw her there,
and silently he cried.

## The Nobel Prize

I'm caught like a beast in a trap,
Somewhere there's freedom, people, light,
but the hunt is after me,
and there's no way out.

The dark forest and the pool bank,
a log of a felled fir tree,
My way is completely cut off,
I am resigned to my fate.

What came over me,
am I dirty and evil?
I made the whole world cry
about the beauty of my land.

The ring of hunters tightens . . .
My guilt hurts another –
I have lost my right hand,
my heart's friend is not with me.

I wish that right hand of mine
would wipe my tears,
when the noose is round my neck
and the hour of death is close.

O Lord, you created the swift swallow
    that burns in the dawn, twitters, flies
and swoops – why did you inspire your appetite
    into a dozen condemned men?
How shall I quench my thirst? How can I force the terrible morning
    to turn red, when there is nothing
but the idol and the fate of the red guard
    in this terrible morning – or?
We forgot the original inspired yellow dawn
    after all this redness.
What are you? What skies have you crossed over to?
    You are not here in these Russian skies.


### The Soul

    my soul, comforter
    of all around me,
    you have become the burial vault
    for those tortured alive.

    You slap myrrh on their bodies
    when you dedicate poems to them.
    You mourn them
    with a weeping lyre.

    In our murderous times
    you are funeral urn
    preserving their ashes
    for conscience and for terror's sake.

    Their combined tortures
    bowed you to the ground.
    You smell of the dust of corpses
    in Egyptian tombs.

    My soul, frail vessel,
    you ground everything you saw,
    like a mill and turned
    and mixed them it all in.

Grind further,
all that happened to me,
for these forty years,
into the soil of the graveyard.

Miracle (*from* Zhivago *Poems*)

He walked from Bethane to Jerusalem,
already tormented by the sadness of forebodings.

Prickly bushes stood scorched on the steep slope,
over the nearby hut the smoke did not move,
the air was hot, and the reeds motionless,
the peace of the Dead Sea was immovable.

And in bitterness that contested the bitterness of the sea
he walked with a small crowd of clouds
along the dusty road to some house in the town,
walked to the city to a gathering of disciples.

And he was so deep in thought
that the field in dejection smelt of wormwood.
Everything fell quiet. He stood alone in the middle,
and the landscape lay flat on its back in oblivion.
Everything was mixed up: heat and desert,
and lizards and springs and brooks.

A fig-tree stood not far away,
completely without fruit, just branches and leaves.
And he said to it: 'Whom do you profit?
What joy do you bring me in your stupor?

'I thirst and hunger, and you are barren
and it is more joyless to meet you than granite.
Oh how offensive and ungifted you are!
Remain so till the end of time.'

A tremor of judgement ran through the tree,
like the spark of lightning on a lightning conductor,
and burnt the fig-tree to ash.

Had it found in that time a moment of freedom
for the leaves, the branches and the roots and trunk,
the laws of nature might have intervened.

But a miracle is a miracle, and a miracle is God.
When we are in confusion, then amid the disorder
it overtakes us in a flash, unawares.

# Bibliography

## Works of Pasternak

JUVENILIA. Six Fragments. Ed. Yungren. 1984. Stockholm doctoral thesis, mostly in Russian. Of great interest.
Michigan edition. Ann Arbor, 1961. Three volumes. This has been the standard Russian text, but it is out of print and unavailable secondhand. A new Moscow edition will soon replace it.
DOCTOR ZHIVAGO, including the poems. Published in NOVY MIR, nos 1 to 4, 1988. In no. 6 the poet's son, Zhenya, discusses the history of the text.
SLEPAYA KRASABITSA [BLIND BEAUTY]. 1969. Russian text of an unfinished play, published in England.
STIKHOTVORENIA I POEMI. Moscow, 1965. Contains almost all the poems and excellent notes on variants.
VOZDUSHNIE PUTI. Moscow, 1983. Shorter prose writings, illustrated with his father's sketches.
POIEMI. Moscow, 1977. Soviet popular, very small. The orthodox Pasternak of the SUBLIME MALADY, 1905, and LIEUTENANT SCHMIDT.
DOCTOR ZHIVAGO. English, 1958. The translation is imperfect but too useful to ignore.
JOURNEY TO THE ARMY (1943) and PEOPLE AND SITUATIONS (posthumous, 1967). Contained in NOVY MIR, SELECTION 1925–1967. Ed. M. Glenny. 1972. Also contains two poems by Pasternak and much other relevant material.
SAFE CONDUCT and other works. 1959. Innovative and fascinating, but for the main work it is better to use Barnes, THE VOICE OF PROSE.
ESSAY IN AUTOBIOGRAPHY. 1958. Excellent notes and introduction by Edward Crankshaw.
I REMEMBER. American, 1983. Essay in autobiography, plus essay on translating Shakespeare.
COLLECTED PROSE WORKS. Ed. S. Schimanski. 1945. The editor was an admirer of Henry Read, whom Pasternak admired, and editor of TRANSFORMATIONS. The blurb says Pasternak is "as yet relatively little known in this country" and does not know Mirsky is dead. Pasternak "will rank with Eliot and Rilke, Valéry, Lorca and Yeats."
SELECTED POEMS. Trs. by J. M. Cohen. 1946. From the same publisher as COLLECTED PROSE WORKS, Lindsay Drummond, and contains the most convincing verse translations ever to appear.
POEMS. Trs. by Lydia Slater. Foreword by Hugh Macdiarmid. 1959. These are by the poet's sister and Pasternak felt they were the best in English. She also did FIFTY POEMS (1963) and POEMS (1984). There is indeed a mysterious whisper of the original in her versions, and they got better. She read him extremely well in Russian, and was a poet in English in her own right. I have come to admire her versions of Boris more, the more I have tried to make my own.

NEW DIRECTIONS. PASTERNAK. 1949. Revised edition, 1958. Contains verse translations by C. M. Bowra and Babette Deutsch. Strangely aesthetic, set against solid hunks of prose.

SELECTED POEMS. Trs. by J. Stallworthy & P. France. London, Penguin, 1984. By normal criteria the best, solidest versions, wide range. Extremely useful rather than inspiring. Interesting introduction.

MY SISTER LIFE and A SUBLIME MALADY. Trs. by M. Rudman and B. Boychuk. 1983. Useful. Unacknowledged help, maybe from Richard McKane.

SEVEN POEMS. Trs. G. Kline. 1972. Brilliant pamphlet.

THE YEAR 1905. Trs. by R. Chappell. 1989. Uniquely useful because it is a bilingual edition of a neglected work.

ZHIVAGO POEMS. Trs. by Donald Davie. 1965. Excellent translations but the criticism unacceptable.

POEMS OF DR ZHIVAGO. Trs. by E. M. Kayden. 1967. Not utterly useless.

KOGDA RAZGULYAETSYA. POEMS 1955–59. Bilingual edition. Spirited version by Michael Harori. The same book appeared with exciting version by Henry Karren (1962) as IN THE INTERLUDE, POEMS 1945–60, but Karren is out of print and extremely hard to find. He may not be photocopied but must be copied by hand in libraries. These two books represent Pasternak's last collection.

THE BLIND BEAUTY, 1969, is his last, unfinished play.

THE LAST SUMMER is a Penguin revised version of George Reavey's 1959 translation of POVEST [A TALE], 1934, which in the 1959 translation had an excellent introduction by Reavey, Pasternak's first English fan, and a friend. The Penguin edition has a brief preface by Lydia Slater.

ZHENIA'S CHILDHOOD, 1982, is the usual four short stories re-issued by a notably fugitive publisher, assisted by the Arts Council, with the copyright registered as their own.

SHAKESPEARE translated by S. Marshak and Boris Pasternak on a Melodiya record, 1979.

## Memoirs and Biographies of Pasternak and his Family

BORIS PASTERNAK, HIS LIFE AND ART. G. de Mallac. 1981. The first part of this thick book is the solidest attempt so far at a biography of the poet. Zhenya Pasternak, the poet's son, has written something better documented which has not appeared. Christopher Barnes had also undertaken a serious biographical study which is due soon. There is a biography in Hebrew, of which there are good reports, by L. Fleishmann. In the meantime, de Mallac's book is fullest, and nearest to being standard.

PASTERNAK. H. Gifford. 1977. Subtitled, 'A Critical Study', but contains much useful biographical information.

PASTERNAK. R. Hingley. 1983. Rather sharp than full, but very well informed.

COURAGE OF GENIUS. R. Conquest. 1961. Subtitled, 'The Pasternak Affair', meaning ZHIVAGO and what followed. A lucid and admirable guide to that labyrinth.

MEETINGS WITH PASTERNAK. A. Gladkov. 1977. The most moving and, I think, the most interesting memoir of the poet that has appeared. Gladkov was a young actor and writer in the circle of Meyerhold, who saw a lot of Pasternak at several times in his life, and recalls him with a restrained intimacy that makes him live.

A VANISHED PRESENT. A. Pasternak. 1984. Thrillingly vivid memoir by Sasha (Alexander), the poet's younger brother. Translated by their neice, Anna Pasternak Slater, with a beautiful introduction. Of the entire family and the long saga, Sasha is the person I would most like to have known.

A CAPTIVE OF TIME. My Years with Pasternak. O. Ivinskaya. 1978. A warm, somewhat confused narrative, with some very important information here and there in it.

PERSONAL IMPRESSIONS. I. Berlin. 1982. Written with a precise focus, an impressive memory and great emotional, intellectual and psychological powers.

MEMOIRS OF LEONID PASTERNAK. Introduction by Josephine Pasternak. 1982. Indispensable guide to the career and opinions of the poet's father. (Some useful sidelights on this in National Gallery catalogue, 'French Paintings from the USSR', 1988).

CORRESPONDENCE OF BORIS PASTERNAK AND OLGA FRIEDENBERG, 1910–54. Ed. E. Mossman. 1982. Charts a lifelong relationship with a scholar cousin in very important letters.

MEMOIRS OF ANNA AKHMATOVA. K. Chukovskaya. 1984. Contains a lot of chatter about B. Pasternak.

MEMOIRS OF ANNA AKHMATOVA'S YEARS 1944–50. S. K. Ostrovskaya (1902–03). With a memoir by M. Aliger. 1988. These surprising memoirs are indirectly relevant but most illuminating.

MEMOIRS. N. Mandelstam. 1985–87. Three volumes. Russian text of this essential and wonderful book; the third volume is unavailable in English. Vol I is entitled 'Hope Against Hope', Vol. II, 'Hope Abandoned'.

LETTERS FROM EXILE. Ariadna Ephron. 1982. Russian text. A few of his letters to her are included.

PASTERNAK'S LETTERS TO GEORGIAN FRIENDS. D. Magarshack. 1967. Contains some very queer mistakes; this is based it seems on the Einaudi edition, 'Lettere agli Amici Georgiani', 1967, which is more reliable. The English edition was produced in a hurry. The letters record a very important literary and personal friendship.

LETTERS SUMMER 1926, Pasternak, Tsvetaeyeva, Rilke. 1986. Exchange of very exalted fan letters between these three writers. Introduction by the poet's son, Zhenya.

WHAT I SAW IN RUSSIA 1905–6. M. Baring. 1908. Calm, lucid description of what Pasternak lived through.

RACCONTI PROIBITI E LETTERE INTIME. I. Babel. 1961. Often interesting and relevant.

MEN, YEARS, LIFE: Memoirs of I. Ehrenburg. Many volumes, various dates. Some good anecdotes.

WRITERS AT WORK. Penguin. Second series. 1977

I have not listed works in German and French because nearly all that they contained was also available in English, except perhaps for EIN BILDBIOGRAPHIE. Gerd Ruge. 1958.

## *Critics on Pasternak*

PASTERNAK. Ed. D. Davie and A. Livingstone. 1969. Modern Judgements series. Useful introductory selection, much of it admittedly useless, but it contains several essays rare in English, including the important one by Sinyavsky.

BORIS PASTERNAK'S TRANSLATIONS OF SHAKESPEARE. A. K. France. 1978. Important though uneven.

THE CREATIVE EXPERIMENT. C. M. Bowra. 1949. An influential and still useful essay.

PASTERNAK'S NOVEL. N. Cornwell. 1986. Competent and amusing *tour d'horizon* of opinions, with some rather forceful critical remarks.

DOKTOR FAUSTUS UND DOKTOR SCHIWAGO. 1976. Thoughtful study.

THE POETIC WORLD OF BORIS PASTERNAK. O. R. Hughes. 1974. Solid and sensible with no nonsense; had I read it earlier I would have thought it original. Powerful in its mild way.

PASTERNAK ON ART AND CREATIVITY. Ed. A. Livingstone. 1985. Invaluable series of texts with acute critical comments. Some of the texts otherwise hard to find in English. A disturbing and fascinating book.

BORIS PASTERNAK. THE VOICE OF PROSE. Ed. C. Barnes. 1986. Volume I only. Useful and accurate set of texts. Notes and introduction meagre. But the intention appears to have been critical, rather than merely editorial. I have not come across Vol. II.

PASTERNAK'S LYRIC. Dale Plank. 1966. Efficient exercise with competent bibliography (fuller than this). Good on individual poems.

HORIZON. Vol. 10, no. 55, Vol. 12 nos 68–9. Contributions by J. M. Cohen and C. M. Bowra writing about, reviewing and translating Boris Pasternak.

THE THREE WORLDS OF BORIS PASTERNAK. R. Payne. 1962. Readable and strong. Good on particular poems.

ESSAYS. Ed. N. Nilsson. 1976. Useful collection.

CHILDREN OF DRANCY. H. Butler. 1988. This contains a most interesting and intelligent piece on Pasternak, pointed out to me by John Bayley.

SHAKESPEARE. Victor Hugo. 1864. Intended to introduce his son's translation. Very important for Pasternak's Shakespeare.

THE FUTURISTS, THE FORMALISTS AND THE MARXIST CRITIQUE. Ed. C Pike. 1979. The notes are full of information.

POETS OF MODERN RUSSIA. Peter France. 1952.

## Other Poets and Theatre People

LIFE OF MAYAKOVSKY. W. Woroszylski. 1972.

LOVE IS THE HEART OF EVERYTHING. Mayakovsky and Brik letters. 1982.

O. MANDELSTAM AND HIS AGE. S. Broyde. 1985.

AKHMATOVA, A POETIC PILGRIMAGE. A. Haight. 1976.

A CAPTIVE LION [Tsvetayeva]. E. Feinstein. 1987.

LIFE OF BLOK. A. Pyman. 1979.

A BLOK, L'INTELLIGENCIJA E LA RIVOLUZIONE. 1978.

THEATRE OF MEYERHOLD. E. Braun. 1986.

I have not listed the numerous and excellent translations of Akhmatova, Tsvetayeva, Mandelstam, Mayakovsky and (to a lesser degree) Blok, or of prose writers like Bryusov, Bulgakov, Bunia and so on, or the innumerable English versions of Rilke. I give an Italian version of Blok's prose pieces only because it is useful and not otherwise easy to find. Many of the translations contain useful introductions.

## Literary History

HISTORY OF RUSSIAN LITERATURE. D. S. Mirsky. 1926. This work is still standard, but it is essential to read it in the old two-volume edition since reprints leave out the political history which is the context of literature. Prince Mirsky lived for many years in England after the Revolution, frequented the London Library, and was a close friend of Maurice Baring; but he converted himself to Marxism and returned to Moscow in the 'thirties, wrote a full political history of Russian which put no emphasis on personalities, and was shot.

RUSSIAN LITERATURE. IDEALS AND REALITIES. P. Kropotkin. 1916. This is the second, improved edition. A short book written with flair and originality, and highly entertaining.

POETS OF RUSSIA 1890–1930. R. Poggioli. 1960. This is a reliable guide to the context of literary movements and the position of individuals within these movements. It represents the received, intelligent view, but it is not exciting.

FROM GORKY TO PASTERNAK. H. Muchnic. 1961. A laborious, detailed, reliable discussion of six writers.

RUSSIAN LITERATURE SINCE THE REVOLUTION. E. J. Brown. 1982. Useful, but I found it heavy going.

THE PROLETARIAN EPISODE IN RUSSIAN LITERATURE., 1928–32. E. J. Brown. 1953. This is an invaluable, detailed study, with documents of the crisis of the 'proletarian movement' and the foundation of the Union of Writers. Its account of literary politics is essential background to Pasternak.

SOVIET RUSSIAN LITERATURE SINCE STALIN. D. Brown. 1978. Interesting, wide-ranging, but not deep, up to date ten years ago.

RUSSIAN LITERATURE. M. Baring. 1914. Brief, brilliant and perfectly readable, ending in 1905.

THE RUSSIAN REVOLUTIONARY NOVEL. R. Freeborn. 1982. Excellent, pointed and challenging, therefore extremely useful. Covers novels from Turgenev to Pasternak. Particularly good on minor figures like Ivanov.

## Anthologies

They are innumerable, some charming, some terrible, very few actually useful.

PENGUIN BOOK OF RUSSIAN VERSE. Ed. D. Obolensky. 1962. Excellent and fundamental, with introductions (general and to each author) and translations.

OXFORD BOOK OF RUSSIAN VERSE. Ed. M. Baring. 1925. Enlarged by D. P. Costello, 1948, but retaining Mirsky's notes on the poets from Derzhavin to Blok. No translations, but the collection is unsurpassable in taste. Costello was a Communist New Zealander who had some connection with the Oxford Press. He used to call on Boris Pasternak to entreat him to join the Communist Party.

SHALFORD BOOK OF 20th CENTURY RUSSIAN POETRY. (In English). Translated by Richard McKane. 1985. The translations are fresh and remarkable.

PENGUIN POST-WAR RUSSIAN POETRY. (In English). Ed. Daniel Weissbort. 1974. Extremely useful as an introduction.

RUSSIAN POETRY: THE MODERN PERIOD. (In English). Ed. J. Glad and D. Weissbort. 1978. Iowa Translation Series. Various translations. Remarkable for its range of emigré poets.

## Russian History

UTOPIA IN POWER. M. Heller and A. Nekrich. 1982. Covers 1917 to now, often in wide swathes, but it does make sense of events.

RUSSIAN REVOLUTION AND SOVIET STATE 1917–21. Documents ed. M. McCauley. Improved edition, 1988. Invaluable.

MOSCOW: A TRAVELLERS COMPANION. Ed. L. Kelly. 1983. Fascinating, wide-ranging and unexpectedly useful.

FIRST RUSSIA, THEN TIBET. R. Byron. 1933. An illuminating witness. Contains (p. 62) a fine photograph of the demolished Cathedral and an 18th century church about to follow it, with a glimpse of the windows of the Pasternak flat in Volkonka.

TOLSTOY. A. N. Wilson, 1988 and TOLSTOY. Martine de Courcel, 1988. Both deal sufficiently for my purposes with late 19th century and early 20th century history. For the years 1910–1917, I relied on articles by Igor Vinogradoff and others.

# Index